Born Nov. 1-1942
Died Ma[...]

MW00682413

Ralph Klein

Ralph Klein

A Maverick Life

Frank Dabbs

GREY**S**TONE BOOKS
Douglas & McIntyre
Vancouver / Toronto

Greystone Books
A division of Douglas & McIntyre Ltd.
1615 Venables Street
Vancouver, British Columbia
V5L 2H1

Canadian Cataloguing in Publication Data

Dabbs, Frank, 1947–
  Ralph Klein

SEMINOLE LIBRARY

ISBN 1-55054-443-8
  1. Klein, Ralph, 1942– 2. Prime Ministers—Alberta—
Biography. 3. Alberta—Politics and government—1971–
I. Title.
FC3675.1.K63D32 1995   971.23'03'092   C95-910495-X
F1078.25.K63D32 1995

Editing by Nancy Flight
Cover photograph by Canapress Photo Service/Ray Giguere
Cover and text design by DesignGeist
Typeset by Vancouver Desktop
Printed and bound in Canada by Friesens
Printed on acid-free paper ∞

The publisher gratefully acknowledges the assistance of the Canada Council and of the British Columbia Ministry of Tourism, Small Business and Culture for its publishing programs.

LORNA FRANCES GASTRELL DABBS

Flowers for the Living

Contents

Preface ix

Acknowledgements xii

1   *Home Country 1*

2   *Rootless Years 8*

3   *The Invention of Ralph Klein 16*

4   *Epiphany 24*

5   *The Miracle in October 35*

6   *The Inauguration 44*

7   *The Feel-Good Mayor 53*

8   *The Winter Games 62*

9   *Choices 72*

10   *The Ecotrap 79*

11   *The Hijack 90*

12   *The Restoration 99*

13   *Miracle on the Prairies 107*

14   *Extraordinary Remedies 116*

15   *The Rivals 124*

16   *The Duel 132*

17   *The Failure of Opposition 140*

18   *The Long Haul 149*

19   *The One-Issue Government 158*

20   *The Eclipse of the Populist 167*

Epilogue 173

Chapter Notes 182

Selected Bibliography 186

Index 187

Preface

*Yesterday's news is tomorrow's
history. Meanwhile there is today,
when it is deemed unfit for either
category—for the one too old; for
the other still unripe . . .*

—Blair Fraser, The Search
For Identity Canada: Post
War to Present 1945–1967

The story of Ralph Klein, Alberta's twelfth premier and its most
recent and colourful anti-politician, illuminates the most important trends in contemporary Canadian life: the politics of fiscal
responsibility, the death of twentieth-century liberalism and the transition from democracy that defined itself by government spending on wars,
high-risk industrial expansion and social programs to one that will be
known, and measured, by the way it conserves public resources and ref-
erees rather than manages the economy.

The unexpected 1995 election of Conservative Premier Mike Harris
in Ontario and the reelections of two other budget-balancing premiers,
Tory Gary Filmon in Manitoba and Social Democratic Roy Romanow
in Saskatchewan, indicate that the sustained popularity of Premier
Klein's tough, austere government is more than just the eccentric restoration, in quirky Alberta, of the patent-medicine politics of Social
Credit's founder, William Aberhart, merged with the social conservatism
of his successor, Ernest C. Manning. For the sake of the long term, Canadians are prepared to lower their expectations in the present.

Canadian governments no doubt will remain constitutional and representative, but this change is of the first order of magnitude; consequently, we had best know the men and women who are making it, for
destiny is not an automaton; it is the human hand. Thus, it is of more
than passing interest to study the man who has become the synonym for,
the revered icon of, and the pejorative for this new science of government. Who is Ralph Klein? When did he discover and define himself
as the person and leader he now is? What are his values? Where do his

ideas come from? Why has he the power and public following he now
wields? How has life marked him thus?

Klein can no longer be comprehended through daily media coverage,
which he so carefully orchestrates and manipulates to his own advantage.
The longer opinion pieces, news documentaries and magazine articles
are notable mostly for the prejudices and predisposition of their authors
and the flawed regionalism of Canadian journalism and are, therefore,
of limited enlightenment. He is still a work in progress, and the main
elements of his political agenda are either incomplete or unformed, and
the ultimate consequences unknown. Therefore, social, political and economic scholars would be wise to wait to deliver their verdicts, and academic historians ought to bide their time. Since we cannot rely on the
news and cannot wait for history to understand and reckon with Klein
and others with similar agendas, this book needed to be written.

The purpose of these pages is to know Ralph Klein. The book's
focus is to describe the making of an iconoclast and renegade, for it will
be men and women of his ilk who will break the old vessels and, on the
potter's wheel of public life, give the future its shape. They will not look
like or act like the politicians of North American's post-war era; they
come from different life experience and take their cues from different
values. These are things that we need to understand.

Yet just when we most need to scrutinize them, politicians, Klein
included, have disappeared behind a temple veil; we are excluded from
knowing them except as they are presented to us in electronic images
and carefully considered sound bites doled out by their handlers and
manipulated by the media. This book attempts to tear the veil in two,
revealing what lies behind. It inspects Ralph Klein's entire life, not just
his current public persona. It examines his roots and explains the political
culture that preceded him and to an important extent defined him as a
premier whose influence extends beyond the borders of his province.

As the acknowledgements, chapter notes on sources, and bibliography indicate, this book is a compendium of the thoughts, reflections and
experiences of hundreds of people who have known Ralph Klein all his
life or in one of his incarnations and have been affected, for better or
worse, by his conduct and decisions. Although Klein refused to be interviewed for this book, he has been, until recently, transparent, and it
has been possible, from primary sources, to identify his own thoughts
about and insights into many of the important events of his career. All
of this has been put in its proper historical context, for without the past
the present is blind. In telling the story, I have tried to be faithful to the
examples and standards of Canada's great political biographers. In the
end, however, this is my book and the opinions expressed in it are my
own; no one else is to blame for the content and conclusions.

I have known Ralph Klein since September 1967, when I was a student at the University of Calgary targeted, along with my three thousand or so fellow undergraduates, by one of his masterful media blitzes for the United Way of Calgary's annual fund-raising campaign. I met and competed with Klein as a journalist covering Calgary's city hall. We were neighbours; he invited me to his home to meet Colleen and their baby daughter, Theresa. He gave me lifts in his signature Volkswagen Beetle with the canoe strapped on top.

When he became mayor, I wrote about him for magazines and CBC Television, and he kindly narrated a fund-raising audio-visual presentation I produced for the Calgary Multicultural Centre. The relationship was cordial but distant. When he was preparing to move into provincial politics, he consulted me twice in 1988; once, by appointment, over beer with his political alter ego, Rod Love, and once, by chance, with Colleen at a Christmas party. Since then, we have spoken once. Although we barely know each other, like many Albertans, I feel I know him like a cousin or a friendly neighbour.

As much as I admire the man and believe that he is doing the obvious, I fear his enormous power and some of the outcomes of his decisions. It seems to me that the responsible citizen should always approach political leadership with healthy skepticism and deep apprehension. The price of continued liberty, as Klein and others take us through the transition ahead, is to live with constant foreboding. But since someone had to do what has been done in Alberta, and given the paucity of the alternatives, I'd rather it had been him.

Acknowledgements

Books are created by teams, nonfiction especially so, and authors are sometimes haplessly carried along by the others. I thank, and am thankful for, Peter C. Newman, who introduced me to Douglas & McIntyre; Rob Sanders of Greystone Books, who is most things that other, less fortunate writers say a publisher never is; Nancy Flight, whose editing was simply extraordinary; and Leah Jahn, the gracious keeper of the electronic bridge between Calgary and Vancouver. I am especially indebted to Florence Erion Murphy, who provided encouragement and practical help at every step of the way.

Friends provided contacts, sources, hospitality, ideas, pasta, wine and a sense of direction and occasionally held my feet to the fire. These included Gus Christopher, Ted Matthews, Jamie Deacey, Paul Boeda, Douglas Cass, Tag Watson, Manny Martin, John Shiry, Robin Farquar, Betty K. Cooper, Gillian Steward, R. Campbell Todd, Don Currie, Jim Munroe, David Dempsey, Heather Roberston, Dean Christopher, Karen Maria Tratt, Neil Richardson, Yvette Alongi, Tim Christison, Ted and Mike Byfield, Julia Jones and Tom MacLaughlin.

Writing a book about a man who declines to be interviewed is challenging. My sources included material drawn from articles and columns I have written in the past about Klein, Calgary and Alberta for *Calgary Magazine*, and two documentary scripts—one written for the CBC and one for the Calgary Multicultural Society. I obtained published speech texts, broadcasts and print media commentaries. *Alberta Hansard* and many government publications also proved invaluable. The Calgary Public Library staff, especially in the Local History Room, were very helpful, and I also thank the University of Calgary for access to its library. In addition to primary sources, I followed Klein's media coverage; sources are attributed in the text. I had several luncheons with Rod Love and Thompson MacDonald. I am especially grateful to the more than 175

Albertans and other Canadians who talked to me about Ralph Klein over a year and a half. Several deserve particular thanks: Ralph's father, Philip Klein, Rod Sykes, Gord Shrake and Andy Philip. I also relied on other authors. A bibliography is provided, but I would like to particularly recognize the work of John Barr and the late Ernest Watkins. Klein wrote a series of columns in 1979 and 1980 for *Calgary Magazine*, which I found helpful; they also are cited in the text. CFCN Television's Dale O'Hara found and allowed me to view Klein's 1977 documentary, *The Blackfoot: 100 Years*. I am indebted to the City of Calgary Archives, the Glenbow Archives, *Alberta Report*, the United Way of Calgary, the southern Alberta division of the Red Cross, the *Edmonton Journal* and the *Calgary Herald* for help with photographs and access to microfilm and other files.

Finally, there are the teachers. My sister, Amy, taught me to read long before I started school. It was on some Georgian Bay summer afternoons in the side yard under the silver birch. We were playing school and sat at orange crates for desks. I think she was all of ten years old. The late Alistair Freisen told me I could write, and should. Mollie Brien taught that there were things worth writing about, and the late Richard Benner said that I had to do it with craft so that people would want to read it. My thanks to them all.

Home Country

Plains of gleam, palace of hills,
blue slopes and rocky mountains
chiseled with valleys and tributaries.

—STEPHÁN G. STEPHANSSON,
"MY REGION," TRANSLATED
BY KRISTJANA GUNNARS

Ninety years ago, a restless and gregarious German chef named Andrew Klein fell in love with a modest and clever British domestic named Kate Drury, who worked in the same hotel in London in which he plied his trade. The handsome and lively Klein was a deeply religious man and a conscientious objector who had gone into exile from his native city of Reutlingen, 40 km (25 miles) south of Stuttgart, at the age of fourteen to avoid the draft and wandered through Europe. He learned six languages and became a chef, working in all the great cities of the Continent. Having tasted life's sweet possibilities, he was determined to rise above the economic station that he appeared constrained to occupy forever in the rigid class structure of Edwardian England. In the last years before the First World War released the twentieth century onto Europe and swept away the notions of destiny and class that fettered ambition, Andrew Klein determined to find a home where he, and no other man, would set his course and where religious freedom would be secure.

There was only one place that offered the alternative—North America. In 1907, Andrew sailed for New York, where he hoped to find a position in a great hotel. He suffered, however, from a breathing disorder, so he joined the 1.25 million Britishers and Europeans who, between 1896 and 1911, responded to the invitation of two political architects, Sir Wilfrid Laurier and Sir Clifford Sifton, to come to Canada and take up free land—and clear air—in the western provinces.

Andrew Klein found the new Jerusalem of his Christian faith at the edge of the Alberta foothills, a week by ox cart west of the nearest railway at Red Deer. He staked his homestead on land that is now part of the town of Rocky Mountain House and sent to London for Kate. After she had endured the long train ride from the immigration sheds of Montreal, he met her on the crowded platform of the CPR train station in the rawboned city of Calgary. The young couple paused only long enough to marry before going on to the Red Deer staging ground, where homesteaders flooding into central Alberta disembarked from the train, acquired the supplies needed to start a new life and continued on by wagon or buggy to their land. The Kleins climbed into Andrew's ox cart and continued west for 100 tortuous kilometres to Rocky Mountain House, to the rich black soil of the aspen-scattered parkland that divides the central prairie from the rampart palaces of the foothills. They built a log cabin and Andrew cleared the mandatory 10 acres required to receive his title to the land; then he went into the booming timber business as a sawyer.

Few places on the British colonial map at that time could have been further removed from the kitchens of Europe's five-star hotels. Since the migrations of late ice age aboriginals, Rocky Mountain House had been an important campsite and meeting place on the North Saskatchewan River for Athapascans, Blackfoot and Cree. More recently, it had been a principal frontier establishment for the Hudson's Bay Company, after Rupert's Land was chartered to it in 1670. The fort was still nothing more than an outpost when it was transferred to the Dominion of Canada as part of the Northwest Territories in 1870. After Alberta became a province in 1905, agriculture and immigration became the thriving forces of the region, and Rocky Mountain House began its transformation into a farming centre, though it was a backward and forgotten place, nonetheless.

When Andrew and Kate Klein took up their land, the taming hand of civilization had not made much of an impression, but the remote, isolated past was ending more rapidly than anyone at the time could realize. The Kleins found a rich land on which cattle and horses thrived, hay and the hardier grains such as rye grew heavy, and the kitchen gardens were supplemented by wild roots, mushrooms and berries. The streams were thick with trout; the dense foothills forests from which Klein drew his living were also profuse with game—grouse, waterfowl, bear and moose; the slopes were covered with hundreds of species of wildflowers, from the crocuses of April to the Indian-paintbrush of September. The Klein household, which grew to include three daughters and a son, was endowed with a lively European intelligence, including the conscientious objector's inevitable interest in community and politics and restless determination to master his own fate. To this was added a profound attachment to the land, the natural things that grew on it and the uses to which a resourceful and energetic family could put it.

Many homesteaders preferred Alberta's open wheat lands of the prairies or the ranch lands south of Calgary, but, in the long haul, the central parkland proved to have distinct advantages, in addition to its wild and rugged beauty, especially when autumn ignited the fiery gold of the aspen thickets and turned the wild rose, bearberry and wild cranberry to an undercarpet of a richer and deeper red than scattered blood. The rain was more reliable where the Kleins settled than on the prairies; during the dust bowls of the thirties, there was no drought. There was plenty of wood for building, and the foothills held a generous share of Alberta's ubiquitous coal seams for fuel. Government-established dairies in central Alberta provided steady cash income to the prospering farms and towns. In this strong economy, Andrew Klein built a good business, supplying lumber for the building needs of both farms and new businesses in the town.

Andrew's and Kate's son, Philip, was an industrious and gregarious lad with a builder's hands and eye. He grew into a burly youth, not large but strong and tough—tanned from long afternoons in the sun and crinkly eyed from smiling out at life. He loved the outdoors; he hunted and fished. He was charming to his seniors and a leader with his peers. He was also as restless as his father had been as a youngster, and he chaffed under his parents' strict regimen in which children were expected to be both obedient and silent. Philip was easygoing, however, and got along well with Andrew and Kate and with the other adults in his life. As an indication of his early maturity and rapport with the adult world, Philip became close friends with his schoolteacher, Alf Hooke, and they have remained lifelong friends.

When the Social Credit political movement swept across Alberta at the outbreak of the depression, led by Calgary high school principal William Aberhart, Hooke became its most doctrinaire insider and a career cabinet minister from 1935 to 1970. There were so many pedagogues in the early movement that a historian referred to it as the School Teachers.[1] Hooke fed Klein's growing passion for politics, and the youth became "dyed-in-the-wool Social Credit." The two men most influential in his life, his conscientious objector father and his Social Credit teacher, thus planted the seeds that made Klein an astute, lifelong political volunteer and junkie.

At the age of fourteen, with the depression under way and not much work for a youth in Rocky Mountain House, he decided to kick over the traces and left home at the same age that his father had been when he left Reutlingen. Philip Klein drifted at first, riding the rails and relying on the Salvation Army for meals and a place to sleep. When he could find work, it was as a farm labourer or driving trucks. He learned to box and made a few dollars in the rough and bloody sawdust rings of Western Canada. As the depression deepened, he found himself on the fringes of the relief camps—government-run work camps where men, mostly single, could find food and shelter in exchange for building roads or railway beds. Historian John Archer captured the life that Philip Klein and thousands of his fellows lived in those years:

> There was a certain discipline among these unemployed. Some were looking for work. Most were too restless, too independent to remain in relief camps. Few got into serious trouble. In summer time they lived in box cars, or in "jungles" adjacent to the railway. By working a little and begging a little they got by—on about 30 cents a day. Green teenagers were made to wash and to keep their clothing clean. There was a spirit of comradeship. But there was little purpose to such existence.[2]

Klein was a man who needed a purpose, so in 1935 he made a decision that resembled the one his father had made in 1907 in London when he immigrated to North America. The beckoning vista was South America, and Philip Klein and a buddy decided to go there. Embarking on the roof of a boxcar, they arrived in Regina in June and went to the local work camp, where they found a band of about eighteen hundred men who were riding the rails on quite another pilgrimage; this was the On To Ottawa trek, organized in British Columbia by Marxist Art Evans and the Communist-dominated Workers' Unity League. The purpose was to confront Prime Minister Richard B. Bennett on Parliament Hill and present grievances over the harsh and meagre conditions in the federal relief camps and to demand a remedy for their plight. Bennett thought differently; he believed these tattered men to be the vanguard of an armed revolution. When sympathetic Reginans organized the Citizens' Emergency Committee to provide voluntary aid to feed the workers after the federal government cut off food supplies to the camp, Bennett ordered the RCMP to break up the trek.

On July 1, in the city's downtown Market Square, baton-swinging police waded into a fund-raising meeting of fifteen hundred men, women and children. The melee spread like wildfire, with pockets of demonstrators throwing bricks and using pipes to club back at the police. One detective was struck and killed. The police fired on the crowd with their revolvers, and seventeen demonstrators suffered bullet wounds. At least twenty-five others were injured, but so many were treated secretly in the homes of sympathizers to avoid arrest that an exact count was never made.[3]

Klein and most of the men in the work camp had hoped to avoid the confrontation by going to a baseball game in the Regina Exhibition Grounds, but the police struck there as well. They were tear-gassed and rounded up at gun point by police armed with revolvers, rifles and machine guns, and then locked in the camp without food for four days before being shipped out of the city on those ubiquitous box cars on July 5. His dream of emigration to South America died in that riot, and Phil Klein landed up in Souris, Manitoba, where he spent the next four years. But the tear gas and the hunger and the blood of his encounter with the Regina Riot have been an indelible part of his life, and he has passed on to his sons a sense of public responsibility and fairness, a hatred of injustice and a propensity to side with the underdog.

In Souris, Phil Klein began his career as a builder. He learned the trades of concrete finisher and road paver and how to drive heavy equipment and trucks. He added wrestling to boxing in his repertoire as a semi-professional athlete. His hard-fisted, tough-guy disposition in the ring belied his soft-hearted, openhanded capacity for friendship and affection. He charmed his pals and wooed the ladies. He had a talent for leadership and managing men and developed a reputation as an able foreman and supervisor. In 1939, he moved to Calgary.

Phil Klein was a recruit soldier for all of two days at the beginning of the war. He enlisted at Calgary's red brick Number One Fire Hall, under its copper cupola, and joined the out-of-step, shuffling march of volunteers through the downtown crowds to the Mewata Armoury for his medical exam. He was stunned to learn, the following day, that he had been rejected because he had a goiter condition. Since he was in perfect shape, he went to a private doctor for a second opinion and was given a clean bill of health. He was shattered to realize that he had been turned down for racial reasons: he was German and would not be allowed to fight for his country in Hitler's War. Politics, it seemed, was the constant of his young life: the politics of a depression lived on the rails, the politics of the Regina Riot and now the politics of race in a war he badly wanted to fight.

Instead, Klein went to war in the construction business, building the airfields, oil field plants and roads that the military needed on the prairies for home defence. His cheerful disposition made it possible for him to accept the reality of his situation with equanimity. During and after the war, he became a supervisor and foreman for the biggest contractors in Alberta—outfits such as Mannix Construction, Brown & Root and Bechtel. He loved enterprise and operated much of the time as an independent business, travelling across the west and later to Québec and Labrador to contract his skills to the big companies. He laboured on airports, dams, gas plants, sidewalks, curbs and gutters. He continued to wrestle as a semi-professional, adopting the theatrical bad-guy roles of the sport, with monikers such as Killer Klein.

As often as he could, he returned on weekends to Rocky Mountain

House, and, one Saturday night at a dance, he met Florence Harper, a bookkeeper and sometime waitress from Calgary who was visiting her cousins. She was the daughter of quietly respectable working-poor parents, Hollins (Harry) and Christine Harper, who lived in Calgary's North Hill community of Tuxedo Park—a suburb of blue-collar families, schools, churches and corner stores.

Harry Harper's homesteading roots were on Alberta's southeastern border country near the remote village of Oyen, where farming was tough and most families got by on meagre means. The region's beauty was breathtaking. Its broad blue wetlands were crowded with ducks and geese, and its wide fields were choked with prairie crocuses in spring. In summer the fields of wheat and grains were lush and thickly green. The infrequent river coulees were crowded with deer, rabbits and porcupines. Even in the bone-cracking cold of winter, these broad, flat steppes were hauntingly beautiful—the black slashes of the poplar and elm stands like charcoal against the clean snow, the ice crystals like icing on the windows and roofs, and long blue moonlight nights when the vast stretches of snow looked like the roof of heaven heaped over with stars and echoing to the cry of coyotes and, occasionally, wolves.

The economy was virtually without cash, however, and almost devoid of opportunity for young families. In 1920, Harry Harper came to Calgary to work for the Cockshutt Plough Company and moved into a bungalow at 3406 Centre Avenue North, in the neighbourhood that was to become the Harpers' and later the Kleins' community for the better part of two generations.

Life in the city may have been better for the Harpers than at Oyen, but it wasn't easy for a labourer with little education. After six years with Cockshutt, Harry had to find another job, going to work as a labourer in the Canadian Pacific Railway freight yards. He struggled through the depression, sometimes working for the Robin Hood flour mill and at other times getting piecework as a carpenter or day labourer. After the depression he got on permanently with the Robin Hood mill as a janitor, until he retired in 1956. But his means were limited. After his retirement he and Christine took on some of the responsibility to raise his grandsons when their parents divorced. To make ends meet, he occasionally returned to work as a janitor for the Shop Easy stores and he and Christine lived for several years with his son, Ralph, a firefighter, and Ralph's wife, Ila.

Harry and Christine may not have had money, but they had depth of character and saw themselves as linchpins of the family in which the children, and later the grandchildren, were the most important aspect of life because they were the future. For all their lives, they were parents that Florence and Ralph could always count on, and the family shared its economic and emotional resources seemingly without ever counting the cost.

Whereas Ralph was solid, modest, dependable and predictable, Florence grew up ambitious, passionate and restless—an unquenchable flame that consumed some hidden and inexhaustible fuel yet was never satisfied. She loved to dance; to her friends she was a vivacious, gay spirit. She was bright girl who was ambitious to advance. Yet she seemed somehow unsettled and had a dark, brooding side even when she was young. She flitted through life like a butterfly, bookkeeping or waitressing, but she never seemed to be tied down by the drudgery of life that was endemic to young women of the the depression in Canada's small prairie cities—as child-bound housewives or as single working girls trapped at home with their parents or living in cheap flats and trying to eke out a pair of stockings from impossibly small wages so that they might dress well if a gentleman invited them to a dance, an event that occurred all too infrequently.

When Phil Klein and Florence Harper met at that dance in Rocky Mountain House in the early years of the war, the spark between two outgoing and intense people was inevitable. Although the magnesium brilliance that welded them together soon turned out to have its blistering, burning side, they married and bought a house a few blocks from Florence's parents. On November 1, 1942, thirty-five years after Andrew Klein first saw his future homestead, they had their first child, a son, named Ralph for Florence's brother and Philip to honour his father.

The infant inherited a legacy much richer than land, treasury or title, none of which his parents or grandparents had to give him. He received the best—and the worst—of the political passions, the family sentimentality, the mercurial brilliance, the religious sensibilities, the restlessness, the charm and the seething, brooding darkness of his people. He also received in his patrimony a sense of place in a home country that would shape and direct his adult life.

2

Rootless Years

*I have ransacked my oldest dreams
for keys and clues ...*

—Vladimir Nabokov, *Speak,
Memory*

Ralph Klein's boyhood oscillated between sweet, brilliant sunlight and dark, bitter shadows—unsettled and unsettling, rootless and disconnected. When he was born, in 1942, his parents were still happy together, and they lived modestly, in a bungalow at 3401 - 1st Street NE, in Tuxedo Park, Florence's neighbourhood, with her parents and her brother, Ralph, living close by. It was also a welcoming and promising place for Philip, with his dreams of becoming a prosperous contractor. Two years after Ralph was born, the couple had a second son, Lynn.

Calgary's frontier exuberance could not overcome the unspoken, rigid divisions between the the old-money upper class, the ambitious and upwardly mobile middle class and the largely non-British, immigrant blue-collar workers. The downtown core was demarcated by the Bow River and the CPR tracks. To the south, the older part of the city, were the best neighbourhoods, with their tree-lined streets, large gardens, well-developed parks, large churches and graceful schools. In the north were the ethnic neighbourhoods—Italian, Polish, Ukrainian—and the modest duplexes and cottages of those who worked for the CPR and CNR, in the oil fields, in the factories and in the service industry. The war and the post-war oil boom knocked some of the British stiffness out of the community, but in 1942 people knew their place and kept it. The Kleins were outsiders; a city lad like Ralph might aspire to being a teacher, but an education for any other profession was almost beyond reach because of the cost of a higher education. He had fewer prospects than if he had been born into a farm family. However cashless, some farmers were prosperous in land and were able to send their sons to school.

There were two avenues out of Tuxedo Park, both equally enticing to two young brothers growing up in the bustling prairie town. One was

Centre Street, a couple of blocks west of the Klein home, which led to the city. Taking the streetcar downtown meant leaving the rows of modest, tidy bungalows, going past the Beacon Hotel at the intersection of the highway, passing the shops and restaurants on the side of the North Hill, going over the Bow River on the Centre Street Bridge, with its imperious British lions, through Chinatown to the CPR station, with its freight sheds, and past the Palliser Hotel, the city's most princely building. To go south on Centre Street was to find a boy's paradise: trout fising in the Bow, pool halls and boxing gyms, restaurants crowded with cowboys and soldiers, and the zoo.

The second avenue out of Tuxedo was a trackless one, going eastward down the hill behind the house and about a kilometre across the open prairie grasses to Nose Creek, where Ralph and Lynn fished for suckers, looked for duck eggs and found arrow points and tepee rings from the not-so-distant past when this had been a sheltered wintering-over site and buffalo-hunting camp for the Peigan. The boys loved to ramble along Nose Creek and up the rampart of Nose Hill to picnic at Split Rock, a huge glacial erratic worn to a shiny sheen by the buffalo that used it as a scratching post.

Nose Hill, named for an incident in which a Peigan cut off the nose of his unfaithful wife, is a river- and glacier-carved abutment sharply rising 100 m (350 feet) above the creek. There are Blackfoot buffalo kill sites, campgrounds and medicine wheels eight thousand years old on Nose Hill, and the boys could look for porcupine and long-tailed weasels or stalk the grazing mule deer and coyotes. Harriers, merlins, kestrels, Swaison's and red tail hawks and the occasional peregrine falcon scoured the skies and argued with magpies and crows over the prime nesting sites in the aspens and willows of the draws carved into the hill. At night the great horned owls hunted for rabbits and mice, and the breezes carried the scents of wild rose and fireweed back down the creek and up the hill to the window of Ralph's bedroom.

Nose Hill became Ralph's school of nature and refuge from the confusing world of adulthood, where his parents were increasingly at odds with one another and a deep unhappiness was taking over the household. There are two sides to every marriage breakup. Florence continued to be brooding, and Philip had no capacity to deal with conflict or with close feelings. He was away a great deal. He worked on construction projects, spent a lot of time in the boxing gym and was involved in semi-professional wrestling. When Philip and Florence fought, they fought bitterly and had no idea how to cope with one another.

When Ralph was just five years old, his parents split up and his father moved to a house on the west side of the downtown core. Initially,

Florence kept the boys and the house on 1st Street NE and got a job as a waitress in a lunch joint called the Blue Derby Café. Philip stayed in Calgary for two years and then, deciding, "it would be best for all concerned if I got out of town," he moved to Edmonton.[1]

For a time as she struggled to adjust, Florence drifted and her life became uprooted and turbulent. Florence had a difficult time being a single mother. As an adult, Ralph described the years until he was seventeen and joined the Royal Canadian Air Force as "pillar to post." Without warning he would be moved from one household to another.[2] His grandparents, Harry and Christine Harper, and his Uncle Ralph began to take more and more responsibility for his upbringing. His mother married a train engineer named Gordon MacBeth, and moved to Rocky Mountain House, a major CNR trans-mountain facility, and Ralph spent a couple of years there.

He also spent two years with his father in Edmonton. It was a Hemingwayesque experience. They fished together and went to the boxing gym above the beer parlour in the old Alberta Hotel on Jasper Avenue. "You had to kick the cockroaches out of the ring before you worked out," Philip recalls. Ralph went to his father's wrestling matches and earned some silver as a water boy. He asked his father to teach him how to box; on Saturday after Saturday, he pulled the gloves onto his pasty pre-adolescent hands and doggedly plodded around the ring. "But he was just no good at it," Philip says. "To be a boxer, you have to have a killer instinct, and face it, Ralph just liked people too much."[3]

With his father, Ralph received his first, tentative introduction to politics. Philip never discussed politics with the boy, but politics seeped into his house through his long-standing friendship with Alf Hooke, now the member of the legislature from Rocky Mountain House and the closest thing to a rebel in the cabinets of Premier Ernest C. Manning. Hooke never gave up the fundamentals of the Social Credit faith. During the Aberhart years, he was a shadowy figure behind a caucus insurgency involving men who thought the premier was drifting away from the strict principles of the movement. He became alienated from Aberhart's successor, Ernest Manning, when, according to Hooke, Manning abandoned the orthodoxy to become simply conservative. Hooke served as a valuable counterbalance to Manning, holding onto much of the government's support with unrepentant rural Albertans who wanted to bust the monopoly of the banks, institute the Prosperity Certificates, the "funny money" promised in 1935, and rewrite the Canadian constitution so that the province could become the master of its own fiscal destiny. Hooke ultimately became a grand old man of the party and toyed with, but rejected, the idea of running to replace Manning in 1968.

In those two precious years living with his father, the impressionable

Ralph Klein absorbed the idea that the maverick of the Social Credit party and its apostle of fiscal conservatism was admirable and trustworthy and that he was the model of what a responsible politician should be. After Ralph became the environment minister in Premier Don Getty's government, a month before Alf Hooke died at the age of eight-nine, Philip took him to the legislature to meet his son. A former Social Credit cabinet minister and now a caucus mate with the younger Klein, Ray Speaker, stood in the House to introduce Hooke and Philip to the assembly. "It was the best kind of tribute, and it made an old man's day," Philip says.[4]

Philip also remarried; Ralph has a half brother, Darren, and half sister, Cindy, from that second family. Throughout his adult years, Ralph has spent every New Year's Eve in Edmonton with Philip and his family.

During his formative years, however, the anchor for Ralph was his grandparents' home, back in Tuxedo Park, because Harry, Christine and his Uncle Ralph provided a reliable emotional anchor; he could always rely on them. From time to time, he and his brother, Lynn, were together there and Ralph became the younger child's protector and keeper. Lynn did not cope as well as his older brother with the family's unhappy circumstances. He became a hellion, and Ralph would frequently cover up for him and take the rap for his misdeeds.

Ralph learned to mask his feelings because he found he could not deal well with people close in. Like his father, he was transparently warm-hearted and gregarious, but he shared his mother's darker, brooding side. To those around him, he was the easygoing leader of the pack, its centre of gravity. He organized the things the boys in his circle did: the fishing expeditions, the hikes up the creek, the pranks and playing marbles in the schoolyard.

He entered school the year after his parents split, at Buchanan Elementary on Centre Street, three blocks from 3401 - 1st Street. Later, when he lived with his grandparents, he attended Tuxedo Park Elementary. He graduated to Crescent Heights High School, where he completed his junior matriculation.

At school, he showed his inscrutable side, keeping his feelings and his counsel to himself. "He was an unassuming student; not that he was any trouble, he just didn't seem to have much to offer the world," recalled his physical education teacher, Ran White. "You know, we spent a lot of time trying to predict where a student would end up, to help them get there. Boys like Ralph are proof that we didn't do a very good job of it. He was completely unpredictable."[5]

What was really going on inside Ralph Klein's head as he slogged through his phys ed classes under Ran White's tutelage was an adolescent longing for a haven, a secure place where the world would be orderly and he could learn discipline. In November 1959, after his seventeenth birthday, he quit school to join the Royal Canadian Air Force and become a fighter pilot.

In 1960, the RCAF was the romance service for young men and women seeking a career in the military. As the role of the other branches of the military diminished, post-Korea, the exigencies of the Cold War brought the air force to its apex, appropriately marked in 1959 with the combined thirty-fifth birthday of the RCAF and the fiftieth anniversary of heavier-than-air flight in Canada. Aircraft were a part of the landscape of Ralph's early years; Split Rock and Nose Hill looked down over McCall Field (now the Calgary International Airport), a base for bush pilots, military flights and TransCanada Airlines. The city had been an important British Commonwealth Air Training Plan centre in the Second World War and boasted a military airfield, Lincoln Park, on the Sarcee army base.

In 1959, no boy of sixteen could not be enchanted by the Red Knight, a solo RCAF acrobat flyer barnstorming the Prairies with his devil-red T-33 (later a newly minted Tutor) jet aircraft. Around the same time, for the golden anniversary of the 1 km (half-mile) flight of the Silver Dart pioneer biplane in Nova Scotia, the air force established the Golden Hawks, a precision team of Sabre-5 fighters, which flew the air shows and garnered hundreds of column inches of newspaper coverage. The heart-stopping displays of the Red Knight and the Golden Hawks encouraged hundreds of young men to join the air force, just as the air marshals had intended, and in the nation's summer skies of 1959 the RCAF reached the pinnacle of its post-war ascendency. Klein was one of the many young men swept up by the sheer excitement of it all.

The air force was serious business. In the year Klein joined, the federal government made the controversial decision to arm it with BOMARC missiles, which were made to carry nuclear warheads, as part of the North American Defence system. In an even more contentious judgement, Prime Minister John Diefenbaker also decided to scrap the Canadian-developed, futurist AVRO CF-105 Arrow jet. Although the seeds of the air force's decline lay in those decisions, for boys of Ralph's age, the disputations simply underscored the desirability of joining up.

What attracted Klein the most, however, was the prospect of belonging to something important and stable. Recruiting posters promised "an adventurous life in service to Canada ... the finest in aviation and executive training ... [and] flying experience that develops leadership and a high sense of responsibility." Ralph had a nacsent sense of public service and leadership; executive status and high responsibility appealed to him. The posters also promised that he would, "share the comradeship that comes with teamwork."[6] Perhaps the air force could replace the family that had been taken away from him, a dozen years earlier, when his parents separated.

The RCAF hustled Klein through the Personnel Selection Unit and his twelve weeks as a flight cadet in pre-flight school, where he was introduced to aviation mathematics, physics and aerodynamics, air crew knowledge and officer development. Then Leading Aircraftman Ralph Klein was posted to Advanced Flight School at Portage-la-Prairie, Manitoba, for thirty weeks of training in Harvard and T-33s, the T-birds that the Red Knight so successfully promoted.

As things turned out, the RCAF was Klein's first and only career failure. The sticking point was the personal discipline that he had so avidly sought by joining. He told his father that "it was not the life for him."[7] His officers speculated that a chip on his shoulder, carried over from the emotional chaos of his boyhood, caused him to be at loggerheads with regimented, regulated life. He developed a reputation for being undisciplined and in conflict with both his superiors and other leading aircraftmen At the end of flying school he washed out.

Serving in the RCAF was probably not time wasted; he went away an adolescent, driven by dreams, and came back to Calgary a man, motivated by adult concerns—to marry, to raise a family and to make something of himself. He had learned lasting lessons, such as the meaning of the badge and motto of Training Command Headquarters, under which the prairie flying schools were organized and administered. The badge features two torches issuing from an astral crown, symbols of learning and leadership. The motto is *Exercendum usque ad optimum*: One must train to the highest standards. Klein absorbed the ideal; in every subsequent step in his career, he sought to master new skills and then to be the best. Although he was easygoing by nature, the air force taught him to compete.

He was not offered a commission, and he returned home to Calgary, at the end of 1960; he had just turned eighteen. He brought with him his first serious girl friend, Hilda May Hepner, whom he had met in Portage-la-Prairie. They were married on April 29, 1961, in Calgary. The marriage lasted only ten years. Ralph and Hilda had two children, Bradley, born in November 1961, and Angela, born in February 1964.

The Kleins lived for several years in Tuxedo, and for a time Lynn, who was still a student, stayed with them. As the marriage grew increasingly rocky and there were periodic separations, they moved around the city, never staying in a neighbourhood for more than a couple of years. Initially, Hilda waitressed at the downtown Caravan Motor Hotel, a place of faded respectability known in the oil patch as the Heartbreak Hotel because it was designated for extramarital assignations between bosses and secretaries. She was determined to improve herself, however, and eventually joined the Royal Bank of Canada, where she has made a career.

In the meantime, Klein needed to complete his education; without senior matriculation, his only choice was to attend private business college. It was a common choice for men returning from the services, young people leaving the farm and city kids without the money or qualifications to attend Mount Royal College or the Normal School for teachers. He enrolled at the Calgary Business College in the Canadian Vocational Training Program, where he studied accounting and business administration.

There were three commercial training schools in the city, owned by local business families; "Old man" George Henderson's was the most prominent and bore his name, Henderson's Business College. The Hussey family owned the other two. When Ralph signed up at the Calgary Business College, its founder, Francis Hussey, was retired, which undoubtedly made his life easier, because his wife, Elizabeth, preferred to run things her way. Her son, Michael, with whom she differed, had set up his own shop, the Modern Business College, which he and his wife, Lucille, ran.

Many of the teaching staff at all three establishments were part-time and not well paid; therefore the requirements for getting a job were informal. Mrs. Hussey was a sound judge of ability and saw in Klein a young man who should not waste his life clerking in some accounting office. She offered him a job as a teacher. He was a success with her students, and eventually she made him principal. In addition to teaching and paperwork, he recruited students and supervised their post-graduation job placements.

Klein was a favourite of the students; he communicated clearly and simply, listened attentively, responded helpfully to students' problems and put in extra hours to assist students, and they trusted him. He worked doggedly to get his students jobs. Judy Howard, now a public relations consultant, went to see Klein when she decided to drop out of accounting. He told her that she had one of the highest IQs they had ever seen around there and asked her if there were something they could offer her. Although she quit, the concern Klein showed made a deep impression. When he ran for mayor in 1980, although she had had no contact with him for fifteen years, she was one of the first half dozen to walk into his campaign office to volunteer, and she became a charter member of what would eventually become the Klein Gang.

In spite of his success at the Calgary Business College, after three years Klein was restless. The low pay was one issue. He had also gone as far as he could go, and he had greater ambitions. One day in 1963, Klein saw a posting at the Canada Manpower employment centre for a director of public relations in the Southern Alberta Division office of the Canadian Red Cross. He lined up a letter of reference from Gordon Grayston, locally a well-known and popular professional boxer who was a pal of his father's, and applied for the job.

Like the RCAF, the Red Cross offered an opportunity to serve. And it was part of the mainstream, raising more than $1 million in its high-profile annual Southern Alberta financial campaign. These were attractive features for Klein. His credentials with the college stood him in good stead for a rather vague job description and the equally vague qualifications it demanded. After a brief review, he was hired.

<u>3</u>

The Invention
of Ralph Klein

We had a lovely magic time ...

—ERNEST HEMINGWAY,
A MOVEABLE FEAST

There are two Ralph Kleins, the public one and the private one. At the Red Cross, in 1963, Klein began the process of inventing the public man. During the next six years, including three at the Calgary United Appeal, he grew in confidence, mastered the art of media management, connected with the highest circles in the city and learned how the invisible networks of power in the small-town milieu of Alberta's cities works.

The rebelliousness that abbreviated his air force career was caged, controlled and channelled into energetic work habits; he became a workaholic. To his friends and Red Cross associates, he was also the gregarious, open and happy guy, the man in control of his life who liked to start and lead the parties, even if he had a disconcerting habit of drifting off to sleep after the first few drinks. He dropped a curtain over his private life. His marriage was failing but few in his professional circle ever knew or guessed.

Six years can be a lifetime for a young man in his twenties, and his growth as a public figure took a long time. At first, he was simply as green as grass. He inherited the job at the Red Cross from Mary Biner, an independent, hard-nosed young single mother and journalist. She was moving on to the newsroom of the *Calgary Herald*, where she became a women's page columnist. Mary was a remarkable person: tough-talking when necessary, astute about public affairs, able to drink and smoke with the most case-hardened denizen of the Press Club. Yet she was moved by a higher set of values than was common in the shabby newsrooms of what was still, in newspaper terms, a prairie backwater.

She was Klein's first important mentor. Burdened with the responsibility of aged parents and preoccupied with her child, after a few years she scarcely remembered the things she had done for Klein and was more surprised than most that he had been so successful. But she introduced him to the Calgary media. He never forgot her kindness and thoroughness in showing him around to the small establishment of men and women, volunteers and professionals, who operated Calgary's charitable establishment. She "compelled" him to join the Canadian Public Relations Society.

Red Cross management quickly recognized that Ralph couldn't write at the level needed for the endless stream of news releases on water safety, fund-raising canvasses and blood banks. Biner put in a quiet word to Merv Anderson, a *Calgary Herald* editor responsible for training, and Klein was enrolled in the newspaper's in-house writing course for beginning reporters. Klein never satisfied his bosses with his writing, although his news releases quickly became clearly written and smoothly styled; they found him too young to be credible. When he moved on to the United Appeal, it was, in part, because he was weary of the endless editing and rewriting to which his news releases were subjected.

At the Red Cross Gil Gilmet, the director of water safety and later the Alberta commissioner, took the inexperienced Klein under his wing, making made sure that he obtained experience in all aspects of the Red Cross's communications program. Klein was put in charge of the library of 150 films available for public bookings. He was also dragged along to spend weekends with water safety volunteers, learning for the first time of the kind of dedication, and camaraderie, that could be found in the world of civic affairs.

He was asked to make speeches and presentations. During this time, he was beginning to establish his reputation for having trouble getting up in the morning, perhaps because of his troubled home life. One Sunday morning he rushed into a volunteer seminar having forgotten to put on his belt. He was talking about something that excited him, and as he characteristically got swept up in what he was saying, he began to wave his arms, windmill style, and his pants began to slide down. Without dropping a syllable, he grabbed his pants with one hand while his other hand continued to flail. Pretty soon both hands were knifing the air, and again, his pants slipped and he grabbed at them without skipping a beat.

This happened several more times, until the members of the audience could no longer contain their giggles. "Hey, Ralph," said one of his listeners, "where's your belt?" For a long time, "Hey, Ralph, where's your belt?" was the inside joke at Red Cross House.

Gilmet also introduced Klein to the way small-town Alberta operated. Until the Red Cross, his only experience of small towns had been the short time he had stayed with his mother and her second husband at Rocky Mountain House and his time off the base at Portage-la-Prairie.

"He was a city boy when I first knew him," Gilmet recalled. "Shortly after he came to work with us, I took him on the road, and we got to High Prairie [a northern community in the Peace Country].

"I asked him, 'Do you know where the weekly paper is located?' He said that he didn't. 'Let's go look for it,'" Gilmet said to his young protégé. They found the publisher, and his small Webb offset, in the basement of his home. It was Klein's first wide-eyed inkling of such a world. "Before High Prairie, he'd get frustrated because his releases would go out and he'd never hear back from these small town papers. He learned that day that everything isn't big city dailies and one call definitely doesn't do it all," Gilmet said.

For all his naiveté, Klein worked hard, had good judgement and learned to get good results. He learned to be diplomatic with his superiors and with the community leadership. He developed the knack of how to "hype" a story—to work up media enthusiasm, particularly when news merit was absent.

The kind of work he did depended on an ability to make doing good seem like a lot of fun to volunteers and contributors, and Ralph was good at celebrations. He developed the philosophy "Have some fun, do some good," which became the mantra of his political campaigns.[1]

He also learned about controversy. In 1964, the Alberta Chapter of the Canadian Cancer Society was nearly ruined when a new executive secretary blew the whistle on the misappropriation of $191,000 and a popular member of his staff was prosecuted. The executive secretary was fired, essentially for breaking the "old boys" code decreeing that that kind of dirty linen in a charitable organization should be laundered privately to avoid embarrassing the prominent professionals and business figures on the volunteer board.

Calgary's normally complacent media, which were usually willing to do as they were told by the city's establishment and not make a fuss about this sort of thing, gingerly pursued the matter. Although by later standards the coverage was mild, it took a lot of time and effort to smooth over the relationship between the newsrooms and the "ivy league" agencies, including the Red Cross. For Klein, it was an early taste of the potential for the media to shape public events and set the community agenda, although the potential lay fallow until the 1970s, when Klein participated in detaching the media's behaviour in such circumstances from the fiats of the privileged and influential.

As the months at the Red Cross passed, Klein was restless and uncertain about his future. He had no career plan, just a vague, ill-defined commitment to the community. The Red Cross seemed to him a big, stodgy organization with too much that shaped it taking place outside Alberta in, to Klein, a hazy place called the national headquarters. He was frustrated because the commissioner's office didn't seem to take him very seriously, always second-guessing his work and redoing his news releases, even after three years of experience had turned him into a passable scribe. He was also ambitious and more confident of his prospects than in the past.

In 1966, Aileen Ellis, who in 1964 was the first woman to head the public relations unit of a Canadian United Appeal organization, resigned from the Calgary United Appeal, the omnibus public fund-raiser for thirty-five social agencies in southern Alberta. Klein moved across the street, figuratively speaking, to take her place. In Calgary, the Red Cross and the United Appeal were Bobbsey twin organizations and dominated the secular charitable sector. They raised, combined, $2.5 million a year, had interlocking boards and depended on the same group of community leaders to oversee their affairs. In effect, because of the close relationship between the two agencies, and because the United Way was the senior, more prominent organization and the staff better paid, Klein's appointment to direct the United Appeal's public relations was a promotion.

He now rubbed shoulders with everyone who mattered in Calgary's establishment: the heads of the oil and land development industries, the railway and trucking bosses, the intelligentsia of the university and colleges, churches, the Calgary Exhibition and Stampede, the school boards, city hall and the media. He had access to the best professionals in advertising and public relations, who volunteered their time to help him plan and execute his ideas. The United Way became the vantage point from which Klein got to know how the town really worked, who were the movers and shakers, how the dots connected to the invisible points of power at the highest level of the community.

Less impeded in his decisions, he made an immediate, positive impression as a "comer" in the communications business. "He was very good at what he did, very professional, and knew the game, knew how to use the media," remembers Gordon Reid, then with Foster Advertising and later an independent consultant. "The corporate and institutional participation was extraordinary, at a level that's gone now."

The autumn donations campaign was full of pep rallies and crazy events: executive bed races, powder puff football challenges, Little Miss United Way, combined Boy Scouts and military parades. "The spirit was incredible," Reid reminisced. "Klein hyped it to heaven, and the media unconditionally loved everything he did."

In 1967, summer lingered through September as the United Appeal put the finishing touches on frenetic plans for the October blitz to raise $1.365 million. The harvest moon hung low over the high school football games played at downtown Mewata Stadium, the pigskin temple in a city that still took the game only slightly less seriously than religion. In those mellow, vanished years, Calgary was still a city of quiet streets at night and the smell of leaves burning in back yard incinerators.

The feel-good month that was about to unfold, with its crisp, sun-drenched mornings, long, hot afternoons and nights filled with good music, good food and good booze, were to make the strongest possible impression on Klein. They became the source of much nostalgia, representing a place that as a politician he wanted to restore. It was, he said, "one big band wagon; the kind of place where you'd want to be born, live and die, without ever stepping a foot beyond the city limits."[2]

On September 21, he hosted a reception in the Malt Room of the Calgary Brewery for thirty reporters, editors and news directors. It was the traditonal advance thank-you to those on whom he would be relying to beat the drum. He was the organ grinder and they were the tame monkeys, and it took a lot of beer and camaraderie to dress up the relationship, to make it appear less crass.

A week later, four days before the kick-off on the steps of city hall, with the mayor, the Catholic bishop, the chief of police, Miss United Way and the oil executive chairman for the year, Klein wrote, in what had become his deliberately old-boy, hayseed prose style, "I think we are in for a darn fine campaign."[3]

After the October 2 formal launch, Klein disappeared into an accelerating blur. Every noon hour, downtown, there were street promotions patterned after Calgary's legendary Stampede Breakfasts in July. At the two local television stations, he was managing a revolving door of news-hour live interviews with the local prominenti, who had to be briefed, and their shaking hands calmed, before going on camera.

He attended powder puff football games, assisted an amateur, matronly chorus line that jazzed up half time at the Calgary-Vancouver Canadian Football League game. He sent thank-you letters to school-children who forwarded their pennies and nickels to his office. His friend Sam Switzer, a successful hotelier, threw a party in the revolving dining room at the top of the Sheraton Summit and donated the cover charge to the Appeal. Now that was a party! The Summit was a dance and dining club to which, by common agreement, oil men did not take their wives. To hype the event, Klein wrote a press release promising, "This may be the most exciting night of your life."[4] Because of the radio plugs, a few men broke with tradition and brought their wives, but that put no damper on the celebrations or shenanigans of the lampshade-on-the-head variety. The following weekend, to balance off the mischief, Klein arranged for most synagogues and churches to plug the United Way from the pulpit.

On October 31, he organized the news conference that announced the campaign's target had been exceeded and $1.385 million raised. He wrapped up with the Have You Been Missed? radiothon, during which Calgarians called in belated pledges and the members of the city's three major car clubs toured the streets, picking up the dough.

Klein participated in two full United Appeal campaigns, in 1967 and 1968, from the spring news conference to announce the fiscal goal, through the summer buildup, to the winter follow-up to tell how the money was used in various agencies. After his 1967 triumph, however, he had only one more important lesson to learn: the use of television production. His mentor was a semi-retired James Lovick & Co. advertising hand, Neville York, who was seasoned in radio, television and film production. A volunteer, York took Klein's job when he left to join CFCN News. Klein schooled his protégé to use images and words to move people, to influence them, to get them to make decisions.

Annually there was a new film to back fund-raising, produced by the U.S. or Canadian federations, or in Western Canada, with a local creation every second or third year. Klein's confidence as a novice documentary producer, and his intimacy with Calgary's commercial television companies, is illustrated in a letter written three months before he resigned. John Meeker, a vice president at British American Petroleum, was the chairman of the public relations committee. Klein wrote him to suggest they obtain a film produced in Regina:

> It was produced specifically for shock and emotional appeal and it has it. The Regina film is exceptionally good and would easily be re-edited to suit our needs. Personally I wouldn't give you two cents for the national film. Last year's was a mundane presentation with absolutely no appeal.
>
> I personally think it is a good idea to have a yearly change in visual material and this year before we make any commitment for expenditures through a professional film company, I would like to feel out the TV stations to see if one of them would want to do a film for a special program, then turn over the production to us, for campaign and public showings.[5]

Klein was now seen as a young man with an executive future. He had his entrée, if he wanted it, into the best circles. He did not take it. He had no desire to be a "suit." The corporate world did not nurture his maverick side, and, besides, his ambition now stretched to politics and to television.

The ambition started modestly, as a compulsion for election campaigns. In 1967, he helped Gordon Reid by writing his news releases and

advising him on his media relations in an unsuccessful campaign for a
seat on the school board. "And he wasn't just doing it for me; he'd offer
a hand to anyone he considered a friend," said Reid.

In 1968, Klein volunteered to work for engineer and lawyer Peter
Petrasuk, who was running, in that year of Trudeaumania, as the Liberal
candidate in the Calgary North federal riding. This constituency em-
braced Klein's boyhood home of Tuxedo Park and the schools where he
had earned his education. Now, on his first foray into politics, he found
himself supporting an outsider running an anti-establishment campaign.
Many of his friends were dismayed; they did not hold Petrasuk in high
regard and told Klein he was making an error in judgement about the
man's character. Klein, loyal to a fault, plunged ahead.

Alberta had been the bastion of prairie conservatism since the Second
World War. In 1968, Robert Stanfield was the new Tory leader; in Calgary, John Diefenbaker was the prevailing deity. Tories joked that Liberals were protected only by the hunting laws that prohibited the shooting of endangered species.

Petrasuk was a tough Ukrainian kid from Calgary's northeast end.
His neighbourhood, Bridgeland, was even lower down the pecking order
than Tuxedo Park. He said there were two careers for boys like him,
the police force or jail. He had started his career as a bellboy in the
Palliser Hotel and loved to tell scandalous tales of the oil men who after
the 1947 Leduc oil discovery virtually took the place over as the base
camp from which they built the head offices of the Canadian oil patch.

Petrasuk was a driven man, terrified that he would get no further
in life than his boyhood chums. He gained degrees in law and engineering, held a prominent job in a Venezuelan electric utility and returned
to Calgary to build a respected legal practice and, in the 1970s, a successful career as an alderman.

Calgary North was one of the safest Tory seats in Canada. During
the Diefenbaker years, it had been held by the defence minister, Douglas
Harkness. Harkness was a soldier, but the riding had been held, vari-
ously, by lawyers, oil executives and the vaguely employed sons of old
money. Petrasuk, the poor bohunk from the river valley, was as much
of a social and political outsider as a man could be on the North Hill.
His campaign as a Liberal defied the political laws of gravity.

He did not recruit Klein because he was a Liberal. In fact, no one
was quite sure of Klein's politics. Rather, his work for the Red Cross
and United Appeal had earned him a reputation as an excellent public
relations manager. After the campaign started, he quickly took control
of the communications portfolio. Klein, said Petrasuk, was a natural political organizer and campaigner. He managed the media flawlessly,

wrote exceptionally good materials and handled communications problems quickly and painlessly.

The Liberals were on the losing side in Calgary North, not surprisingly, given the riding's history and Petrasuk's outsider background. But the campaign taught the young public relations manager valuable lessons. Charm and ability had limits, including the city's social strictures and its popular prejudice against Liberals. He discovered that he didn't like to lose, and thereafter he would not pursue lost causes. When the provincial Liberals courted Mayor Klein, in 1988, for a career in provincial politics, the lessons of 1968 were a factor in his decision to become a Tory. Maverick he might be, but he would dance with the high-brow devil to win.

The Liberals gained four of Alberta's twenty seats, including Calgary South, the swing riding in the city in 1968. The next four years were a brief moment in the sun for the province's Grits; when Prime Minister Trudeau tumbled into a minority government in 1972, he lost all his MPs in the province. Through the long Liberal drought of the 1970s, Ralph turned up occasionally to assist federal candidates who had become friends, including Nick Taylor, later the leader of the provincial wing of the party. As a newsman, Klein worked in a Prairie media culture, founded by men like John Dafoe of the *Winnipeg Free Press*, that allowed journalists to quietly assist friends in political campaigns.

After the highly successful 1967 United Appeal campaign, Ralph decided that he needed to round out his public relations skills and that he ought to spend a few months working in a news room. He began to distribute his résumé but invariably was told that he lacked experience or that he wouldn't want to take the cut in pay he would face. He let things slide until the summer of 1968, after the Petrasuk campaign, and then resumed his search for a media job in earnest.

Once again he was rebuffed, until he contacted Joe Hutton, the news director at CFCN-TV. Hutton was one of the men turning Calgary journalism on its head, as the hoary news room guard changed for young, aggressive men and women. When Hutton agreed to hire Klein, initially to read farm reports and the news for radio, he introduced Ralph to city's top news team and its first truly independent operation, free from the constraints of serving the business and political elite.

4

Epiphany

*He could feed his heart with the
heart of a continent,
Insatiate, how noble a wounded
animal,
Who sought for his wounds the
balsam of adventure ...*

—DOUGLAS LEPAN, FROM
"COUREURS DE BOIS"

T he village of Gleichen, Alberta, lies several kilometres south of
the TransCanada Highway on the broad, sweeping plain east of
Calgary. This is dryland country of cattle ranges and enormous
prairie irrigation systems. Gleichen is a white enclave, a reservation town
adjacent to the lands of Alberta's largest community of the Blackfoot—a
First Nation that calls itself the Siksika. More than one hundred years
of European agriculture that has altered the surrounding territory has
bypassed the Blackfoot, who live on the ground of their ancestors, the
terrain virtually unmarked by ten thousand years of civilization.

On the long, hot days of summer, the open plains and the flawless
blue sky take on an ethereal quality. The sudden, severe summer storms,
often accompanied by sheets of relentless hail, contain the voice of a thousand ancient spirits in the wind, in the rain, in the thunder and in the
keening of the hawk and harrier. In the afternoon, one may see an ancient Siksika widow dressed in black, walking on ancient pathways
across the open ground, a mirror of, and a metaphor for, the almost
invisible people who occupy a mere sliver of the once endless land of
their forebears.

The prairie horizons invite and encourage the vision quests, the
coming-of-age rituals for young Blackfoot men that took place during
uncounted generations before the Europeans. Standing on the dry
grasses, feeling the feather of the wind and hearing the cry of the falcon
on a hot spring day, one requires little imagination to embrace the spirit

of the deeply religious and political culture that thrived here in the days of the buffalo.

In 1977, Gleichen was the service centre for the Blackfoot—a source for groceries, gas and a beer in the newly integrated tavern that had recently ended its ban on non-whites. It was a thirsty, forgotten little place, its most prominent building an old mission school. In earlier times, this imposing, three-storey structure had represented the great Catholic hope for Christianizing and anglicizing a new generation of compliant aboriginals, the first step on the road to assimilation. A newer generation of white liberals had turned it into a satellite campus for Calgary's Mount Royal Community College, the better to bring urbanization to the Indian, or the Indian to urbanization. The building also functioned as a recreation centre; on Saturday nights, families gathered here to dance, eat and drink and to let the frustrations of reservation life sometimes spill into fist fights on the vast, dark prairie.

Only an hour's drive from Calgary, this world was more than a century away in human experience. There was for most of this century, really, only one significant point of contact: the Blackfoot were important participants in the Calgary Exhibition and Stampede. The Stampede parade and the Indian Village on the grounds were the one opportunity in the year for the Blackfoot and the other aboriginal groups of southern Alberta to be noticed, respected and honoured for their culture. More often, the young men and women of the Blackfoot left home for the lure of the city to find that their dreams dissolved in the cheap rooming houses and the dowdy beer parlours of Calgary's east end. When the oil boom rocketed Calgary into prosperity and sophistication, its urban Native people were left behind with no education and no opportunity to join the mainstream. The only change that Calgary's new affluence brought to them was access to heroin and cocaine. This was the legacy of an unspoken racism; justice seemed a long time coming.

In 1977, this obscure village became the focal point of a celebration to mark the one hundredth anniversary of Treaty No. 7, through which the ancient territories of the buffalo hunters of southern Alberta and southwestern Saskatchewan had been given over to the Dominion of Canada in exchange for reservation lands and the dubious benevolence of treaty rights. A reenactment of the signing took place on a piece of prairie horizon still called Treaty Flats, with representatives of the Blackfoot, Stoney, Peigan, Blood and Sarcee Nations. Prince Charles, heir to the colonial throne, agreed to attend—fitting because the ceremony would reaffirm a pact made with the Crown that purported to guarantee aboriginal land, education, health and welfare.

It was a splendid event, certainly for the whites who had been the winners in the pact between the Crown and the Indians of Treaty No. 7. At best for the Native Canadians involved it was an opportunity to rise above the daily invisibility of their lives, to demand respect and recognition. The paradox between the promises made a century earlier and the daily lives of the Blackfoot in the city, beset by alcoholism, prostitution, sickness, imprisonment and early death, were obvious to journalists at CFCN-TV in Calgary. It was a field ripe for investigative work.

CFCN, the local CTV affiliate, was a combined radio and television outlet and had the city's top news ratings. The station had a sense of its history, dating back to radio days, as the self-described Voice of the Prairies; William Aberhart broadcasted his religion and his politics on it. One of the station's fortés in the 1970s had become the preparation of prize-winning television documentaries into which many months of effort were often poured. The budgets were generous for a city of Calgary's size and reflected the pride of place that CFCN's management felt.

News director Thompson MacDonald decided to commission a work that would probe how the Blackfoot felt about the past one hundred years of their history and document life under Treaty No. 7. Ralph Klein, who had been at CFCN for eight years, got the assignment. He had good connections with urban aboriginals and a solid reputation for thorough reporting. He had developed into a gritty, street-wise "down and dirty" reporter not likely to be impressed by the rhetoric and fine display intended on the day of the hundredth anniversary.

Klein was assigned a camera man and for several weeks simply disappeared from CFCN's radar screen. It was not unusual for senior newsmen on special assignments to be away at length and to be out of touch in this time before cellular phones. Klein had often vanished while on assignment, always coming back with stories that were worth the wait. Nevertheless, MacDonald began to worry.

Nothing was heard from Klein until he called to say that he was in jail, thrown there by the RCMP to cool down after a brawl in a beer parlour. Klein had developed good contacts and was getting below the surface of life on the reserve. After work one afternoon, he had been invited by a group of his Blackfoot friends to have a few beers. Another white man had come into the tavern and begun to take Polaroid photos.

Klein's hosts explained that this man was a government employee and regularly recorded who was spending time and money drinking. The newsman saw a story and confronted the official. Sticking a microphone into the man's face, Klein introduced himself as a reporter and asked what the fellow was doing with the camera.

There are various accounts of the next few seconds and who threw the first punch, but a fight quickly erupted; Klein and the nameless bureaucrat were the chief protagonists. The RCMP decided that swift

paternal justice was best; several of the pugilists, including Kle
the night at the Queen's expense to sober up and cool off.

The incident reassured MacDonald that Klein was doing his job and
might even get to the bottom of the story, and so he left him to get on
with it. Something much more important than writing and producing a
documentary was going on in Klein's life during those long weeks at
Gleichen, however. In a manner of speaking, he got religion.

As his research progressed, he opened himself up in an unexpectedly
personal manner to Blackfoot religious, linguistic and cultural life. While
he was filming, he was also being initiated into the worship and ritual
of his new friends. He was given a spiritual adviser and introduced to
the central ceremonies of the Siksika, including the sweat lodges, where
the men spent long hours meditating and praying, and the ritual of burning the sweet grass, which formed an important part of the prayer life
of the Blackfoot. He began to study the language and the tribal traditions
of his hosts. In the rather ecumenical fashion that suited the Blackfoot
tradition, he adopted portions of their beliefs.

The documentary was an incisive and moving portrayal of the gap
between white intentions and aboriginal realities on the treaty reservations of Alberta. It aired on June 6, 1977, and Klein's tautly written script
narrated with empathy by Alberta's best-known news anchor, Darrel
Janz, ran the gamut of emotions. The words seethed with anger as Janz
reported on extended families of twenty-five crammed into battered
shacks as part of a parsimonious housing program. In his writing, Klein
vividly captured the scars of a lifetime inflicted by the nuns of the mission
school on Sunday "pay day" when children were paid with a lash on the
behind for each time they spoke or sang a song in their own language.
He was coldly indignant as he unfolded the frustration of Native con-
stables patronized by the authorities, who would not allow them to carry
service revolvers, as he described the sun dance ceremony, lost forever
when it was outlawed by the Europeans, and as he recounted the disap-
pearance of half the sacred medicine bundles of the band's secret societies.
And he injected the humour of the old Siksika legends of Napi, the
trickster whose Paul Bunyon–like incarnation is said to be buried on the
band's land.

Klein found the highest of human hope in the graduation of eighteen
young men and women from the Old Sun College and the acceptance
of the elderly into the tavern to which they had formerly been refused
admission. "These are good people," bartender Tony Roman said on
camera to Klein. Like everyone else, they just want to be treated like
human beings.

"Once these people were prisoners on their own land, requiring a
permit to leave until the early 1940s," Klein wrote with barely disguised

contempt. "I would like to have the last hundred years back," a young man named Rex Catface tells Klein, who concluded that had Chief Crowfoot known what was to come, he never would have signed the treaty in 1877.

Klein's political insights were both unexpected from so young a man and also annoying and disturbing to the organizers of the hundredth anniversary celebration, but the deepest and most moving portions of the documentary had to do with religion. When he asked one holy man, Nat Owlchild, to whom he prayed, and was his God Anglican, Catholic or Mormon, Owlchild replied, "I pray to the Creator. He made the sun and the moon; he is the one that made us to live in the world. Of course, we did not know that He had sent his son to die for us until the Spaniards came in the fourteen hundreds and the fifteen hundreds." Pressed by Klein to explain himself in conventional theological terms, Owlchild said, "My own religion . . . is not publicized. I can't speak it, but I know it."

Klein was finding a religion of which he, too, could not speak. He filmed the Blackfoot praying, and he filmed their ceremonial sites, but not their ritual, because they forebade the documenting of such activities as the sweat lodge. The point at which Klein's journalism and his personal response to the Blackfoot met was recorded and included in the documentary. He had eaten a modest lunch of beans and bannock with a man in his simple, spartan kitchen. After the meal, the two stood at the wood cook stove, both dressed in denims and plaid shirts, as the man gave thanks and sprinkled sweet grass on the hot stove top until it smoldered. Klein was absolutely silent and visibly on the verge of tears. The silence spilled over into the film, and it seemed that there was a third presence, the Creator, standing with them in the quiet.

Whereas some politicians boast of being the honorary chief of an aboriginal nation, Klein never brags of his experience or of the lifelong bond he formed in those weeks with the Blackfoot. Outside of the film script he kept the experience private, sharing it only with his closest friends. There is nothing honorary or symbolic about his relationship to the Siksika. He continued to visit them for spiritual instruction and to gain greater skill in the language They had given him a life-shaping experience that put a foundation under, and brought balance and purpose to, a previously rootless and aimless life.

The message of the documentary and the essence of Klein's epiphany was his encounter with a form of spirituality and a connection with the Creator that he could accept and practise. Equally important, the practice of this new faith demanded political involvement, and Klein set out on what proved to be an agonizing pilgrimage of three years to fulfill this new obligation.

The epiphany transformed a politically passive journalist, a professional observer of events, into a man of action committed to shaking up politics. In the weeks and months following Gleichen, sparked by quiet outrage at the inequities, unfairness, irresponsibility and human waste of contemporary political culture, Klein the politician emerged.

In retrospect, Ralph Klein's journey to power was inevitable with his first news assignment to cover civic affairs, shortly after he arrived at CFCN in 1969. He had a short apprenticeship to learn which buttons to push on a tape recorder and how the news room functioned. Then Klein was on the street, filing stories.

Before the 1970s, reporters in Calgary were summonsed and sent at the discretion of the city's powerful and influential. In the post-war economic boom, reporters were uncompetitive; socially they were captives, and their work was easily influenced by the free drink, the free lunch, the Christmas remembrance, the junket, the five-dollar bill wrapped in the press release. They spent most of their time with their competitors; they got each other to press conferences, covered for one another when assignments overlapped, shared copy and the beer cooler in the city hall press room and ate lunch together at noon in the back room of the Modern Café, half a block from city hall. The reporter in Calgary was expected to mediate between those on high and the unquestioning public—to be a ministering angel of the establishment. The reward was to be a favourite bauble on the mantlepiece of the privileged, to have access to the fringe of power.

The great media proprietors of the city—publisher Max Bell of the *Albertan* and broadcaster H. Gordon Love of *The Voice of the Prairies* (CFCN) were important businessmen first and communicators second. The news room was expected to march to the drumbeat of commerce and the community. In the late sixties, however, Max Bell and Gordon Love were at the end of their lives and influence.

A new CFCN executive named Ted Chapman arrived to question and challenge the order of things. To command respect and to meet its responsibilities, the television news should be vivid, exciting and provocative, Chapman said. Reporters should be aggressive and persistent; they should no longer respect the taboos and dictates of the city's social, commercial and political masters.

Klein went to work at CFCN in the midst of the transition and was assigned to the city beat in time to begin reporting on the new mayor, Rod Sykes, an anti-establishment politician who bulldozed to power through barricades erected by the powerful and privileged men who maintained city hall as a quiet club.

The city beat focussed on municipal politics but included the whole range of civic affairs: crime and police stories, school and hospital boards, the courts, the communities. Klein proved to be a savvy apprentice. He liked the street and was quick to gain people's confidence, so his network of contacts grew.

His best work came in long, gritty pieces of research on the urban underclass, the rejects and the outcasts of a rapidly expanding city. He spent weekends with outcast motorcycle gangs, producing clear, unambiguous news documentary material. He got to know "the often despairing life of booze and petty crime that begins at the city limit" for young Natives migrating from the surrounding reserves. He reported on prostitution, the drug trade and gambling with the insight provided by a network of sources that included police detectives, madames, drug kingpins, social workers, clergymen and pimps.

His reporting on the political struggle to save Chinatown from destruction in the name of urban renewal overturned a racial taboo that had long infected the media. White people might go to Chinatown for the local colour, but they assumed that the main purpose of the community was to hide illegal immigrants, promote illicit gambling and protect secret drug rings. For too many people, there was just enough drug-related prostitution to confirm the rumours. Chinatown was socially unacceptable, but Klein built strong and highly visible relationships with its leaders and shaped a more accurate and generous view of the Chinese people.

He paid a price for his interests. Other reporters gossiped about Klein's relationships with his sources. The bikers, for example, frequently turned up at the CFCN news room on Saturday morning to drink coffee, smoke and talk with Klein for hours. He was not abashed to skinny-dip with them at their hot tub parties. Yet he produced biting criticism of the gangs and their drug and prostitution connections, and other reporters could not understand how he could dig so deeply into the seamy side—living and partying with the gangs so intimately—without compromising himself. The gossip, which he shrugged off, was fuelled by the fact that his beat included downtown beer parlours and the after-hours Chinese restaurants, where he drank rye ordered as "cold tea" and brought to the table in tin pots because Asian proprietors could not get licensed to serve alcohol.

Ralph's biggest indiscretion, however, was to refuse to join the media pack. His status as a rising star at CFCN provoked jealousy; he routinely failed to make the 8:30 A.M. assignment meeting; often during the session, someone would call his home and put him on the speaker phone while he splashed in the tub.

"He ran his own show; he'd disappear and people would say, 'Where's Ralph?' but he'd turn up every afternoon with a story," recalled Grant Howard, a newsman and later a public relations consultant.

"Every news room has a class structure; the thing I noticed first about Ralph is that he wasn't bothered by it, even though he was a rising star."

Klein was generous with younger reporters, helping them as they struggled with their assignments. He developed a few strong friendships, usually with men older than himself, like Andy Philip, the city's dean of radio reporters, who kept a paternal eye on city hall's press core. But he spent a great deal of time away from the cozy, incestuous circle. He worked alone and often disappeared to go fishing; for a long time there was a canoe strapped to his Volkswagen Beetle from early spring to late fall.

Klein's intention to spend a few months in journalism stretched into more than ten years. He honed his political journalism with what was to become characteristic patience. He invested long hours of time and effort to master and then stay on top of the issues. He had time for everyone and anyone connected to civic affairs, including police officers, school board members and hospital administrators.

Although he worked the phone exhaustively, he mostly dealt with people face to face. City hall, the public and separate school boards, the police and the provincial courts were all headquartered on a three-block stretch of Macleod Trail. Most civic affairs journalists seldom ventured far from those comfortable, companionable environs and the nearby St. Louis Hotel. In contrast, Klein built up strong connections throughout the city.

He became well versed in the direction and detail of civic policy and its impact on people's lives. He developed a flawless memory and worked without detailed notes, filing stories with only the sketchiest of scripts. Arcane matters absorbed him, whereas other journalists saw them as incidental and trivial. He once amused his colleagues by reporting on the expropriation of a pet cemetery. They regarded it as a story of no interest to anyone but a small group of eccentrics—until they saw the volume of mail and calls he received in response. At the same time, he began to build, in his reportage, a well-defined portfolio of larger issues. The common topic was the impact of urbanization on people.

The inner city seemed to fascinate him most: Chinatown and the older blue-collar communities of Victoria Park and Inglewood. People who lived in them were without strong representation on council; electoral boundaries weakened their influence on aldermen by pitting them against more prosperous communities in the same ward. Klein became their spokesman; although he detested advocacy journalism, his stories became weighted against the establishment.

In the early 1970s, most political journalists in the city press core were trying to crack open the wheeling and dealing surrounding the very competitive plan to develop a major convention centre. One alderman, the late Tom Priddle, was feeding the media with some substantive leaks and even more speculation.

Klein, who had his own access to inside sources, became concerned that the story would break prematurely, preventing a thorough investigation. One night, he went around to see Mayor Sykes to warn him that the CBC's reporters had been bragging about breaking the story within days, or even hours. Sykes fired off a telegram to the Canadian Radio and Television Commission alleging a media conspiracy. The fallout from the telegram cooled the story.

Klein's role became known to the conspirators. They shunned him completely. One day he arrived at city hall to find that his typewriter in the press room was in pieces and abusive notes had been left on the bulletin board, signed "The Conspiracy." Never again was Klein even close to the mainstream of Calgary's news media. Nor did he seem to care much.

He was once invited by two police officers to break the story of a drug bust in which Mayor Sykes's thirteen-year-old son would be arrested in possession of marijuana; the implication was that the drugs would be planted. Klein tipped off the Sykes family. He eavesdropped on city council, was barred from police department media briefings and was charged with obtaining and publishing the contents of the wiretap of a secret civic commission meeting, but he had his limits, and a drug plant on an innocent kid exceeded them.

Meanwhile, as he became more prominent and respected in the community, his marriage to Hilda was in complete wreckage. Two strong-willed people, they bickered constantly, fed by too many accumulated resentments. He was unfaithful, and they separated several times, signing a separation agreement in early 1970 before one final, unsuccessful reconciliation. The marriage finally broke up in May 1971 and they divorced formally in April 1972. Hilda took custody of Bradley and Angela; Klein began child support payments of $100 a month—12 per cent of his annual gross salary.[1]

Klein remarried shortly afterwards. His second wife, Victoria-born Colleen Evelyn Hamilton, was an accounts clerk with Imperial Oil and a single mother with two daughters, Christine, who was twelve when Colleen married Klein, and Lisa, who was six. Colleen was the survivor of an abusive thirteen-year marriage to Fred Pinder, from St. Boniface, Manitoba. In October 1970, Colleen left home with her children and, in order to obtain a restraining order, swore in an affidavit that Pinder drank heavily, threatened her on at least two occasions with a revolver, beat her, verbally abused her in front of their girls and was frequently unfaithful. The divorce followed a month later.[2]

Until she was able to put her life back together, Colleen was forced to rely on social assistance on at least one occasion. She had grown from these experiences into a tough, compassionate, wise woman who understood the demons that shaped and drove Klein and his gritty journalism. Colleen was more than a survivor—with Klein she was an emotional rock, a perceptive confidant and the linchpin of a tight-knit marriage that was a pact to make good out of life as well as to create a family that astonished people like Philip Klein for its warmth and humanity.

The Kleins had a daughter, Theresa, in 1973. And Colleen began the slow, patient task of settling Klein down; she became his best friend and the stabilizing force in his life, according to Klein's father. Friends watched, somewhat astonished, as she gently moulded him and brought him around to the maturity he would need for public office. Colleen deserved much of the credit for the fact that Klein was receptive to the world he found in the Siksika Nation when he did his 1977 documentary.

When Klein returned to Calgary from his Gleichen epiphany, he entered what his colleagues described as his spiritual phase. He was detached and disengaged, seeming to disdain the ordinary world. He spent hours on the phone, in the news room, conversing in Blackfoot. Briefly, when the 1977 civic election revved up, he considered running for an aldermanic seat but decided not to seek office, at least not yet, and lapsed back into his dreamy world.

Then, at the beginning of 1979, he resumed his pursuit of civic affairs and politics. But he was no longer the "down and dirty" reporter. He spent long hours with Grant Howard and others; he wanted to talk and he needed listeners, sounding boards. He was disturbed that governments were leading people instead of being led by them, in the process destroying people's individuality and sense of responsibility. "It was not power that seemed to interest him, it was a vision of what society could and should be. And he wanted to become someone who led rather than someone who talked about what other people were doing," Howard has said.

"He talked about what was right and what was wrong, about getting the greed factor out of city hall and making people the priority. This was a real shift from digging through garbage cans behind city hall for torn-up bits of scandal. Artists go through phases; suddenly they find peace, and it shows in their work. Nineteen seventy-nine and 1980 were agonizing years for Ralph; he was a man who needed his soul to be soothed. It took politics to do it," Howard observed.

As he swung suspended between his past and his future, boredom and frustration ate at him. Even with Colleen's steady hand, his drinking became a problem, at least for his friends. At the Victoria Park community association Christmas party, in 1978, he arrived late and already inebriated. He became insulting and offensive. One of the aldermen drove him home and walked him to the front door; Colleen was waiting. The next day, the alderman met Klein, who said that the rest of the night had gone badly; he had had a row with Colleen and driven away from the house, only to be picked up by the police, who put him in jail for the rest of the night to sober up. There he got into an altercation with the guards.[3]

He turned up at the city hall press room the next morning begging for coffee, bruised, rumpled and dirty. Characteristically, he suggested that one of his colleagues, radio reporter Candi McLean, accompany him back to the police station, where he was to be processed on an impaired driving charge. "Oh, Ralph," she said, "who would care about that?"[4]

5

The Miracle in October

Who supported me? Why, the vagabonds, misfits and beautiful people.

—RALPH KLEIN

The issue that focussed Klein's frustration in the first half of 1980 was the blockbusting of properties on east 8th Avenue to make way for a new civic centre. The plan was to build an opulent city hall surrounding the historic sandstone clock tower. Alger and his city council had moved to consolidate a land holding covering three city blocks and build a sweeping low-rise structure around a public square. Another two square blocks west of city hall were to be razed and replaced with a grand performing arts centre.

Standing in the way of the ambitious Alger scheme were the brick and sandstone storefronts of a historic quarter of two-storey walk-ups, pawn shops, secondhand furniture stores and bookstores, modest apartments, blue-collar eateries and beer parlours in the downtown. It all had to go. City council had taken only five minutes, in 1978, to authorize the purchase of the five-block area, as Klein said, "without the benefit of a development plan or a social impact study."[1]

For two years, the city's land department ruthlessly broke the landowners one by one. In one case, the department acquired a Salvation Army citadel and leased it to an inner city project that took care of transients. When the boiler broke down, in winter, the city refused to fix it and sent the bulldozers instead. For months the lot was a vacant, windswept piece of dirt, and the homeless and needy were without a haven.

Klein detested the kind of politics he saw in action. "It finally got to the point where I hated even going down to city hall," he said.[2] As the civic centre plan unfolded in the early months of 1980, Klein pondered a response that would be stronger than the objective restraints of journalism allowed him.

Meanwhile, a second issue was developing—the expansion of the city's light rail transit system. The expansion route favoured by the civic administration crossed the river to the university and the burgeoning communities of the city's northwest. A corridor had to be cut through a series of politically alert communities opposing the project, however. The administration was pushing ahead, often covertly, to crush or short-circuit the resistance and get the line built.

Klein saw that no one recognized that political reality should override bureaucratic fiat. The city's oldest, most established residential neighbourhoods were fed up with the pressures of growth and were angry that city council was complying with the land developers, who were making hundreds of millions of dollars by extending Calgary's urban sprawl.

Klein started to write about his ideas in a monthly column in *Calgary Magazine*, a thriving city life magazine that was widely read. The columns are as close to a political testament as exists for Klein, because his electronic journalism has largely evaporated into the ether. Written before he had made the final decision to enter public life, they were prepared without the intervening hand of the minders, handlers and image managers of conventional politics.

The columns, entitled "The City," were the reflections of a political challenger, an outsider disturbing the comfortable status quo. They were deliberately salted with anecdotes about prostitutes and cops, about the mayor hiding secrets in his executive washroom, about destitute urban Indians, about the tricks of investigative journalism. Whereas most prudent, aspiring politicians would avoid expressing their frank opinions, Klein used the columns to shape and test a new political agenda that departed from city hall's accepted wisdom.

He unleashed his anger at the civic administration's vicious blockbusting tactics. "When private developers engage in the practise of blockbusting, there are defences for those being threatened. But when the city itself—armed also with the power of expropriation—becomes involved in blockbusting there is no defence, and that makes it an insidious proposition indeed," he wrote.[3]

He wrote with passionate fury about the pollution of the Bow River. He reported an interview with a long-time fisherman who quit, "vowing never to return," because the smell of the river and of the fish he caught made him sick. "That man is angry, and so are thousands like him. They can't understand how the local politicians were able to ignore something for so long," Klein said.[4] Calgary had been named for the river's clear running water, but the city's inadequate treatment of human sewage had destroyed the recreational value of the river, making the fish inedible and the water unswimmable and creating downstream health threats: kidney infections and prostate cancer.

He dissected transportation planning for the future as the city staggered under the load of its oil-boom growth—but his column was not as dull as the topic. He regaled his readers with the tale of a bus driver who abandoned his vehicle and his passengers in rush hour, after announcing he had had enough of the city's traffic. Klein tried to find reason for optimism—as he usually did in his columns. He urged his readers to take some time to examine the city's efforts to construct better roads and a light rail mass transit system: "you might see a better Calgary down the road," he wrote.[5]

Klein pried beneath the surface, looking for what had gone wrong with the political process. He dissected the electoral reform and wrote gloomily about the high cost of the 1980 mayoralty races. It appeared that the winning candidate would have to outspend rivals; the price tag for the chief magistrate's office would be $100,000.[6]

He gave a witty self-exposé of his investigative techniques for political secrets, describing how city officials ran a Keystone Cops–style investigation to find a news leak for what was in fact a simple case of keyhole eavesdropping. "In retrospect it all seems so ridiculous," he wrote in the column, "but it does point out that the inevitable election talk about freedom of information legislation is mostly bunk. Those running for election usually talk up a storm about open government and the public's right to know. Once elected, however, council members seem satisfied to sit behind closed doors . . ."[7]

Vaclav Havel, the Czech politician, playwright and political philosopher, wrote about this kind of "anti-political" politics, morality and civility in his 1991 *Letni premitani*, published in 1992 in English as *Summer Meditations*. He advocated the practice of politics subordinated to conscience. "Despite the political distress I face every day, I am still deeply convinced that politics is not essentially a disreputable business; and, to the extent that it is, it is only disreputable people who make it so," he wrote.[8]

Havel also put his finger on the qualities that were to make Klein stunningly successful in his first venture into politics. "An education in political science, law, economics, history and culture is an invaluable asset to any politician, but I have been persuaded, again and again, that it is not the most essential asset." Qualities like fellow feeling, the ability to talk to others, insight, the capacity to quickly grasp not only problems but also human character, the ability to make contact, a sense of moderation—all these are immensely more important.

"[A politician] need only be sensitive and know when, what, to whom and how to say what he has to say," Havel writes. That's a pretty reasonable checklist of Klein attitudes, style and qualities as he stood on the threshold of public life in the 1980 summer of his own meditations.

One consideration that held Klein back from a decision to run was the candidacy of university professor Phil Elder, a New Democrat who had pulled together the progressive, reformist and mildly leftest Calgary Urban Party in 1977, unsuccessfully running half a dozen aldermanic candidates. After that defeat, Elder decided the focus of the campaign had been wrong and that his party should have first sought the mayoralty. Klein agreed. He believed he was seeking the same basic constituency as Elder and made up his mind not to split the vote. Then Elder withdrew from the race in the early summer when his party organization failed to gel. Klein had quietly raised the possibility of seeking the mayoralty with Colleen and a few friends; when Elder pulled out, the pressure on Klein to make a decision increased.

Meanwhile, he continued to cover the campaign. Former mayor Rod Sykes was in the Modern Café near city hall one day when the owner told him that a film crew was in the back lane filming an actor costumed as a bum, scavenging through the trash cans for food. Ross Alger had been making an issue of bums on the street: the east end needed to be cleaned up, and the new civic centre would accomplish that. Sykes correctly surmised that the film crew was preparing a television ad.

Sykes called the CFCN newsroom. Within minutes, Klein was on the scene with a news camera to capture the simulation. The film crew was, in fact, working for an advertising agency, which, in turn, acknowledged that Alger was the client. Klein broke the story on the 6:00 P.M. news. In 1980, in Calgary, audiences were not prepared for negative political advertising, especially fiction. The Alger "bums" ad was seen as cynical, manipulative and misleading, seriously harming Alger's credibility.

On the morning of August 20, Klein walked into the CFCN news meeting, on time for once, and dropped a bomb. He told his boss, Thompson MacDonald, and his colleagues that he intended to run against Ross Alger. He was greeted with swift, unthinking laughter.[9]

His colleagues thought he was joking about a campaign that had already generated a great deal of black humour over the mediocre quality of the two protagonists. The more he insisted, the less they believed him. Stung, he called reporters at the *Calgary Herald*. They were more receptive, and his announcement was on the front page of the afternoon paper.

His father was equally skeptical when Klein called him for advice. "I'm running for mayor," Ralph said.

"Are you nuts? Are you sober?" Philip asked. "And how much is this going to cost me?"

His son replied, "Whatever you can afford." Philip lent his motor home and a few bucks, but he didn't think Ralph could win. "I always thought he'd be a preacher or in public relations, never a politician," he later recalled.

His father's skepticism and that at CFCN, however, was hardly his worst problem. He had no money, no manager and no organization. The campaign kick-off fund was $300 out of his own pocket—all he could afford. He had his father's motor home for the campaign but wasn't quite sure how best to use it.

He had been counting on Alderman Nomi Whalen to organize his election bid. Whalen was a one-term council member who had proved to be wacky, off the wall, funny and committed—a wonderful anti-politician who used effective guerrilla tactics to force council to address social issues it would rather ignore. She was also the wife of news and CFAC-TV sports caster Ed Whalen, a CFCN competitor. Ed and Nomi were among Ralph and Colleen's strongest friends. Ralph's maverick nature, however, disturbed them.

"I'll run your campaign if you get rid of the Indians and stay away from the St. Louis [a favourite watering hole for Klein in his off-hours]," she told him. Klein told her to get lost.

He turned to his father's old boxing buddy, Gordon Grayston, who was incredulous. "Lie down until the feeling leaves you," Grayston said. Finally he persuaded a labour organizer, Ted Takacs, and a criminal defence lawyer, Webster MacDonald Sr., to co-chair, but they were ineffective. They did not know how to raise money, deal with the media or make effective use of volunteers. Things bumbled along with no one or everyone in charge, depending on the day.

Klein was on thin ice; in contrast, his main rivals, Mayor Ross Alger and Alderman Peter Petrasuk, had large well-funded volunteer committees. Klein pondered withdrawal into an aldermanic bid for one of several possible wards where he knew he would find good volunteer help.

On Monday night, August 25, he canvassed about twenty people, the heart and soul of his support. When he proposed dropping down to an aldermanic race or dropping out, he hit a brick wall. His supporters insisted that he stay the course. That was the night, four days after his first campaign limped out of the gate, that the Klein Gang was born, the cadre of die-hard Klein people who would stick with him all the way to the Alberta premier's office.

Klein operated for a few days from a nondescript storefront, east of city hall on 8th Avenue SE across from the St. Louis Hotel. The street was an out-of-the-way, blue-collar enclave of secondhand stores, rooming houses, a barber shop and a gas station, untouched by redevelopment. Wealthy, well-connected businessman Jack Singer provided the space.

A generous, likable entrepreneur whose family was a pillar of

Calgary's Jewish business establishment, Singer was a shrewd judge of character and an honourable man. He was one of a small cadre of civic-minded men who liked Klein's journalism and were keen to see him succeed politically.

The makeshift office, with a telephone and a few battered tables and chairs, was virtually the campaign's only asset. For a few days, Klein was the entire full-time staff. The candidate's $300 seed fund was quickly spent.

The cash never did roll in lavishly; various accountings place Klein's resources in 1980 as no more than $22,000. Most of the funds were raised by Jo Buck, a no-nonsense friend of the Klein family who hit the street every day to con, browbeat, sweet-talk and—if all else failed—appeal to the reason of potential contributors. She would walk into the campaign office every afternoon and dump the contents of her purse on the table: bills, silver and the occasional cheque.

His campaign was impoverished, but Klein had the issues and a grasp of the city's people. He sensed a shift in the political winds that only he seemed to have detected. He managed the media well, in spite of the inauspicious reception his announcement had received at CFCN. And he counted on attracting a few more good people to help out, to swell the ranks of the twenty folks who were with him on day one.

Shortly after the campaign kicked off, a political junkie named Rod Love turned up. He had dropped out of the University of Calgary's political science department because he was being taught nothing about practical politics—nothing about the grit and sweat, the back rooms, the money, the deals, the compromises. He picked up work as a waiter and maitre d', drank beer, chased women and got very bored, very quickly.

Love has told several versions of how he joined the Klein Gang. In one, he stopped by the campaign office on a rainy day because he couldn't go golfing. In another, he heard Klein in a radio interview and it struck a spark. Love called the campaign headquarters. A man answered the phone. When Rod asked about volunteering, there was a long silence; then the voice said, "Come on down," and gave him the address, still the 8th Avenue storefront.

Love parked his Volkswagen Beetle in front of the headquarters. From the outside, the place was ominously quiet. Inside, it was deserted except for a stocky man in casual clothes who looked only vaguely familiar. Love said he had called about joining the campaign and asked for Ralph Klein. "I'm Ralph," the man replied, looking straight into Love's eyes with that trademark candour that Rod would get to know very well over the next fourteen years.

Love asked what he could do to help. Klein said he needed a driver. No, not a driver for the campaign—a driver now. He had decided the headquarters was too far off the beaten track, and he was on his way to meet Jack Singer to arrange a better location. He had to change into his suit, which was in the motor home out back. Would Love mind driving so that he could dress?

In a minute, Love was at the wheel of the vehicle, headed along 8th Avenue, while Klein rummaged around in the back. "Gotta light?" Love heard Klein ask. He looked back over his shoulder to see the man who would be mayor, buck naked, with a beer bottle in his hand and a cigarette dangling from his lips. Klein grinned at Rod, his big, lopsided trademark grin; clearly, thought Love, the candidate was enjoying himself hugely.

Singer gave the campaign a better, more central location, on 12th Avenue SW across from an old YWCA. But the place was dreary, an old warehouse with no washrooms, no hot water and light bootlegged in from an adjacent premise with extension cords. Workers crossed the street to the YWCA to use the toilet.

Klein's gang took shape as political buccaneers from outside the system. Of course, no one took them very seriously. In September, Mayor Alger's polls showed he had a comfortable lead, with the anti-incumbent vote split between Petrasuk and Klein. The pollsters concluded that "Alger can only lose if he self-destructs."[10] Talking to people on the street, Klein heard a different theme: anger at Alger and Petrasuk, and the old politics. It was the crack, and Klein would widen it.

For most of the campaign, Klein was a novelty. A symbol of the style was the battered white campaign van with its stark black and white "Ralph Klein" posters plastered on its rust-specked sides; it looked like a hippie flashback. The members of the campaign were oddballs, but they were quietly pulling into the lead. Office manager Isobel Grayston knew he was going to win from the outset. In the blue-collar Forest Lawn district, Social Credit stalwart Ella Ayers, one of the city's smartest and toughest political organizers ever, was working for Klein and told friends before Labour Day that "Ralph was winning from the start."[11]

His friend Grant Howard, a reporter who was assigned to the campaign, started betting on Klein and found lots of takers; election night proved quite profitable for him. In the Alger camp, some workers had sensed a shift in public mood because Klein was in the race; they warned Alger he was in trouble. The mayor refused to believe them and declined to adjust his strategy to deal with the "Ralph" factor.

Meanwhile, Klein's long-standing political relationship with Petrasuk was turning out to be a costly one. Desperately, in the second half of the campaign, Petrasuk's people began a whispering campaign based on sketchy research into legal matters surrounding Klein's 1972 divorce. They implied that Petrasuk had inside knowledge of the case and claimed he was disturbed by what he knew of Klein's character; messy gossip spread about the reasons for the divorce. It was an unsuccessful move; Petrasuk finished third, and later it turned out that he was financing his political ambitions from client trust funds, for which he was prosecuted and jailed. However, the experience opened a Pandora's box of rumour and innuendo about Klein's conduct, and the public record of the proceedings became one of the most-thumbed-through files at the Southern Alberta Court of Queen's Bench.

As the campaign entered the final stretch, Klein stayed with his instincts, more certain than ever that the old-style campaign—big budgets, organizational charts, floods of lawn signs, ad agencies, platforms offering more of the same municipal government—was out of step. "I knew people were looking for the alternative, that people were really focussing on me as that choice," he said. He felt the voters wanted an outsider to get into city hall and shake the place up.[12]

So he talked about getting back to feeling good about Calgary as a place to be born, and to make a decent life, where everyone could enjoy the opportunities and take on the responsibilities of the community and where it was possible to die with a measure of contentment and satisfaction. He made only two vague promises: to communicate and to act like a politician, by which he meant to be accountable and to do the things that the people wanted done.

He was no barn burner; his speeches rambled and never took rhetorical flight. But he had a firm handshake, he looked you right in the eye when he talked, and he left the impression of plain talk from a straight shooter. When he promised to be a politician, he meant to end the cronyism and elitism that was the day-to-day modus operandi of the clubby establishment that ran the real estate board, the Exhibition and Stampede, the university, the hospitals and all the other public institutions orbiting city hall.

During the weekend before the vote, Klein believed he was very close but not ahead; his own polls showed that Alger and Petrasuk were destroying each other, alienating one half of the city and splitting the vote of the other half. Klein believed he was most likely to be successful with former mayor Rod Sykes's constituency of outsiders: a combination of liberal, blue-collar, non-anglophone and immigrant voters that crossed over to include service professionals: teachers, nurses, accountants and social workers. An endorsement from Sykes would be decisive in moving uncommitted voters into his column.

Klein called Sykes and asked for a favour: a public endorsement in a television news interview. Sykes declined a direct endorsement because he had already told Alger and Petrasuk that he would stay out of the campaign. If he were asked a direct question, however, he would say that Klein stood a chance because the other two candidates were turning off the voters. Ralph jumped at the offer and arranged a CFCN television interview. Sykes was asked, "Do you think Ralph has a chance?" His answer was yes.

After the election, Sykes received another call from Klein, to thank him for the endorsement. For about two years, the two men frequently dined to discuss politics. Sykes has recounted that Klein always thanked him for the endorsement and said, "I owe you."[13]

On Monday night, thirty-six hours before the polls opened, the three candidates attended a final mayoralty forum. The debate provided the *coup de grâce* of Klein's campaign. Alger and Petrasuk squabbled over the soaring city budget; Petrasuk hammered at the increases during the Alger administration, and the incumbent defended the increases. Klein ignored them both. He talked quietly and simply about accountability, access for every citizen to processes and decisions of city hall, and the need for politicians to make people feel good about Calgary again.

For reporters dividing up election night assignments, the Klein headquarters was the last choice. The movers and shakers would be elsewhere; Klein would soon be back in the press room himself, they were sure. Besides, the word was out that there was barely enough money in the campaign treasury for beer and pizza for the volunteers and journalists expected to turn up to wait for results.

The results were a thunderbolt. Within an hour after the polls closed, the outcome was clear. Almost at once, someone coined the phrase the Miracle in October. Within minutes, the loyalist crowd at Ralph's headquarters was swollen with a flood of opportunists and hangers-on. The first through the door were the bewildered political money men who had refused to contribute to the campaign and had taken their dollars elsewhere, where there would be markers to call in. Now, chagrined, they tried to quietly corner the mayor-elect and hand him a cheque. Klein regarded them as claim jumpers; to most of them, he smiled icily and said no.

Thompson MacDonald called Philip Klein to say his son had won a landslide. The elder Klein didn't believe him at first. And in a corner of the crowded headquarters under the glare of the television klieg lights, Florence Gray, Klein's mother, was holding court with reporters and telling them that Ralph was too thin-skinned to be a politician.

6

The
Inauguration

... tomorrow comes saying,
We are born of the yesterdays ...

—CARL SANDBURG, "MAN THE
MOON SHOOTER"

R alph Klein was sworn in as Calgary's 32nd chief magistrate on
October 27, 1980. The ceremony took place in the windowless,
flag-lined council chamber, with Mr. Justice Aza Milton Harradence presiding. Colleen, wearing a stylish, almost brash broad-brimmed
hat, held Theresa's hand as Klein took the oath and began an eight-year
apprenticeship in power. On October 28, the then federal energy minister, Marc Lalonde, rose in the House of Commons and pulled the rug
out from under Calgary's soaring economy by imposing the National
Energy Program (NEP) on the petroleum industry.

The withering impact of the NEP on Calgary's growth preempted
much of Klein's agenda. The political conflict that erupted ensured that
his first months in office would be overshadowed by the clash between
two titans: Alberta Premier Peter Lougheed and Prime Minister Pierre
Trudeau. The "oil war" gave Klein a long honeymoon without a single
severe test of his capabilities. When he had a profile, mostly on the radio
talk shows that he instituted and hosted early in his tenure, he talked
about positive, feel-good changes at city hall, in sharp contrast to the
tension and conflict of oil politics. His perfecting of the talk show as a
political tool, a decade before it was fashionable in North America, was
the singular accomplishment of his first term and cracked open access
to city hall as if it were an overripe nut.

On the day of the swearing in, Klein was at his gregarious best,
setting the tone for his feel-good agenda. Gone, or at least well masked,
was the intense rage of conscience and the preoccupation with the city's
future that had powered his three-year march to the mayoralty. Taking
the oath of office in style provided the opportunity to start the feel-good
party that was to become the hallmark of his apprenticeship.

Milt Harradence was a reassuring presence for the thirty-seven-year-old novice mayor. As a criminal defence lawyer, Harradence had a simple rule of thumb for his relationship with journalists: "Lose a case, but never lose a reporter."[1] Consequently, the judge had the trust of most, including Klein. He was a quiet mentor to many, including Klein. Although Harradence's status as on the bench now precluded Mayor Klein from seeking much in the way of direct counsel, no one missed the weight the judge added to the occasion, weight that Ralph badly needed.

Harradence was another outsider, politically and socially. His lawyering was unorthodox; he defended criminals and at the same time was the favourite counsel for police and the police union. He didn't cut much ice with Calgary's establishment, because he was too close to the street, and that engendered suspicion. He had a good prairie pedigree as an anti-politician in his own right. He revered John Diefenbaker, having grown up under his influence in Prince Albert, Saskatchewan. Partly because of Diefenbaker's influence, Harradence and his brother, Clive, entered the legal profession and practised Diefenbaker-style criminal defence. This entailed brilliant courtroom rhetoric, cunning use of the news media and the aggressive selection of the toughest and often most hopeless cases. It also included winning: Diefenbaker and the Harradences shared a knack for out-of-the-jaws-of-defeat courtroom triumphs.

As a politician, Harradence was stamped with the Diefenbaker style: a crusading image, a polished platform speaking style, an instinct for underdog causes, a visionary's approach to policy making and the liberal application of charm and warmth. He had a brief career at city hall as an alderman, and he was constantly a thorn in the side of the political establishment. Then he headed the Progressive Conservative Party of Alberta in the mid-sixties, before Peter Lougheed. He conducted his leadership without a seat in the legislature. He was unsuccessful against the Manning hegemony, but he successfully injected flare into the province's grey flannel political life by conducting his election campaigns from the cockpit of a Mustang fighter aircraft painted in Tory colours.

It was Harradence's capacity to communicate, to convince an audience, that indelibly impressed the new mayor. Klein's speaking style was, and is, usually the hyperbolic prose of his United Appeal press releases and letters, ranging from the florid to the colloquial but always stilted and cumbersome. Although Klein never matched Harradence's gift for spoken language, consciously or unconsciously he cloned his public style: wry humour, terse dismissal of opponents and an intense eye-to-eye contact that charmed the wary and reassured his true believers. Klein mastered the judge's clarity, dramatic timing and conviction. To the extent that Harradence copied John Diefenbaker, when Klein speaks, the old ghost stirs.

Klein felt the need for political role models and relied on the advice and example of older men. Among the most important influences on Klein's mayoralty was Rod Sykes, the abrasive, combative former mayor who once said that his religious upbringing taught him not to expect to be happy in this life and that politics confirmed the truth of this. Sykes feared no special interests and transferred his personal parsimonious style to public life. "A politician should spend every cent as if it belongs to someone else, because it does," said Sykes, contradicting the prevailing political culture of a city awash in the riches of rapid urban growth in the 1970s.[2]

Rod Sykes dominated civic politics from 1969 to 1977, a period that coincided with Ralph's preeminence as a television journalist; the two men, who stood astride civic affairs of the day, enjoyed an ambivalent relationship. Sometimes they cooperated, and at other times they clashed; they always held each other in high regard, however.

"Klein often said to me in the first few years that he was modelling himself on me, and trying to do what I had done because he admired me as a forthright mayor. I was always rather taken aback that what resulted might be my style, but a compliment is a compliment," Sykes once said. And Klein always spoke highly, and wrote in a complimentary fashion, of Sykes's "new broom" approach to shaking up city hall.

Like Klein, Sykes was from outside the municipal establishment. He rode to power over the wreckage he had made of the existing political machine, destroying the hold that the Calgary Real Estate Board, the Calgary Exhibition and Stampede, and the civic coalition that was created and run by a wealthy cadre of businesspeople who resided in the exclusive Mount Royal district had over the city. Klein intended to be the same kind of tough guy on important issues.

Sykes had given the city's outsiders a voice when he tore the door to the mayor's office off its hinges at his first photo opportunity in 1969. He ran the city personally and controversially. He reduced taxes twice and allowed increases in spending. He affronted the insiders and the establishment. He told the unions they couldn't have pay increases because the money wasn't there.

In 1972, when the provincial government legislated wage rollbacks, civic workers who were members of the Canadian Union of Public Employees marched on city hall. Skyes stared down a thousand angry workers on the front steps. He told them they would get nothing from him by resorting to confrontation, but he would see that they didn't get docked a day's pay so long as they went straight back to work. They did, and Sykes kept his promise.

Klein, who stood with other members of the media on the fringe of the crowd, took careful note and did not miss the significance of the flood of approving calls that came into the mayor's office, the radio talk shows and his own news room over the next few days.

Klein is a student of Calgary's history; his mayoral style and political agenda contained key elements from Andrew Davidson, the mayor Klein claimed to admire most. Andy Davidson ran city hall from 1930 to 1945 and never lost an election. Klein said Davidson embodied the "city's unquenchable spirit" and nurtured it through the dark years of the depression and the bitter years of the war.[3] During the 1930s, Davidson built the huge Glenmore water reservoir. It was a project of visionary dimension, ensuring a water supply adequate for nearly half a century of constantly accelerating growth. What dazzled Klein most, however, was that Davidson had refused to use heavy machinery and built the dam and reservoir works with human muscle. The project employed three thousand men. It failed every test of government efficiency, but the hire these men earned fed and clothed three thousand families through the devastating depression years.

But however much he relied on the experiences of others, Klein marched to a different beat. He brought his own strengths and weaknesses to his mayoralty. He wanted be more than a composite; he wanted to be his own man and to make his own mark. He was exceptionally bright; his lack of opportunity for a formal education masked his intelligence and discipline. He was a quick study. He knew the workings of city hall intimately and had a strong grasp of the realities of power. If his agenda was a bit inchoate, it had some clear touchstones; Klein talked about pioneering a new, greater civic accountability and being the focus of it. He devised a regular series of radio talk shows on which callers took him to task for anything from potholes on the streets to tax hikes.

Klein had the weaknesses of an outsider. He was insecure about his lack of education. At first he avoided debate with the commissioners in public on the financial, engineering and technical issues that are the bread and butter of civic debate, fearing that they would exploit his lack of sophistication. Although he owed no one, he quickly came to rely on a circle of confidants and advisers that has widened with time. Chief among these in 1980 was Rod Love, who soon emerged as Klein's close friend and shadow. Calling himself "Ralph's air traffic controller," Love became part minder, part keeper, part valet.[4] Observers thought, incorrectly, that he was the brain behind Klein's success; it is Klein who is the brain behind Love. Love became the only constant influence on Klein's strategic thinking, however.

At first, Klein gingerly pushed the envelope of his power with the commissioners. The issues he raised were surprisingly trivial. He was scheduled, in the early days of his administration, to travel to a national meeting of municipalities in Montreal. Travel arrangements were made and an airline ticket sent to his office. Klein called the commissioners' office at once and demanded to know where the ticket for his wife was to be found.

"In this city, the mayor's wife does not travel with the mayor," he was told. "This mayor's wife travels with this mayor, or this mayor does not travel," Klein shot back. In short order a second plane reservation was made, and thereafter Colleen was assumed to be included in travel plans, unless the mayor's office advised otherwise.[5]

Later, Klein set the important rules for the relationship between the mayor and commissioners. The commissioners would bring forward ideas on policy and projects and would provide the information to assist in reaching decisions. But decisions would be made by the elected members of council. The mayor was very clear about this.

The commissioners were to stay out of the debate and were not to manipulate or manage issues on the floor. The mayor was the chairman of council; it was his most powerful lever in a system in which he held just one vote and had no control over the aldermen. So the commissioners would not preempt his function as chairman. The mayor was also very clear about this.

When decisions were made, the commissioners were to execute them, whether or not they agreed. If they thought a council decision wouldn't work, the job of the commissioners was to find a way to make it work. If the commissioners left politics to the politicians, the politicians would leave the administration to the commissioners.

The relationship between a diligently political mayor and an extremely powerful administrative board of commissioners worked because of the successful relationship between Klein and George Cornish, who became chief commissioner in May 1981. When Cornish assumed the post, he was regarded as the most adept bureaucratic politician in the city's brief history. The aldermen and the media called him the shark's shark and the piranha's piranha.

He was as different from Ralph as night from day. Once, at a Christmas function hosted by the commissioners for the media, Cornish hurried in late and stayed only a few minutes for a soft drink. He did not remove his coat, leaving as quickly as he had come. He had left his wife outside, waiting in his car with the engine running. Klein was the gregarious, hard-drinking journalist, Cornish the reserved, abstemious engineer; Klein was the open, accessible politician whose power base was the trust of his public, Cornish the back room civil servant who marched by night and seldom left traces on his victims. Yet the two formed a bond of common public interest and genuine friendship as rare for its warmth as it was for its combined power.

They found strong common ground on two points: a passionate love of the city, and an idealistic sense of political values and morality. Both men had grown up in Calgary and could not imagine living anywhere else. Neither cared much for money; they were equally incorruptible. Cornish was rivaled only by Rod Love in his influence on the mayor.

Initially, Klein was the weaker of the two, undermined by his own lack of self-confidence and dependent on the savvy of others to make up for his vulnerability and naiveté. Thus, he may have been drawn into the relationship with Cornish out of vulnerability—for advice on things like protocol, administrative process and relations with the province. What triggered the rules of the relationship, however, quickly became academic, since both men gained from it while giving up little that was fundamentally important to them.

Although Klein was fascinated by the details of civic administration, he had other priorities and soon lost his compulsion to control council's legislative agenda. Leadership on this he left to the commissioners, who over time developed a sense of the things that would not fly with this powerful mayor and therefore should be left untouched.

In return, the mayor obtained the support he needed for his role as the communicator and representative of the city. He had support for steady increases in the mayor's budget, which was so meagre to start with that his senior staff made less money than long-serving secretaries in minor positions in the bureaucracy. He also had backing for initiatives such as the powering of the city's economic development authority, a joint venture with the chamber of commerce.

As Klein's mayoralty moved on, past two successive reelections, Cornish increasingly ran city hall. Once, at an awards ceremony in which Cornish was being honoured by an engineer's association, Klein in his own well-lubricated tribute told the audience that not only did George run the city, he even called the mayor on the carpet from time to time.[6] The grain of truth in that boozy hyperbole was that Klein was glad to be relieved of some of his responsibilities and to be protected from being made to look bad by public servants ruthlessly protecting their turf.

In a succession of subtle bylaw changes, the commissioners were seen to be disassembling the mayor's accountability for the administration. In helping to reorient the mayoralty function to one of public leadership, they usurped some of his administrative responsibilities. As a result, the mayor's office was less informed in the making of policy and less engaged in implementing it. Although the mayor's job was less tedious, involving less time behind a desk and more in public, it was also subtly pushed toward the periphery. Once given up, the power would be all but impossible for subsequent mayors to regain.

Council, too, was weakened. The politicians, however, were rewarded with larger offices, budgets and travel accounts, and even executive assistants. While Klein was augmenting his personal power by strengthening his electoral constituency and shoring up his image as a civic booster, ombudsman and prophet of hope, behind him the traditional basis for the mayor's institutional power was eroding as the commissioners acquired more responsibility internally for keeping the machine running under less supervision.

It was an anti-politician's remedy for politics. More traditional politicians thought Klein was abdicating his responsibilities. He thought otherwise. Administrative mayors were unresponsive to constituents between elections. In the proper order of things, their chief function was to ensure that the civic administration responded promptly to shifts in public opinion. Leaving the details to a faceless public service fit well with Klein's evolving conservatism; he distrusted intervention and believed in the moral limits of politics.

All of that was an uncut page on October 27, 1980. The inauguration was, for the most part, carefree and unconcerned with weighty matters that might lie ahead. There was a foreshadowing, however, of a different Klein. In addition to the predictably easygoing man, there were moments—when he fussed over protocol, for example—that he exhibited flashes of a new serious and formal demeanour. This was surprising because it seemed paradoxical to his gritty style. He had discovered that he could not presume on the good will of his former colleagues. Many of the same city hall news room denizens who were boasting of their close personal ties to Klein were sharpening the knives.

In the twelve-day transition from election day to swearing in, the new mayor had experienced the dark undertow of public life. A coup d'état makes for bitter enemies, and in Calgary's civic politics, there are no graceful losers. These embittered foes—Alger and Petrasuk, their backers, the city's civic establishment who regarded Klein as an outsider and a handful of journalists who were beside themselves with envy—now fed the frenzy of scrutiny. Klein's personal life underwent its first fumbling evaluation, fuelled by rumour and plain old news room gossip.

Very little of the rumour generated by the media and political investigations into his personal life gelled into print or broadcast, either during the transition or at any time up to the present, because it lacked credible substantiation. The corrosive innuendoes, however, circulated on the cocktail circuit. Klein's street research into television documentaries on heroin, prostitution and motorcycle clubs were hyped. The talk that the Petrasuk camp had started during the campaign about his first marriage—that it had been violent and unseemly—had no basis, but reporters who couldn't substantiate it with research and go into print nevertheless repeated the gossip, and it spread.

There was speculation that the Kleins, who had little money, would not be able to cope with the financial demands of public life. Colleen's intention to keep her job as a cashier for the Calgary Cooperative food stores was taken as a sign that the two intended to live beyond their means, particularly since the mayor's paycheque was modest. Colleen was depicted as a clotheshorse, Klein as a guy with a penchant for expense account living. Neither was true, but this mattered little to wagging tongues.

Klein was wounded by the rumours, which robbed the heady victory of some of its sweet savour. He maintained his characteristic poise, however. "People say I'm a kid with a new toy," he mused. "But really, it's the city that has a new toy. Me, a young journalist become mayor. I think people just want to know if their new toy is breakable."[7]

In fact, Klein was learning quickly how to shape his media coverage, to turn liabilities into assets. If people wanted to think he drank too much, well, he'd take advantage of the fact that they would underestimate him as a result. He was learning to be everything that people saw in him and none of it.

He exploited the myth that he haunted the St. Louis Hotel precisely to cultivate a rumpled, beery image that masked his intensity, focus and occasional ruthlessness. The St. Louis is an old-style beer parlour in the basement of a working-class hotel about a block from city hall. For years, the "Louie" had been a watering hole for civic employees, news people and politicians. Occasionally, on days city council met, Klein joined the crowd in the St. Louis during lunch and supper breaks. Occasionally, but not often.

For the most part he steered clear of the media pack. He was, in fact, more often downtown in the Queens or the Alexandria, two other blue-collar haunts, than at the St. Louis. When he put up his feet for a drink, it was in the relative quiet and seclusion of Frank's Caffé dello Sport, across the street.

Rod Sykes, however, showed him the advantages of politicking in Calgary's beer parlours. "A great political institution, although a little hard on the liver," Sykes said of Alberta's huge beer barns, now mostly disappeared, where in a single afternoon a mayor could create the illusion of political intimacy with several hundred gregarious patrons. So, in the campaign of 1980, Klein started to spend more time in the St. Louis.

Immediately after the victory, news writers looking for an angle seized on the St. Louis as the symbol of the rumpled, boozy "mayor of all the people" caricature they were crafting for Klein. The negative side of the image was unsettling, but the new mayor seized on a good thing and began to play up his connection to the grungy basement tavern, with its huge paper platters of fried chicken and thick potato wedges.

He discovered the political edge of being underestimated as a good-time, beer-drinking guy without serious substance. Time after time in those early days he won the nasty little street fights of political life, most of which took place out of the public eye, against opponents who didn't expect much from Klein.

Meanwhile, in the first exuberant weeks after the election nothing overshadowed the energy of the moment. Everyone in the office was inexperienced, but the sheer fun of what they were doing papered over the mistakes. Late on Friday afternoon, a young woman whose name, regrettably, is lost to history, arrived at his office and asked to see Klein. She claimed a passing acquaintance with the mayor, and in the open style of the place gained an audience. Once in his office, she stripped naked and offered to "do" the mayor.

A secretary later recounted that he burst out of his office—as if the door weren't even there—sputtering, red faced and incoherent. "He really is a prude, you know," she said. He wanted some help, but no one knew what to do, and besides they were all laughing too hard to call security or ask her name. In the midst of the hilarity that bordered on hysteria, the woman dressed and quietly retreated.

Klein's style did little to dampen the impression that he regarded his new office as more fun than work. One morning, a radio reporter arriving early at city hall found the mayor crawling around on the ground, looking for his car keys. Klein had been on an all-nighter and was finding his way home. The reporter got him inside, gave him some strong coffee and arranged a discreet ride home, where the mayor could take a long, sobering bath before starting his day.

7

The Feel-
Good Mayor

> *. . . the perfect munchkin mayor,*
> *brought to power by rainbow*
> *dreamers and backfence schemers.*
>
> —RON WOOD, "THE CITY,"
> *CALGARY MAGAZINE*

When Ralph Klein moved into the mayor's office, in the shadow of the sandstone clock tower on the southwest corner of the second floor of Calgary's city hall, he was expected to fall flat on his face. The media expected it, the city commissioners expected it, to a man and woman the aldermen expected it and the city's social and business establishment not only expected it, but wanted it.

For a time, Klein seemed perfectly willing to cooperate. His office was in chaos; there were no job descriptions and Rod Love, now his chief of staff, was bullying his way to the top of the circle of key staffers. Love had the younger women on the staff in tears, and he owed a lot of money around town but refused calls from creditors, ordering the secretaries to take messages that he never returned. He was also cracking the whip with reporters, doing gossip damage control by buying drinks, picking up the tab and then, in effect, saying, "Let he who sins not cast the first stone." He put the right spin on the new mayor—that he was capable, diligent, hard working and intelligent, not a boozy bozo. When charm and reason failed, there were angry phone calls to editors and thinly veiled orders given to news directors.

Even though Klein had made Isobel Grayston his appointments secretary, Love told people, "You want to see him, come through me." Grayston, alone among the women, stood toe to toe and went blow for blow. She was responsible for the schedule, so she insisted that Klein come to her for his itinerary and forced people to see her, not Love, for appointments. Klein is great with people at arm's length, but he does not like to get close. He could not deal with the conflict. When asked to deal with an the office tempest, he would plaintively ask, "Why can't everybody just get along?" Or he would say, "Why can't the other women stand up to Rod the way Isobel does?"[1]

If the rest of the day was chaotic, mornings were anarchy. Klein would just not show up for early meetings, or if he did, he would be grumpy on a good day and unbearable on a bad one. His staff learned that the best time of day to meet him was at the end of it. Bruce Planche, son of Hugh Planche, a former cabinet minister in the Lougheed government who was briefly an understudy to Love, became the artist of excuses and Grayston learned to write imaginative letters of apology.

Once, Klein failed to show for a Calgary Real Estate Board breakfast. The host called and Planche spun a story while, on another phone, another staffer tried to reach Klein at home but couldn't and called Colleen at work. She drove home and dragged the dozing mayor out of a tepid bath. After that, for the really important appointments, one of the staff drove out to the Kleins' to pick him up.

Klein was getting twenty requests a day for appointments, and he hated to say no. But he would often just disappear. Once, when a group of German investors arrived for a late afternoon meeting, Klein had been missing for several hours. Bruce Planche reassured the delegation for almost a half an hour, weaving a wonderful tale of the mayor's progress from an imaginary previous engagement. The investors had a plane to catch and were watching the clock. Just as Planche was about to launch into an amazing account of why the mayor, regrettably, would be forced to cancel the meeting, Klein burst into the office, looking for a cigarette, completely oblivious to the crisis he had created.

When his staff threw a surprise party to mark his sixth month in office, they invented an appointment with a fictitious ambassador from a far-removed, minor nation and made an appointment for him to sign the city's guest book late one Friday. Protocol demanded that the chief magistrate be present at such an occasion, but Klein argued for days about the appointment and no one was sure he would make it until he came through the door.

Klein was an instant success in the ceremonial and social tasks of the office, suprising no one except himself on that score. In developing policy, he was a detail nut. He had a tireless capacity for briefings, a flawless memory and a knack for knowing the right thing to do. His weakness was his propensity to consult far too widely, until he would doubt his own good judgement on a matter. Colleen emerged as the one who kept him focussed and relatively free of distracting influences. She encouraged him to rely more on his own judgement, warned him against unreliable advisers and counselled him on which projects were worth his time.

Beneath his laid-back façade, Klein was a worrier. He agonized when decisions led to conflict or forced him to chose between people. He worried when issues got out of control. He once spent a night pacing the floor of his office when a city union was on a strike deadline. He talked about "the families of these guys having to do without their wages." Outside his office, he was the tough, hardheaded boss who cussed out a group of demonstrating union members when they confronted him on the steps of city hall. In the sanctum of his office, he was on the other side of the issue.

The spacious, high-ceilinged office, with its heavy brocade curtains framing the towering windows, its hardwood floor lavishly carpeted with oriental rugs, the glass-fronted bookshelves, the executive washroom and the acre-sized desk did not seem to suit the man at first. From the third-floor press room he retrieved the battered typewriter on which he had once hacked out his cryptic news scripts and placed it on a corner of his desk. It was the only obvious thing that connected him to his past. As the shelves, coffee tables and broad windowsills filled up over the years with the bric-a-brac of office, the mementos and memorabilia that politicians accumulate, the office became a statement of the gulf that came to divide the political phase in his life from everything that went before it.

In both the substance and the style of political office, Klein at last found a task equal to his capacity for unbridled enthusiasm and to his zest for experience. When challenged about his hard partying, he shrugged and admitted he was human and had hangovers. He did not let raised eyebrows deter him from the focus of his mayoralty agenda: to be the chief communicator of civic hopes and dreams, the chief salesman of Calgary's future.

He set about redefining the mayor's job. He made the job more political by identifying himself as the official responsible for city hall's public accountability. He also took on the role of chief booster and salesman for opportunity and growth. Colleen, meanwhile, became a new kind of political wife for Calgary. She was front and centre at social occasions, and she travelled with Klein whenever possible. She became a stellar community volunteer, even cleaning toilets and shovelling snow at the Salvation Army Children's Shelter.

The thin-skinned, insecure side of his political persona kept him alert and wary. More than most politicians, he seemed aware of his limits. He was the pretender to the throne who had overthrown the legitimate monarch. He had upset the established political order. The aldermen regarded him with intense suspicion and distrust. The administration regarded him as an unpredictable maverick, an accident of history, a loose cannon. Many news reporters assigned to the city beat envied him with a corrosive passion; they sat in the press room for hours, regaling one another with fictions of his incompetence and stupidity. Until he was first reelected in 1983, they proclaimed him a one-election wonder.

Klein was on a high wire. He knew that his foes wouldn't bother with the subtleties of political ambush; they would knock him off the first chance they got. He intended to give them no opportunity. Klein wanted to conduct politics on the high road. As much as any politician, he wanted to be liked. He wanted to be the good news mayor. By taking on the roles of civic booster and public communicator—the guy who made people feel good about the future and helped them understand and gain access to the process—he avoided confrontation and conflict. By concentrating on these strengths, he consolidated his power base and built his credibility.

The strategy fit the times. There was no bad news to deliver—not at first. Things were good; the city was rich and full of opportunity. People behaved as if the boom would go on forever. Klein could be a feel-good mayor in feel-good times.

When he was uncertain about his ability to win debates in council chambers on substantive issues against the sophisticated and well-informed commissioners, he fell back on the time-honoured process of brokering blocs of votes on issues about which he cared. In the legislative process he was one vote of thirteen; he did not have the kind of confidential advice from public service professionals that a cabinet minister enjoys. He was good at the back room game, so he played it when his priorities needed support. The legislative agenda became less important to him than his work as a communicator and super salesman for the city.

He slowly found his feet. In early 1981 he and Colleen travelled to Europe in a group chamber of commerce and civic officials on a British Airways promotional tour. Klein had been the mayor of Calgary for just three months. Through an excess of courtesy and bad protocol, the airline had decided not to withdraw the invitation it had extended before the election to former Mayor Ross Alger and his wife, Lois. No one had expected Klein to unseat Alger, and the Kleins were not a hot social commodity. With his chamber of commerce connections and his tactlessness, Alger was easily able to hold onto the plum.

The Kleins were uncomfortable, and at first they were treated poorly. Alger, with characteristic bullheadedness, took advantage of the situation to play at being mayor one last time. The Kleins, however, found friends on the trip—Harold Millican—a prominent independent businessman, former political aide to Premier Peter Lougheed and later president of the chamber of commerce—and his wife, Donna, started to look out for Ralph and Colleen. They ensured that the Kleins sat at the correct tables, were introduced properly and could enjoy the trip a little.

Quietly, Harold told Alger to be gracious, to stop acting like the mayor and to let Klein make the pronouncements and give the greetings.

Slowly, Ralph gained confidence and began to assert himself. He seemed to get to the point where he said, "Hell, I'm the mayor now and Ross Alger isn't. I'll speak for the city." As the trip wound up, Klein was fully in command and Alger properly positioned as the elder but not interfering statesman. Others on the trip remember Alger becoming the uncomfortable one at the end.[2]

Klein was also learning to make the compromises of realpolitik. He had campaigned, for example, against building a the new civic centre attached to city hall in 1980. After the election, former mayor Rod Sykes pointed out to him that it was too late to undo the project. Klein was simply powerless to reverse a commitment against which he had strongly campaigned. The construction of new office space was unavoidable. Not only was it needed to accommodate an administration swollen by the city's growth, but the cost of lease and rental arrangements in private buildings had become untenable. The commitment to put the bureaucratic complex beside the historic sandstone city hall, with its landmark clock tower, had already cost taxpayers millions.

Klein simply let his vociferous opposition to the project die. This embittered the defeated Ross Alger, who viewed Klein's management of the issue as cynical and self-serving. Alger received little credit for the new city hall when it was completed. Nor was he credited for his role in the successful bid for the 1988 winter Olympics. Klein was learning quickly that politics, like journalism, is a game for winners. He massaged opinion in his radio talk shows and public appearances until it was favourable, then emerged, grinning, to cut the ribbon.

He seemed to know intuitively when to turn and hold his ground. The historic Burns Building, across Macleod Trail from the new city hall, was to be demolished as part of the redevelopment. Largely because of Klein's new power, it was preserved. The Burns Building was lavishly refurbished and tied into a magnificent new performing arts centre, which also preserved a federal building as the regal façade of the Jack Singer Concert Hall. The performing arts centre was part and parcel of Alger's grand vision for downtown; most people only remember Klein at the ribbon-cutting ceremonies.

The *pièce de résistance* of the redevelopment of the two square blocks west of city hall was the creation of Olympic Plaza, which became the venue for the Gold Medal ceremonies at the 1988 Winter Games. The pre-mayoralty Klein railed against the blockbusting that opened up development of this most opulent civic monument in western Canada. Then, Mayor Klein, the home-town booster, played a key role in selling the redevelopment to city taxpayers as a jewel of public pride.

His second reversal came on the construction of the northwest light rail transit (LRT) line through the community of Sunnyside, in the inner city, across the Bow River from downtown. The LRT was a political dilemma for the new mayor. The proposed extension of the system into the northwest was bitterly opposed by communities through which it would run. In the eyes of these neighbourhoods, that was a quality-of-life issue, too. The toughest activists lived in Sunnyside, where Klein had received support when he was elected in 1980. Klein's council knew that it might take months or even years to get the northwest expansion approved, so it decided to expand to the northeast, giving time for the opponents of the northwest LRT to exhaust themselves.

In 1981, when the city was named host of the 1988 Winter Games, the politicians found the rationale they needed to go ahead with the northwest line, running it exactly along the route that had caused so much controversy. Council astutely bided its time until after the 1983 election, however, before it pressed the advantage and developed the line. By then the games had broad support across the city, affording the political strength to proceed.

During the 1980 campaign, Klein had created the impression that the route would slice through Sunnyside only over his dead body. But he did not use his power to preempt the route, and he gave the project his blessing and support when it became part of the infrastructure for the 1988 Winter Games.

The cachet of the Olympics pitted the resisting community against the entire city and made the objectors appear petty and self-centred. Klein defended the route as an inevitable reality and a "soft" intrusion with little negative impact. The Sunnyside political establishment was stunned.

Klein's Sunnyside LRT flip-flop signalled that Ralph, the anti-politician and outsider, would belong to no political hierarchy except his own. He was beholden to no one, not even activists who used the sanctity of neighbourhood empowerment to oppose larger developments. This was the first indication that although he could be innovative and progressive, he was not the liberal many assumed him to be.

The political fact was that as opposition to him as mayor became more clearly and sharply defined, it proved to be in the minority. He marginalized contrary opinion by being persuasive and transparent. People said they agreed with him often enough to trust him when they didn't.

And Klein launched his persistent, aggressive salesmanship of the city. He travelled at every opportunity to promote the diversification of Calgary's economy. He looked for businesses and investors to bring to the city and strengthened the city's economic development authority.

His greatest successes, as a civic salesman, came in Hong Kong and China. He turned Calgary to face west and started people thinking of the city as a member of the Pacific Rim, in competition with Vancouver for Asia's top immigrants and investors. During his trade missions, he quickly learned to woo the Chinese. Businesspeople watched in astonishment as he charmed the pants off officials, shortcutting by months and years the normal requirements of business courtship in China. The years of absorbing Chinese culture and some sociable scraps of the Canontese language, over tea pots of whiskey in the after-hours joints of Calgary's Chinatown, were paying off.

Fighting the election of 1980 had given him an even broader grasp of the city's rapidly changing demographics. Calgary was joining Toronto and Vancouver as Canada's most culturally diverse communities—the centres of immigration. By the time Klein took office, more than half the city's inhabitants were first- or second-generation immigrants from 135 backgrounds with mother tongues other than English. The success of his trade missions abroad strengthened his credibility with the ethnic constituency back home.

Klein had few visible enemies, and only one was able to get under his skin. Brian Lee, a Ross Alger protégé, viewed Klein as a one-term inconvenience to be disposed of as efficiently as possible. Lee should never have been more than an annoyance. A precocious, brash political opportunist, he won a seat on council in 1977, while still in his mid-twenties. His glib tongue and aggressive style gave him a media profile and ambitions that outran his abilities. Lee curried favour with Mayor Alger, built up the appearance of a power base and in 1980 struck a deal with Alger not to challenge him in that election in exchange for an assurance that Alger would back Lee's mayoralty drive in 1983.

When Klein blew Alger out of the water, he also damaged Lee's carefully prepared career plan. Lee never forgave him and immediately launched an abrasive, taunting harassment campaign. The assault became classic guerrilla warfare. Klein wanted to stay on the high road, but up there he made a perfect target. Outgunned although he was, Lee discovered he could provoke the mayor.

Brian Lee gleefully dragged Klein into the kind of fractious, bickering exchanges that he had wanted to avoid. Never Klein's equal, Lee was successful because during Klein's first year in office, long before most others, he discovered just how thin Klein's skin could be.

The two men hacked away at each other with such animosity that a peace conference was arranged by some older and wiser politicians. Alderman Gord Shrake presided over a dinner of steak and stuffed potatoes at Romeo's, a favourite haunt of city politicians in Klein's North Hill boyhood neighbourhood. It was the Christmas season and the rivals were in rare conciliatory form. They agreed to lower the temperature. The pact held for less than a month.

On January 7, 1982, Klein gave a routine lunch-hour speech to a women's club. It would have gone unreported except that an *Alberta Report* writer, Bob Bettson, happened to be present. The entire city was in a surly, uncharitable mood. The Canadian oil patch was in serious economic trouble; companies like Dome Petroleum were going under. Even though the fountain of oil field jobs had dried up, the city continued to be flooded by young Canadians from the Maritimes, Ontario and Québec looking for work. The social problems—rising crime, the escalating welfare tab—that accompany resource booms were now fully exposed, and politicians were taking the heat. The costs were starting to pinch city hall's pocket. After his speech, with a venomous tone rare in his entire career and in a characteristic shoot-from-the-lip response to a question from Bettson, Klein blamed "eastern bums and creeps" for the city's economic and social ills. The underlying message was: go back home.

It was a serious blunder. Canadians, especially municipal politicians, in Central and Eastern Canada were apoplectic, and Klein was nationally vilified as the spoiled Albertan who had lived well during the boom and did not have the guts to resume the circumstances in which the rest of Canada had to live all of the time. Within days, the mayor realized that the remarks had undermined his sales effort to attract business and investment from the rest of Canada.

At home, his pellets had hit many supporters, including campaign workers and people whose votes he needed in 1983 to gain reelection. He had forgotten one of his own rules for the 1980 campaign—to woo the people who had arrived most recently. So recently an outsider himself, he was now castigating outsiders. He had also broken the code in a city that prided itself on its hospitable reputation and marketed the annual Calgary Exhibition and Stampede throughout Canada with the message that everyone was welcome in Calgary.

Brian Lee was elated; he poured on the scorn and pummelled Klein mercilessly. His attack looked very much like the early, opening salvo of the 1983 mayoralty election campaign.

Klein acted with what was to become characteristic speed and decisiveness. In a matter of hours, he apologized. He exhibited repentance and chagrin. He said that he was human and made mistakes. He said that although the bums and creeps who were robbing banks and pimping young girls were not welcome, people who were looking for a future and were ready to help build a great city were welcome even in hard times. He went on the road to talk shows and town hall suppers anywhere in the East that would have him. He got great reviews in the rest of Canada and grudging acknowledgement back home.

Klein also kept a record of the damage Brian Lee had tried to do. For if the "bums and creeps" speech proved him to be the master of political crisis management, it also showed him, in the long run, to be a man not to be crossed.

Soon after, Brian Lee moved up to provincial politics, winning a safe Conservative seat in the city's inner core. When Lee faced reelection in Calgary Buffalo, however, he was vulnerable. Klein smelled blood. He quietly and effectively threw his weight, including organization and funds, behind the Liberal candidate, Sheldon Chumir. Chumir was a wealthy lawyer with a strong civil rights record, an idealist and, like Klein a lifetime Calgarian. He was also an outsider—all political elements that resonated with Klein and created a bond between the two men. Although Chumir earned his political spurs and held his seat on his own merits until his untimely death in 1991, from cancer, he won his first term in the legislature thanks, in part, to Ralph Klein.

The temporary alliance with Chumir encouraged the Liberal Party's high-profile courtship of Klein in 1988 as a potential leader of the party. But the Liberals were wrong in interpreting the mayor's support of Chumir as an indication that he was a Liberal. He was just quietly settling the score with Brian Lee and leaving virtually no trace of his hand on the weapon.

What he did to Lee was not characteristic of the friendly fellow most Calgarians saw. The Great Communicator who emerged from the crucible of these first years in office was the affable booster, the politician who made them feel good again about being Calgarians.

His politics were not profound or complex. He was perfecting the art of winning elections, not hijacking the system. For all his maverick values, he had no agenda, yet, for which he would risk himself. Rather, he was serving an apprenticeship, cautiously testing new ideas that were maturing slowly, marking time until he found a challenge fit for his passions.

He once made an appointment to meet outdoors journalists Bruce Masterman and Roger Francis for some early morning trout fishing on the Bow River. After a couple of hours, when it was time to go into his office, he dug out his cellular phone and called in to cancel his appointments for the day. "The fishing is just too good," he said. First things first.[3]

8

The Winter Games

*Did he really influence his times and
the events that surged through them?
Or was he just another great prairie
wind?*

—G. V. FERGUSON, *JOHN W.
DAFOE*

fter Ralph Klein came to power in 1980, those who most resented
his intrusion into their affairs were the backers of Calgary's bid
for the 1988 Winter Olympic Games. Perhaps the most charitable view was that of Frank King, the independent oil man who had
emerged as chairman of the Calgary bid, and Bill Pratt, the rough-hewn
project construction genius who became his highest-ranking general.
They would work with him reluctantly and maintain a united public
front, but they were not pleased with the prospect of dealing with Klein
because they feared he would turn the Games into a political beast.

The impetus for the Games bid came from southern Alberta's most
established elites—the petroleum, ranching, land development, academic
and government leaders. Klein was not their kind of people; he was an
intruder, the kind of man you sent around to the back door. During the
year following his election, socially acceptable folks at the cocktail parties,
to which he was not invited when any other mayor would have been,
spoke of him in pejoratives. They nicknamed Klein Hizzoner, pro-
nounced with a pseudo-drunken slur. Often the slights were vicious; they
called him the the part-time mayor, the boozer who picked his wife up
after work from the battered women's shelter.

Socially the Winter Games became a cutthroat competition—a battle
for position, for the best invitations, for the grace and favour of Olympic
officials—in which gold medal egos played nasty little salon games to
determine who was in and who was out, who sat above and who sat
below the salt. This low behaviour towards Klein was to be matched,
during the course of the Games, by officials in Prime Minister Brian

Mulroney's office, who were galled that "this pipsqueak mayor" out-ranked Mulroney; they could find no role for their boss that was not secondary, and even tertiary, to Klein's.

Klein was also resented because the bid was not his idea; he was perceived as hijacking an opportunity he did not deserve. The political dividend belonged to Ross Alger, the mayor that Ralph unseated, and to Peter Lougheed, then the premier. Most of the Olympic crowd had supported Alger's mayoralty and thought Klein was an upstart who had stolen his chain of office. To add insult to injury, Klein had campaigned against Alger on projects that were deemed essential to the Olympics—the civic plaza and LRT. Alger had encouraged the volunteer group be-hind the effort to persist in spite of earlier failures and the almost uni-versal pessimism that accompanied the early work of the Olympic organizing committee, starting in 1978. Lougheed, encouraged by his Calgary caucus, provided provincial financing and lined up the necessary federal cash, using up a chunk of his rather limited political capital in Ottawa.

And yet the palace guard had no choice but to trade with Klein. In the rigid world of Olympic protocol, the Games are hosted by cities, not nations or provinces; the mayor ranks second only to the chairman of the International Olympic Committee (IOC) in the pecking order. There was also the question of his popularity; neither the Canadian Olympic Committee nor the Organizing Committee for the Calgary Olympics (OCO), could fight it. The disapproving bid-backers regarded Klein as a maverick, and to some extent the prophecy became self-fulfilling. So the backers of the Games tried to sideline him. Lougheed, at times, threw the weight of his office behind the alliance to shunt the mayor aside. They were all unsuccessful.

Once, Klein wanted to take a group of Blackfoot dancers to a critical IOC meeting in Montreal to dance and perform the sweet grass ceremony. The idea came naturally to the mayor, who increasingly was incorporating his spiritual links into public occasions. There was a strong communica-tions objective as well. Klein knew the Blackfoot participation would offer Europeans—who have a great enthusiasm, sometimes to excess, for North American aboriginal culture—a unique perspective on Calgary. He also wanted to continue cultivating IOC chairman Juan Antonio Samaranch, to whom he planned to make a gift of Blackfoot ceremonial dress.

The organizers of the meeting tartly suggested that he leave his ab-original friends at home when he went to Montreal. They got Premier Peter Lougheed's office to send Klein a letter with some fatherly advice to give their request some muscle. Klein snapped back a terse reply: "No Blackfoot, no Mayor of Calgary." With much muttering, Klein's antag-onists relented, but with the implied threat that the mayor would be

personally responsible for the Blackfoot and would be wise to get his
dancers out of town as soon as the ceremonies were over.

With characteristic style, Klein very nearly complied. The aboriginal
ceremonies were an enormous success, and not surprisingly, the dancers
were a big hit not just with the Olympic executives but with the staff of
the Queen Elizabeth Hotel. Early the next morning, when Rod Love
went looking for the Blackfoot to drive them to the airport, he found
them in the hotel kitchen, being regaled with a sumptuous meal and
some of the best wine in the cellars. As a parting shot, with a prankish
sense of humour that was becoming more common, Klein and Love ensured that the bill for the meal went onto the government of Alberta's
hotel tab.

In spite of the early snubs, which Klein had come to expect and
shrugged off, he plunged into the preparations for the formal bid, scheduled for September 1981, with his customary ebullience. He was enthu-
siastic in public—promoting the Olympics as a great boost for the city
as its economic woes mounted in the oil recession—but behind the scenes
there were bitter fights with Olympic organizers and provincial officials—using the muscle of Games protocol and his friendship with
Samaranch—before he successfully wielded the power of his office to
gain his proper place.

Klein's agenda was not very complicated; he wanted the city to be
a good steward of its financial and political responsibilities for the Games.
And he wanted the Games to make Calgarians feel good about themselves.

Ultimately, Calgary took on $1.6 billion in debt for the games; Klein
wanted to ensure that the burden was well managed and imposed the
least possible hardship on taxpayers. Klein recognized that the federal
government, the provinces and many private interests would be forking
out large amounts of money in capital expenditures and for sponsorships.
Even though Calgary was the official host, the city could not go it on its
own, and he wanted it to use its resources frugally.

During the election campaign of 1980, Klein had talked about the
Games bid in the same breath as the proposal to build a new arena for
a National Hockey League franchise, as projects that would get
Calgarians feeling good about their city again. The rapid growth and
sudden wealth brought on by the 1970s oil boom had scarred the city.
Ralph knew that its people were surly; disparities in income were widening, and there was more crime and family crisis. The city needed a
good old-fashioned boost, and the feel-good mayor set the tone for the
feel-good games; the end result would be a better community.

In the months leading up to the selection meeting in Baden Baden,
Klein made several tangible contributions to the outcome. First, he en-

sured that the city would build the Saddledome, an Olympic and professional ice hockey arena that put the city in the serious running for the Games. He did this, figuratively speaking, over George Cornish's dead body, ramming the project through city council on the strength of his ability to stick-handle it past the Board of Commissioners. He also sold the site, on the Stampede Grounds, to the neighbouring Victoria Park community, even further eroding its residential future, which as a journalist he had tried to protect.

Second, he conveyed to the IOC the warmth and hospitality that it would find in Calgary, reprising his role as the charming, unofficial host of old United Appeal campaigns. Third, he and George Cornish marshalled the city's administrative and financial resources behind the athletic facilities that would need to be constructed to host the Games, if the bid succeeded. Taxpayers struggling through an economic trough had to be sold on the idea, but in the end the support was ungrudging and Cornish was resourceful in finding the finances.

Finally, Klein developed a warm personal relationship with the IOC chairman. This was entirely unexpected; the patrician and crusty Samaranch had nothing visible in common with the unpolished, informal mayor. Klein found the invisible link: Samaranch's love of native folklore. At each meeting of the IOC and the city, Klein presented him with a piece of a Blackfoot chief's formal wardrobe. By the end of the Games, Samaranch had the entire regalia.

In September 1981, Klein travelled to Baden Baden with a large Calgary contingent of Olympic volunteers, staff and federal and provincial officials to receive the IOC decision on the 1988 Winter Games of the XXI Olympiad. Klein brought along Bill Kuyt, the city's transportation commissioner, who spoke four European languages and was knowledgeable about many of the technical details of the Olympic facilities, including the new LRT line.

One transferable skill that Klein brought to office from journalism was the ability to be at ease with persons of all backgrounds and in any social circumstance: the sweat lodge, the cowboy beer parlour and even the splendid galleries of Europe. With this skill, he made his final contribution to the Calgary bid. Kuyt sat back and watched the perfect chemistry between Klein and the world's Olympic establishment, which he later described as the most natural fit he had ever seen. Night after night, at the cocktail receptions, over dinner and in the bars, the mayor held court, speaking Blackfoot and giving gifts of aboriginal art and artifacts.

On September 11, 1981, the International Olympic Committee selected Calgary to host the 1988 Winter Games. The image of Klein, at the moment of the announcement, leaping into the air with his arms raised, yelling an unrestrained, barrel-chested "Whoopee!" charmed and even electrified Calgarians back home watching on television. His enthusiasm was infectious; even the more sedate members of the (Canadian) Calgary Olympic Development Committee and (Calgary) Olympic Organizing Committee let down their hair and whooped it up with the mayor.

Many of the more than five thousand volunteers who assisted with the hosting of the Winter Games now recall newscasts of Klein's victory dance, when he bear-hugged others in the delegation or pounded them on the back, as the moment when they decided to get involved. Volunteerism was the hallmark of Calgary's hospitality to the world in February 1988. Maximum community participation was the one thing that Klein agreed on with King, Pratt and all of the Calgary Olympic circle. The mayor's leadership by sheer enthusiasm may have been unconventional, but it worked.

After Baden Baden the resentments against Klein led to attempts to limit his role in the preparations and the event itself. It had taken the efforts of many to win the bid and there were accolades to spare; nevertheless, in the social atmosphere of the times, the hundreds of volunteer members of dozens of committees needed to organize and host the games were avaricious for credit. If some of the people behind the bid could have had their way, the Games would have been hosted without the mayor. As a compromise, they would do their best to elbow him into a minor role. Success did not make everyone gracious towards the man they still scathingly referred to as "Hizzonor."

Meanwhile, it was becoming apparent that winning the bid was a picnic compared with getting the facilities ready and the people in place to host them. Within a few months, OCO was under the gun for almost everything; it was being pounded in the media for issues ranging from the selection of the Nakiska ski hill to the cost overruns on the Saddledome. Klein was pouring oil on the flames by making an issue out of the secrecy-shrouded OCO board meetings. He pushed for an open forum at the same time that sensitive and controversial issues such as personnel decisions on the dozens of well-paid positions the Games created, combined with often negative media coverage persuaded other board members to tighten the lid.

OCO members began to expect Klein to drop a bomb on them at every meeting. When the board started to leak like a sieve, with minutes and documents ending up in the hands of journalists, especially at the *Calgary Herald*, which developed excellent inside sources and became a thorn in the side of organizers, Klein was the chief suspect. It was assumed that Rod Love was passing material to reporters, with the mayor's blessing, so a secret identifier was placed on every scrap of paper given the board. If any leaked document ever ended up back in the hands of the OCO, security officials could pin down the offender who was tipping off the media.

Klein also fought bruising battles on the Saddledome cost overruns with Bill Pratt, the general manager in charge of delivering the facilities on time and on budget. He was quite unfair to Pratt, exposing the general manager to harsh public scrutiny and criticism. Pratt soon felt that city hall and the media were out to get him. He was too willing to shoulder responsibility for things; he had a "damn the torpedos" attitude to getting his job done and tended to think that the buck, as well as the bombs, stopped on his desk. What Klein failed to see was that he and Pratt were brothers of a kind under the skin. Pratt, with his cowboy hats and his bluntness, is another maverick who has been given few breaks by the establishments he has served. Both Klein and Pratt can charm the stuffed-shirt establishment, and both are driven by the same need to prove themselves, but they tip their hat to no man. Normally inclusive, Klein should have realized that Pratt was more friend than foe. In the end, both men rose above their unresolved differences to do their best for the games.

OCO did not have a major public relations success until it negotiated the international television rights to ABC-TV for more than US$300 million—an impressive coup that staggered the media world. Although the relationship with the frequently carping media was never smooth, it got more constructive as the games approached.

Meanwhile, Klein slid into his protocol-laden role as host mayor. At the 1984 Winter Games he won the affection of the city of Sarajevo, and at the closing ceremonies the mayor of Sarajevo presented him with the Olympic flag that was to fly in front of Calgary's city hall for the following four years.

The legendary story that came out of the two sparkling weeks in Sarajevo, now made so distant by the war, is of Klein at a cocktail reception summoning the king of Norway to fetch his car. The king was taken aback and asked the mayor to repeat himself; the confusion continued until someone tactfully introduced the two men. Klein was not the slightest bit embarrassed; he explained to the king that his understated blue uniform for the occasion bore a striking resemblance to something that might be worn by a North American limousine driver. The mayor's unassuming candour charmed many national leaders and assured the relaxed gaiety that became the hallmark of the Calgary games; men like the king found the informal tone endearing.[1]

Meanwhile, on more tangible matters, Klein worked hard, with George Cornish, to nail down financing for key facilities. In addition to the Olympic Plaza, where the medals would be awarded each night, and the Saddledome, the city was primarily responsible for the extension of the LRT system to move spectators between venues without the traffic tie-ups that were an anathema for other communities that had hosted the Olympics in the past.

The Winter Games became the political tool used to end the impasse over completion of the northwest leg of the LRT. The well-established residential communities along the route fended off the project, which they said would split their community like the Berlin Wall, until Calgary was awarded the Olympics. Then the onus shifted. The city was no longer the expropriator; the communities were now obstructionists as the city pulled together to host the world. City council was ready to override objections and build the line.

A new problem had arisen, however. In the ten years that had intervened between the first engineering work and right-of-way land acquisitions and the decision to proceed, $138 million in special funding expected and needed from the province had evaporated. Klein and Cornish called on transportation minister Arthur Kroeger. He regretted that Calgary had missed the window. To give it $138 million now would require the department to give an equal amount to Edmonton; there simply weren't the funds for special projects.

Cornish and Klein countered with a proposal for the LRT money to be included in generic transportation grants over three years for an equivalent amount. The ploy, largely one of perception, succeeded; Kroeger used the loophole suggested by the tag team negotiators to ultimately arrange $140 million.[2]

The northwest line was completed in time to bring tens of thousands of patrons to the hockey matches and figure skating competitions in the Saddledome, the speed skating at the University of Calgary, and the opening and closing ceremonies of the Winter Games in McMahon Stadium.

The controversy over the LRT gave false hope to Klein's few serious enemies and to the ambitious hovering around city politics. As the October 1986 election approached, Alderman Sue Higgins, a salty, chain-smoking politically incorrect politician who liked to call herself "the Alderbroad," decided to challenge Klein's hegemony. Her closest friends advised against it, but she was cynically encouraged by journalists assigned to city hall who wanted a hint of drama in the campaign. Higgins's friends were correct; Klein steamrollered over her on his way to winning his third term with his biggest plurality. She had been made the sacrificial lamb in a contrived media story of a contest for power.

Autumn in southern Alberta can be as flawless as a perfect blue diamond. It is a time of fire on the hills, as the blood gold of the aspen pours across the amber of dried grass. After the equinox, the sky on cloudless day after cloudless day takes on a softer blue that darkens to near indigo at the zenith. The soft warm breezes that slide down the eastern slopes of the Rockies carry no undercurrent of the coming winter. It is a time of tranquillity and well-being. Across the plains each night the grain combines raise their clouds of dust, and after sunset the long beams of their headlights trace the caterpillar patterns of harvest until dew fall, which is often long past midnight.

The autumn of 1986 in Calgary was as perfect as it could be—and on the frosty mornings of October, the sun-cast city streets blossomed with a fresh supply of lawn signs that seemed to spring up like mushrooms overnight. The municipal election had attracted a record number of candidates; civic politics was the place to be. Here there were no unpleasant energy wars, none of the excesses and blunders that were beginning to mar the Mulroney and Getty Conservative governments. Ralph Klein, the city's chief booster, had made local politics fun; half a dozen people longed—and *longed* is not too strong a word for it—to become Ralph II, and another few dozen would settle for just being at the same council table. If that weren't enough, the coming term in office would include the perks and privileges of the Olympics.

Klein was at the pinnacle of his mayoral power. The extent of his influence was demonstrated by the quality of men and women who were touted as challengers to his seat but who had declined to step forward because running against him was a pointless waste of resources.

His campaign was characteristically loose, although there was plenty of funding, for a change, and he now had a core of experienced volunteers who were on their third election assignment with him. With the outcome certain, Klein was at his relaxed best around the makeshift headquarters in an abandoned restaurant on 1st Street SW, a five-minute drive from his office at city hall. The black and white signs and buttons bore one word: *Ralph*. A folded, three-panel pamphlet, also in black and white, was as economical in detail as it was in cost.

Each Saturday morning, between thirty and fifty volunteers met before 9:00 A.M. to eat some donuts and pick up bundles of brochures. They scattered across the city to knock on doors and drop their literature into mailboxes. They returned shortly after noon to eat an endless supply of pizza and mark off, on a giant map, using coloured felt pens, the streets they had canvassed. They picked up more brochures to deliver during the week, lingered for a while to visit and then dispersed, usually by 3:00 P.M. These Saturday mornings became known as the children's crusade because so many of the workers were kids. Campaigning for Ralph had become a family affair. For some of the older children, it was a school project to be written up and submitted as a study in civic affairs.

To the baby boomer parents among the campaign workers, the clear

silver of young laughter and voices spoke of a more perfect version of
the politics of joy than had been achieved in the radical student days of
the 1960s. Call it anti-politics, call it the realization of the counterculture,
whatever. If you wanted conventional politics with ambitious young lawyers in suits, banks of telephones, advertising agencies, graphic designers,
organizational charts and intense strategy meetings, you had to go some-
where else—there were plenty of choices around town.

Here the ambiance of success was leavened with the earnestness of
amateurism; here politics was like what the rest of life should be—not
far removed from the vagabonds and beautiful people, the rainbow
dreamers and backyard schemers of the 1980 campaign. Jo Buck still
presided in her corner of the room, Rod Love hovered like a shadow,
and it was said with hushed reverence that Colleen had cleaned the toilets
when they had set up shop.

Dressed in his trademark track suit, the beaming candidate made
sure to spend time on Saturday, usually over the noon hour, in the headquarters. Surrounded by the children, he looked like Father Christmas
at summer camp. It couldn't get better than this, and therein lay the
problem. Klein's ever-watchful, ever-analytical eyes carried the portent
of restlessness and the first hint of the boredom that had helped drive
him out of journalism.

He won the election with more than 90 per cent of the vote, crushing
Higgins. Afterwards he asked himself, "What more can I do?" For the
next year and a half, of course, there were the preparations for and the
hosting of the Olympics. Klein intended to pour himself into the task
with the characteristic passion of a workaholic, and he did. The Olympics
merely postponed the inevitable consideration of his political future.

That Calgary's hospitality at the Winter Games of 1988 resulted in
a brilliant success is a matter of record, well presented and preserved in
other books. A city much hardened by the affluence of the oil boom and
the disappointments of the bust regained, at least for a few weeks, some
of its old informality and warmth, its western openness and charm. In
turn, some of the icy cynicism and predatory ruthlessness that had come
to be associated with the Games themselves melted, at least for a few
weeks in Calgary's balmy Chinook ambiance.

Calgarians wear their hearts on their sleeves at the slightest prompting; there were many damp eyes among its citizens at McMahon Stadium
when Ralph Klein handed the Olympic Flag over to the Mayor of Albertville, France, who would host the Winter Games in 1992. The shin-
ing moment had come and gone too quickly for the young community.
And when Klein left the stadium that evening, he too was moving on
to other things, his mayoralty essentially over.

He had presided over Calgary's public life as the city redefined its culture for life after the oil booms. And the city had presided over his political life as he redefined its politics. At some point on the way to the Olympics, Calgary had become a new, more subdued but more mature city. At the same time, Klein had become a leader. Calgary was now his political home, and he was its most visible political creation.

The Winter Games became the defining event of Klein's mayoralty. And when the Games ended, he knew that it was time to move on. This he did before his third term in office formally ended. The experience of such a major political success had blooded him for a much higher level of politics than he could find inside city hall. He had seen a wider world and could never again be content with the smaller things of city hall.

Dealing with premiers and prime ministers, kings and courtiers had exposed him to the meanest and most noble aspects of high office. He had learned not only that the lure of power was a greed that could drive one to dishonour but that men and women would risk their lives to gain the fruits of corruption. Betrayal of country, embezzlement of millions of dollars and murder were the common stuff of the international politics he had glimpsed through the window that the Olympics provided. Yet through that window he had seen the creation of civilization, the ending of wars and ennoblement of the human spirit.

It is possible that Klein's political career would have been stillborn without the Games. Calgary's frenetic growth subsided as he came to office, so he was never tested on the ideals and issues that brought him into politics. As he learned the ropes and developed his leadership strategies, the only other definition of his regime came from his gregarious appearances on radio talk shows, where he was cast as an electronic ombudsman, to account for city hall's weekly stewardship and to listen to complaints about potholes and water bills.

He was a lacklustre chairman of council's proceedings, and he became disengaged from the administrative process and was still finding his way on other issues and actions that might have redefined the mayor's office. Reinventing the government of sewers and freeways is pretty dull stuff compared with an Olympic bid. Without the Games, the novelty of Ralph Klein might well have quickly worn off, and the intuitive political tactics that allowed him to hijack power would most likely have been successfully challenged in the economic downturn of 1983.

The Games allowed him the chance to mature, to develop his leadership style and to use it successfully. They allowed him to do what he said he would do: to make people feel good about the city again. His enthusiasm for public life was undiminished, his gritty idealism untarnished. His mantra was still "Let's have some fun and do some good." His horizons had been stretched, however. He had been a good apprentice, but the training was over and it was time to step into the ring.

9

Choices

*Tomorrow he shall take his pack
And set out for the ways beyond . . .
An alien and a vagabond*

—BLISS CARMEN, INSCRIPTION
ON THE ENDPAPER, *MORE
SONGS FROM VAGABONDIA*

In the anticlimax after the Winter Games ended, Ralph began to seriously ponder his future. He believed he had done everything he could do as mayor; he showed no interest in hanging on to become part of the furniture at city hall, athough he could continue to be reelected with an easy grace and historic margins. He had become what he wanted to be: the city's chief salesman and spokesman, the chief magistrate and the front line of his council's public accountability. It had come almost too easily.

If he seemed, at times, like a slow-developing political apprentice, his friends detected that it was because, at its most demanding, being mayor did not require the full extent of his ability. Those who endorsed the basic pragmatic decency of his mantra—"Have some fun, do some good"—observed that doing good in civic politics was too much fun to be too serious.

Klein was acutely aware that had he lost either of his reelection bids in 1983 and 1986, he would have been an overnight nobody. He was aware that Don MacKay, the anti-establishment mayor of the 1950s, whose radio broadcasting background and style of boosterism more resembled Klein's than any other mayor's, had gone into oblivion, with no substantial job offers and no prospects. "No one took care of Don," people at city hall often said.[1]

Although Rod Sykes had done very much better, financially, as a private consultant, Klein did not have Sykes's previous business experience and reputation. Moreover, Sykes was a chartered accountant, whereas Klein did not have an education. Except for the brief period when he sought the Social Credit leadership, Sykes was now entirely out of the limelight, busy with his children and grandchildren and immersed in his books and his beloved rock garden. Klein did not want to be sitting in a den reading or on his knees gardening for the rest of his life.

He could start the life of a corporate executive, which had been a possibility at the United Appeal before he decided to go into journalism. The best he could hope for in business, however, was a vice-presidency, probably in the land development or housing industry, probably in marketing or public affairs. He risked becoming the tame pet of some ambitious entrepreneur, to be dragged out on special occasions as the toy ex-mayor and to be used for whatever vestige of acumen and influence he might have over the civic affairs of the company. If there were ever more substantial job offers, Klein never hinted of them.

Then there was national politics. Prime Minister Brian Mulroney sent an emissary to formally offer a cabinet seat to Klein, if he would run in the September 1988 federal election.[2] But Ottawa was too far away for Colleen; she knew such a move would disrupt the family and she laid down the law: no federal politics until Theresa was out on her own. Klein needed little discouragement; the idea of a five-hour airline commute to Parliament did not appeal to him.

Meanwhile, the Liberal Party of Alberta was preparing for a leadership race in which its rock-ribbed, old-fashioned boss, Nick Taylor, was to be challenged by a new generation of younger, more pragmatic Grits.[3] Klein's past relationship with Liberal campaigns, starting with Peter Petrasuk in 1968, and discreetly continued with Taylor in 1972, led some Grits to assume that he would look to the Liberals if he made a move into provincial politics. The impression was reinforced when he helped Sheldon Chumir defeat Brian Lee in the 1985 election. It was well known that his relationship with Premier Lougheed had not been good, and Liberal recruiters took this as a sign that he would have no interest in the Tories. They also assumed that he would not be interested in anything less than leading a party, and the Conservative Party had a leader—Don Getty.

Edmonton mayor Laurence Decore was a certain candidate for the Liberal leadership. His family's Grit loyalties were deep and complex. Members of the media and academe began to speculate about a mayor-versus-mayor battle between Klein and Decore. An amiable rivalry had already been created between the two men, based on the competition between the two cities' professional football and hockey teams. Once the two men had even raced bobsleds down Calgary's Olympic bobsled run.

Although it is hard to credit Klein with having seriously considered the Liberal leadership, he did consult widely with friends and supporters about the possibility. He found that the Liberal Party needed him more

than he needed it. Even he, in his most cocky moments, could not imagine that he could turn a bunch of chronic losers into winners. He also
faced up to the fact that he was not a liberal.

Liberals in Alberta are much like the Russian émigrés of London in
the first half of the twentieth century, living for the restoration of the
czar. Only true believers would carry the flag into hopeless campaign
after hopeless campaign. The Liberals whom Klein might lead were, at
their heart, well to the left of centre, passionately committed to interventionist social policy and centralist-style federalism, which were totally out
of tune with Ralph's own politics of personal responsibility. The mayor
was liberal only in the nineteenth-century John Stuart Mill sense of the
word, and then only with respect to Mill's ideas on fiscal responsibility
and legislative accountability. The greatest good for the greatest number,
in Klein's political philosophy, would be that the greatest number rely
not at all on the government for almost anything.

Klein's more hard-nosed, less philosophical insiders agreed that even
with Klein, the Liberals would never be anything more than an Opposition party. The Trudeau legacy was a poisoned thing and would dis-
enfranchise Grits in the province for a couple of generations. Trudeau
aside, the endless erosion of the current leader Nick Taylor's credibility—until one had to marvel that there was any standing at all left to
be eroded—could not be undone in a span as short as the career of one
leader. To lead the Liberal Party in Alberta seemed, in the minds of his
supporters, to consign Klein to the noble but pointless role of sacrificial
lamb.

One thing was certain—Klein's political career was up for grabs.
The Liberals came calling, and Klein gave them an audience. The news
media began to speculate about his candidacy. The mayor called around
his network for opinions and advice. The Grits began to weigh their
chances against Premier Don Getty, who had taken office in 1985 and
already looked to the Liberals like a man they could knock off his perch.

Klein characteristically procrastinated on the issue, perhaps largely
because there was nothing else pressing on his agenda. He calculated
every angle and talked about the matter to anyone whose opinion he
valued—a very long list of people indeed. Then he announced he would
not be a candidate for the Liberal leadership. The Liberals were griev-
ously wounded. Many had taken his procrastination for tacit consent. In
spurning them, Klein had denied them "Jerusalem next year."

Some Grits harboured the suspicion that the Liberal Party had been
had, that Klein, the closet Tory and clever manipulator, had merely entertained them to conduct a reconnaissance for the Tories. They suspected that the whole exercise was a spying mission that had badly compromised their strategies. Given the transparency of Liberal affairs, there

was hardly anything Klein could have gleaned that would not have been available some easier way; nevertheless, the suspicion lingered.

The Grits' bitterness and venom has been, and will continue to be, expressed in every campaign that Klein has faced and will face in his own constituency for as long as he is a Tory. In rejecting the Liberals, he created the only prize that a Grit, especially a Calgary Grit, values more highly than winning government in Alberta. That prize is to defeat Ralph Klein in his own riding. Its most damaging impact, however, is to cloud the judgement of the Liberals on almost any matter related to Ralph Klein.

Once he had said no to the Liberals, Klein was still left with the problem of deciding his future. The Tories, especially in Calgary, were in a state of near despair over the failing leadership of Premier Don Getty. Many of Klein's closest civic supporters were Tories; they may not have considered recruiting Klein earlier, but his flirtation with the Liberals had put him in play as a potential provincial politician, and this brought him to the attention of Premier Getty.

In 1988 Don Getty was foundering. The Conservatives had made a serious mistake in electing him leader when Peter Lougheed retired. To whatever extent Lougheed himself aided and abetted the succession, he, too, had seriously erred. As a premier, Getty was a misfit. He developed a reputation for being more interested in golf than work. He handled the media poorly and was lax in disciplining his ministers. He was a weak leader; he held no strong ideas of his own and appeared at times to be swayed by the last person out of the room. Then, one of his sons was charged with possession of cocaine; the Gettys closed ranks, and his detractors had a field day using the tragedy to question his political credibility.

The truth of the matter was that Getty had neither the personality nor the inclination to do the job and he seemed short on ability. Some of his problems were inherited from Peter Lougheed, and some were the result of his inability to communicate through the medium of television. Politics is a cruel sport, however, and no matter how laudable his intentions and how upright his private life—and he was an exemplary family man—Don Getty wasn't cutting it.

By 1988, at mid-term in his mandate, he was already in deep trouble and knew that there was more to come—more controversy and scandal. His worst problems concerned a series of large provincial investments in businesses that were made in pursuit of an economic diversification policy. Several deals had gone sour, leaving the government on the hook for hundreds of millions of dollars. The bitterest attacks came over a regulatory failure: the collapse of the Principal Group, a trust and financial institution, had cost Albertans several hundred million in lost pension investments, and the political fallout was overwhelming. In addition, with the collapse of the oil economy, Getty knew he faced the kind of tough economic times that make life for incumbent premiers very painful. At the very least, Getty knew he needed some fresh blood in his ranks if he were to survive the anticipated 1989 election.

Realists in the party were also concerned about the future; they needed to shore up the Tory team in preparation. Ralph Klein was an obvious winner, and he had powerful sponsors within the Conservative Party, men like lawyers Brian Scott and Bruce Green. Scott had been city solicitor under Klein; Green, a land development expert who sat on various civic commissions and boards. These, and other influential individuals, knew that Klein was cabinet material. Several MLAs in the Conservative caucus had been aldermen on Klein's councils.

Getty, with plenty of urging and advice, took the initiative to bring Klein into his cabinet. There is gossip that he did so reluctantly because he recognized Ralph's power base and had no desire to bring men to the cabinet table who might be seen as his own successors. Klein would be on any media or party member's list of speculative candidates to replace Getty.

Whatever the premier's reservations, Don Getty and Ralph Klein met on November 15, 1988, to discuss the mayor's candidacy as a Conservative in an election that was scarcely four months away. Klein later told his father that a cabinet seat was offered, but not necessarily a senior one. Klein would have to earn his spurs. Since Getty had every intention of being premier of Alberta for a long time to come, there was no suggestion that the Calgary mayor would be any kind of special lieutenant or have a privileged position at the right hand of power. After all, Getty had several ex-mayors in his caucus. If none were as prominent as Klein, Getty was not about to let that turn his head.

Nevertheless, the premier was charmed and he told friends later that Klein was a much more substantial and serious person than he had expected. Later the charm wore off. The prudish Getty tired quickly of Klein's jocular, boozy lifestyle.[4] But initially he responded to Ralph's warmth by revealing his own very private side. The battering of office had made Getty reserved and cold. People who remembered him as Lougheed's powerful energy minister in the 1970s—always gregarious and accessible—remarked on the cold wall of reserve that he had thrown around himself since returning to politics as the party's leader.

Getty was impressed that Klein insisted on a further meeting at which their wives would join them. The premier correctly presumed a parallel between Margaret Getty's role as his closest adviser and often his only real friend and Colleen's role in Klein's political life. This was reassuring as well as warming. The comparison was not entirely exact; unlike Getty, Klein had a wide political council of people he trusted. But he would not dream of making a major change in his life unless Colleen had considered the idea and was prepared to make the choice with him.

At this point, Klein began to procrastinate, just as he had in the summer of 1980 when he was faced with the decision to enter politics. He canvassed widely for opinion among friends and associates through the Christmas round of parties, dinners and year-end media interviews. Soon the biggest open secret in Calgary was that Klein was considering joining the Conservative government.

He called his father to seek his opinion. Philip had not forgotten that his son had refused his advice in 1980 when he had discouraged Ralph from entering politics in the first place. "You seem to make up your own mind about these things," Philip said.

His son replied that he had been offered a cabinet seat, which seemed to his father the least that Getty could do. "You can count on my help in any way I can," Philip promised.

Klein received nothing but encouragement: yes, he could win one of several ridings; yes, he could leave civic office in mid-term without a backlash; yes, it seemed the obvious thing for him to do. The Christmas season passed without an announcement, but the matter was all but decided. Klein went on a brief holiday while the final pieces fell together.

On January 10, 1989, Ralph Klein made it official; he was resigning as the city's mayor and would seek a Conservative seat in the coming election. The transition was seamless; Don Hartman, the senior alderman on council and a veteran of two decades in office, was named interim mayor. Klein accepted the Tory nomination in Calgary Elbow, a heterogeneous south Calgary riding of older communities that were neither inner city nor suburban.

It seemed an odd choice of constituencies: Klein was a prized candidate and there were safer seats. Calgary Elbow included upper-middle-class neighbourhoods were he was regarded as an interloper. Their only comfort was that with Klein out of city hall, it would finally be back in reliable hands. The Liberals were gleeful; they were sure that Klein was out of his element and had picked a constituency where he would be most vulnerable.

Calgary Elbow had the singular merit, however, of being available. Few MLAs wanted to leave the political sinecures of their Tory seats in Calgary. Other Conservatives regarded the mayor's entry into the party with distaste. They saw him as an opportunist and a threat to the career ambitions of longer-serving MLAs. They would do what they could to prevent him from crashing the queue. Much of the resistance came from ambitious Calgary MLAs who believed his purpose was to usurp the leadership when Getty retired. They had the knives out for him.

David Russell, the Calgary MLA, had been, along with Getty, one of Peter Lougheed's original team in the years of Opposition to the Social Credit government from 1967 to 1971. Russell had served ably in cabinet but was now getting out of politics while he was still young enough to return to a private career. He was a political moderate, and the cabinet and the caucus under Getty were shifting to the right. Russell preferred private life to that. When he stepped aside, Klein stepped in.

The Liberals, under their new leader, Laurence Decore, threw one of their brightest lights against the former mayor. For a time they were sure that they had beaten him. Gib Clark was a blue Liberal; he had earned his conservative credentials as a federal drug prosecutor and member of the kind of Liberal law firm, Walsh Young, with which Conservatives could be seen socially. At the United Appeal, by coincidence, he had worked with Klein on some committees. Patrician and polished, Clark was the kind of man that the Grits thought could swing important ridings out of the Tory column, especially with the growing doubts that Alberta's business and professional establishment had about Don Getty. Ironically, Clark, the establishment candidate in Calgary Elbow, was running with the renegade Grits; Klein, the outsider, represented the political establishment.

During the late winter election campaign, Klein stepped gingerly around the riding, not wanting to knock on doors in neighbourhoods where he would not be welcomed. It was not that he was without friends. He had joined the winning team. Outsider that he was, he at least had the resources of a strong establishment at his disposal. His constituency president, wealthy land and resort developer Hal Walker, was typical of the kind of influential men and women whom he now encountered as a colleague and Tory fellow traveller.

As it turned out, the Liberals finished third across the province in the 1989 election. Decore had not delivered the breakthrough; New Democrats had the strongest Opposition block of seats in the eighteen-year Tory dynasty. In Calgary Elbow the outcome fit the pattern; Clark went back to the law and Klein went on to Edmonton.

Although Klein had won the seat, his entrée into the Conservative Party was questioned because he was actively disliked by some of the blue-chip Tories in his riding. As far as they were concerned, the jury was still out.

10

The Ecotrap

You will go on, and when you have
prevailed
You can say: at this point many a
one has failed.

—T. S. ELIOT, "PORTRAIT OF A
LADY"

When Ralph Klein was appointed environment minister, in April 1989, a month after winning the seat in Calgary Elbow, covert elements in the Conservative cabinet and caucus could hardly contain their joy. Klein, whom they regarded as a pretender to the throne, had walked into a trap. At late night, boozy cabals, men and women calculating the equations of power speculated that Premier Getty had set it for him, to cauterize his ambition. The Environment Ministry would be the premature but unlamented death of Klein's career. His populist political instincts, soft-edged style and thirst for popularity were all wrong; he would be exposed for what he was: not a Conservative.

Getty's personal defeat in the Edmonton-Whitemud riding had triggered shadowy preparations to replace him, even while he was winning the by-election for the safe Stettler constituency. The premier said he was not planning to step aside, but funds were being raised, organizations were being put into place and incumbent cabinet ministers were squeezing every advantage they could out of their portfolios. The skirmishes between real and imagined rivals were strategic, to establish positions of advantage. These rivals—all of whom were in in the cabinet and caucus—saw Klein as a parachute candidate for a prize that belonged to someone else, someone in cabinet who had soldiered in the trenches and earned a place in the party's establishment. They feared Klein would do what he did best—hijack power.

In the inevitable leadership contest ahead, Klein had a call on Getty's endorsement, or so other prospective candidates feared, since Klein had made it well known that he and Colleen had dined with Don and Margaret before making a commitment to the Conservatives. Even weakened, Getty's power to lay the mantle on a successor was important. Peter

Lougheed was circumspect about a favourite but never dispelled the inference that he blessed Getty's candidacy, in 1985, thus influencing the decisive support of key cabinet and caucus members. Whether this laying on of hands was true ot not, rank-and-file party members believed that it was and voted for Getty accordingly.

Then Klein walked into the ecotrap; he settled for a middle-level portfolio regarded, politically, as a necessary evil. His job, now, was to figure out how to fend off the hard-core environmentalists while the resource industries carried on business as usual, a task that guaranteed that he could satisfy no one. His ambition would flounder on disputes over pulp mills, prairie dams, toxic waste treatment and natural gas drilling in the foothills. Klein had thrown away, prematurely, the leverage of his popularity and reputation.

Yet Klein was pleased with the appointment. Environment was a portfolio in which he could make his mark by changing and moulding it. He would have some freedom because he was overshadowed by more influential ministries, such as energy, health and education, where the big dollars were dealt. It was a portfolio he understood, since it managed issues to which he felt connected, such as protection of Alberta's rivers, and since he had already established a working relationship with ministry officials on such matters as waste management and clean water during his mayoralty.

Klein regarded the preservation of the Bow River as one of the political accomplishments of his eight years in civic government. He brought the Bow River onto the policy agenda and kept it there. The river that bisects Calgary is its heart, its prime recreational facility, and it defines the city's physical character and its beauty. To Klein, it was the place to which he retreated in his canoe or with his fishing tackle and the place that connected him to his spiritual taproot. His political program for the river, which was coordinated with the province, had included protecting it from river-bank development, blocking new freeway crossings, improving sewage treatment and eliminating industrial sources of pollution.

Klein attacked his new post with tireless enthusiasm. "There are no stories in a news room," he once said to explain why he spent so little time, as a reporter, riding the desk.[1] To oversee Alberta's environment, he went to where it was, adopting a merciless travel schedule.

Soon he established a reputation, at least among his cabinet colleagues, for accessibility and a tireless energy. He got into the habit of going to his department's trouble spots, learning the situation firsthand and often improvising both policy and administrative actions on the spot.

"What I liked about Ralph and his approach to politics was his willingness to talk to people wherever they were," writes Boomer Adair, former MLA for Peace River and minister of transportation and utilities when Klein headed environment, in his biography. "During his time as Minister of the Environment, he made three trips to the north end of my constituency [and] he visited Peace River several times to deal with flood problems, the construction of a new pulp mill, and to find out generally what his department was doing in the area."[2]

After the 1992 spring flood that inundated four hundred homes in Peace River and forced the evacuation of part of the town, Klein took Adair and the mayor of Peace River on a hasty trip to Victoria to present a $4.1 million damages bill to B.C. Hydro for failing to lower the flood level of the Bennett Dam upstream from the community, Adair recalled. Klein began to turn up all across the province to deal directly with issues and crises, or to master the details of his department's work.

He softened the government's economic image by opening up environmental evaluations to public processes and gently reigning in the resource sector. Alberta had the reputation of being one-sided—tough on "activists" (the environmental lobbies) and soft on "polluters" (the non-renewable resource sector). Klein moderated the mood by being firmer with resource projects and ensuring that environmentalists had a stronger voice and more influence.

He forced Proctor and Gamble to comply with water effluent standards for dioxin disposal at its Grande Prairie pulp mill. Boomer Adair recounted that people said Klein didn't have the guts to shut down the plant. After a personal visit to meet with officials, however, Klein gave the company a short deadline to remedy the problem or face a plant closure. The company swiftly began to improve its water treatment procedures and complied with the province's standards under the deadline.

Against strong resistance from the doctrinaire, laissez faire Conservatives in the cabinet and caucus, he instituted the broadest, most public environmental impact assessment in the province's history for the Alberta Pacific project, a bleached kraft pulp mill developed in the subarctic softwood forests, northeast of Edmonton. He won the grudging respect of the company and most of the environmental activists on the file, and the plant was built to a high standard of compliance.

The new environment minister found an in-tray full of unresolved problems, none of which seemed winnable, all of which were high-profile political conflicts with small, determined activist groups supported by a sympathetic media. Not all were as easy to resolve as the Proctor and Gamble or Alberta Pacific conflicts had been. One such thorny issue was the escalating dispute between his officials and Opron Construction Ltd. of Calgary involving the building of a clay and gravel dam on the Paddle River in the early 1980s.

The project had overrun its budget by more than four times, not

including legal costs for the Opron lawsuit against the government, cost-
ing at least $43 million and possibly as much as $60 million against a 1974
estimate of $12 million. Opron was claiming that environment department
officials deliberately misrepresented important facts about engineering
and materials, and the case was winding its way through the courts. Klein,
like a total of seven environment ministers before him, was petitioned by
the company to settle the matter out of court but didn't.[3]

Nor could he resolve the escalating costs and controversial toxic
waste disposal issues surrounding the Alberta Special Waste Treatment
Centre at Swan Hills, a government joint venture with a company called
Bovar Industries. The plant, built in 1984 to incinerate the most diffi-
cult-to-dispose-of hazardous wastes, such as PCBs, and to create a powerful waste-handling monopoly for the Prairies, had become a $250 mil-
lion-and-rising sinkhole for public money and was not yet operating
efficiently. Moreoever, use by out-of-province customers had not been
resolved, because of regulations governing the transportation of wastes.[4]

Klein's ability to manoeuvre was handicapped. The responsibilities
of his department were blurry; the powerful Energy Resources Conservation Board reviewed and ruled on the environmental effects of the
province's dominant industry, petroleum. The federal government was
developing the new Environmental Protection Act, which included a
new impact-assessment process directly threatening provincial resources
and constitutional jurisdiction.

The government's loan guarantees for Swan Hills had become a
high-profile embarrassment, and the plant was a target for environmentalists who thought its environmental impact had not been properly as-
sessed before construction. When the province wanted to import and
incinerate dangerous wastes such as PCBs from other jurisdictions that
did not have comparable plants, opponents depicted the proposal, with
inflammatory rhetoric, as a plan to make the province a dumping ground
for other people's garbage. None of the important Swan Hills issues were
resolved while Klein was environment minister.

A prairie irrigation and water management dam under construction
on the Oldman River in southern Alberta was embroiled in a complex
controversy. The province had failed to subject the project to its own
environmental review standards, and that matter was before the courts.
Intervenors were asking judges to halt construction and make the province tear down what it had built.

Landowners whose property was being flooded for the reservoir, including a group of Peigans, were carrying on an emotional and
embittered rear-guard action to prevent the loss of their lands. The
Peigan had been involved in a standoff attempt to throw crews off the
project by force. Shots had been fired, and Peigan leader Milton Born

ABOVE: Klein was 21 years old when he joined the Red Cross, launching his public life. PHOTO COURTESY OF THE CANADIAN RED CROSS SOCIETY ALBERTA-NORTHWEST TERRITORIES DIVISION

RIGHT: Gil Gilmet, Red Cross water safety supervisor, gave Klein his first lessons in public relations. PHOTO COURTESY OF THE CANADIAN RED CROSS SOCIETY ALBERTA-NORTHWEST TERRITORIES DIVISION

Klein was the rising star of CFCN Television's crack news
team that included (*standing, left to right*) David Legg,
Klein, Murray Dale, and (*below, left to right*) John Gulka
and Grant Howard. PHOTO COURTESY OF GRANT HOWARD

LEFT: After three years of agonizing over his future, by the summer of 1980 Klein, here in his Calgary home, was ready to make the switch from journalism to politics. ALBERTA REPORT

BELOW: The 1980 campaign opened in an office amid the rubble of the block-busting for a new city hall. The disadvantages of the site led Klein to obtain a better location. ALBERTA REPORT

Top: The Klein family at breakfast in their modest southwest Calgary townhouse, in 1980. *Left to right*: Theresa, Colleen, Ralph and Lisa. GLENBOW ARCHIVES/NA 2864-41567; CALGARY HERALD COLLECTION

ABOVE: After the polls closed on October 15, 1980, the unexpected mayor-elect, wearing a headset for a TV interview, and Colleen were thronged by reporters, well-wishers and opportunists. GLENBOW ARCHIVES/NA 2864-41501; CALGARY HERALD COLLECTION

ABOVE: As mayor-elect, Klein toured the proposed northwest LRT route signing autographs; he campaigned against the line but as mayor reversed his position, disillusioning the community. GLENBOW ARCHIVES/NA 2864-41640; CALGARY HERALD COLLECTION

LEFT: The former reporter and now mayor-elect, with Rod Love, met defeated incumbent Ross Alger (*right*) in the city hall press room a few days before power changed hands. GLENBOW ARCHIVES/NA 2864-41620; CALGARY HERALD COLLECTION

Top: Mr. Justice Milt Harradence (*left*) administered the oath of office on inauguration day, October 27, 1980. Harradence was a major influence on Klein's journalism and politics. THE CITY OF CALGARY ARCHIVES

Above: Posing on inauguration day for his first official photograph as mayor, Klein knew that the key to his success would be the image he presented as an accountable, accessible politician. THE CITY OF CALGARY ARCHIVES

ABOVE: George Cornish, Calgary's Chief Commissioner throughout Klein's years as mayor, shared Klein's deep love of the city; otherwise, they were complete opposites. THE CITY OF CALGARY ARCHIVES

LEFT: Klein claimed Calgary's depression-era mayor, Andrew Davidson, as his chief political role model and emulated Davidson's labour-movement compassion for working people. THE CITY OF CALGARY ARCHIVES

RIGHT: Mayor Klein spent hundreds of hours at his desk ploughing through the arcane detail of civic policy, but he always appeared laid-back, cheerful and easy-going. THE CITY OF CALGARY ARCHIVES

BELOW: Mayor Klein and his novice political staff (Rod Love and Bruce Planche) refused to let work get in the way of enjoying the thrill of just being in office; at times it seemed the hijinks would go on forever. ALBERTA REPORT

With A Tooth was defending himself against firearms charges in a high-profile criminal case. Environmentalists, who also opposed the dam, wanted the federal government to step in and enforce additional environmental-impact review processes.

When Klein took over the file, he disappointed those in the Friends of the Oldman Society who thought the anti-politician might be enough of a maverick to reverse the government's position. They misjudged both his political convictions and his commitment to the orthodoxy of cabinet solidarity.

He carried the ball for the completion of the dam and defended it in the legal system. Klein had no desire to tear down the looms of Alberta's agriculture industry, which would benefit from the Oldman dam. The activists were also ignorant of Klein's perceptive understanding of support for the project in the region, particularly in the larger cities of southern Alberta, where summer water supplies would be improved when the dam was completed.

With Klein's backing, the dam was completed, but the legal actions against it dragged on like a bad toothache. The facility proved its worth during historic floods in the spring of 1995, when downstream communities would have been devastated without its water-management protection. Pincher Creek, an upstream town, was also the most seriously damaged.

Alberta's pulp and paper industry presented the environment minister with his toughest battles. In one of his major economic initiatives, Premier Getty authorized the granting of millions of hectares of harvesting rights to support the construction of a new generation of giant mills in the north. Overnight, Edmonton became the centre of Canada's fastest-growing forestry boom. Environmental interventionists were outraged; they broadened the attack on Alberta's forestry to include the environmental review of the mill projects and then attacked any forestry expansion.

The conflict was overshadowed by the fight on the coast of British Columbia to interdict the logging of old-growth forest. It was bitter nonetheless and polarized pro- and anti-resource development opinion in the province. Environmental controversy, specifically the pulp mill development issue, probably cost Getty his seat in the 1989 election and contributed to the creation of a New Democrat stronghold in the capital city.

If the environmental movement expected Klein to crack on the issue, however, they were badly mistaken. In his role as a new tough guy on the political block, Klein stood firm. He argued that the environmentalists were misrepresenting the strength of environmental regulation and enforcement, and he continued to be as tough an enforcer as Getty would

allow him to be. He got the industry to cooperate and be patient with
the environmental review process. He became an even stronger advocate
of sustainable resource development, saying that it was possible to have
both economic expansion and clean air, water and land.

As his tenure in the department unfolded, it was clear that he believed the province's resource industries were basically responsible and
that he trusted his department's powers and procedures for impact assessment, monitoring and enforcement. He positioned himself on the
middle ground in most disputes but ultimately always sided with industry and backed his officials. Surprisingly, his media coverage was basically positive; the handful of journalists covering the beat believed that
Klein was the most reasonable, open and flexible minister to occupy the
portfolio in the Conservative years dating back to 1971. Just because he
did not reflexively attack the environmental movement, he was not crit-
icized very severely for always coming down on the side of development.

If he disappointed Alberta's environmental activists, their movement
also disappointed him. He was predisposed to be fair; he was better able
than most ministers to listen clearly to the message, unaffected by con-
frontational style or tactics. In the end, he could not overcome the ad-
versarial nature of a process that defined him as an enemy when he
thought it was his role to be the referee. When he lost patience during
the Alberta Pacific environmental review and flipped the finger at noisy
protesters in a public meeting, it was more than anything that the activists he encountered were not convincing and Klein respected people and
organizations who could present a winning case.

He was, however, far from a doctrinaire "slash and burn" developer.
A chronic toothache for the government during Klein's tenure at Environment was petroleum drilling on the eastern slopes of the Rockies.
The environment minister is out of the play on oil and gas development;
those issues are decided by the independent, quasi-judicial Energy Resources Conservation Board. The energy minister brings those regulatory
decisions to cabinet for ratification, so the environment minister is not
on record on the merits of a development dispute.

From 1989 to 1993, when oil companies and environmental protection organizations clashed on specific drilling projects in sensitive areas,
Klein made it clear that if the industry lost any of these, they should not
expect him to support, in cabinet, a move to override the conservation
board.

Klein had not left behind an image as a successful legislator in Calgary. Nor was he expected to earn top marks from bureaucrats, lawyers,
technicians and scientists who worked in the regulatory mechanism system. His biggest success at environment, however, was to drive a new

Alberta environmental protection act through the legislature after a two-year public review and consultation, one of the largest processes in the province's legislative history.

The new act was expected to be more than controversial. It was to be a minefield for the government. The Opposition expected to waylay the government at a dozen turns. Klein, dubbed the lovable lout by his media detractors, was supposed to fail at this kind of thing. The interventionists had laid in ammunition for a long siege. But in spite of all the hand wringing and the vitriolic public posturing, the bill slid through the legislature and became law when give royal assent by the lieutenant-governor, smooth as silk.

After it was law, Klein and Vance MacNichol helped launch the Natural Resources Conservation Board, a super-regulator that reviews and approves all resource development other than oil and gas. That done, they started in on the environment department and streamlined it until it was running as well as anything in Edmonton.

The environmental profession, especially that segment of it on the corporate payroll, was lavish with its praise. Resource industries, especially oil and gas, were pleasantly relieved that a man touted as a populist had been so reasonable in his dealings with them. The people in the department who worked for Klein said he was the best minister with whom they had ever dealt.

The Paddle River dam file that Klein inherited, however, degenerated into a worse condition during his tenure. Klein compounded the problems by stonewalling the action and all attempts to resolve it before the trial.

The nub of the lawsuit was that Environment's fraudulent dealings—misinforming contractors about soil profiles and gravel supplies near the dam—had bankrupted three contractors. The contractors claimed that the deliberate misinformation had cost them millions in cost overruns at the job site that they could not recover under their contracts. They said the government was prepared to let the matter drag on indefinitely.

Klein's conduct of the file, as environment minister, was uncharacteristically shoddy. He met Peter Hutton of Opron Construction, the principal defendant, only once. He had been drinking, prompting Hutton to ask if he always prepared himself this way for technical meetings.[5] Later, in Question Period, Klein would claim to have met several times with the plaintiffs to seek an out-of-court settlement, but apparently he delegated the file to Rod Love and Vance MacNichol—and if the matter was mishandled during his term as environment minister, it was one of those two men who had dropped the ball.

Perhaps not coincidentally, the two cabinet ministers who, as premier, Klein was to fire in 1994, Deputy Premier Ken Kowalski and
Transportation and Utilities Minister Peter Trynchy, were also caught
up in the controversy because the project affected their ridings and Trynchy attempted to engineer a deal that divided the political patronage
spoils to be allocated between the two men, with Trynchy awarded 75
per cent of the gravy and Kowalski in control of 25 per cent.

The trial court's decision in favour of the plaintiffs was Klein's first
crisis as premier, after the 1993 election. Although Opron appealed the
amount of the settlement, the judge found that the environment department had acted fraudulently and deceitfully. Klein was forced to ask for
an independent report from the attorney general of Saskatchewan to determine whether officials should face criminal charges or other sanctions.
The report, which Klein buried as long as he could, concluded that no
disciplinary or legal action beyond the civil suits against the government
was warranted, but Klein bungled again by withholding a scathing covering letter that chastized several officials and politicians for their conduct in the matter. When the letter leaked out, Paddle River became the
sole issue that Klein inherited from the disastrous Getty years that had
the potential to cause him long-term political harm.

Except for Paddle River, Klein's tenure as environment minister was
widely regarded as a great political triumph. Much of the workaholic
effort he poured into the department went unrecognized because it dealt
with relatively arcane administrative issues and was of little interest to
most people outside of government. In a way that he never had as mayor,
he asserted his control over the bureaucracy. He created a clear understanding of how he wanted to draw the line between external political
issues and matters that could be resolved internally and insisted on being
in charge of the political agenda. He read, travelled, sat through endless
briefings and gained credibility with his deputies. Then he backed them
up.

He succeeded because he had learned from George Cornish how to
build trust and consensus with bureaucrats, and he did that within his
department. Cornish made an incredibly valuable contribution by
smoothing the way for Vance MacNichol, the deputy minister, to meet
his new boss. Cornish called Klein when he heard of his appointment
and told him that MacNichol was the best deputy in the government.
Cornish gave a parallel endorsement of Klein to MacNichol.

MacNichol gave Klein what he never had at city hall: a professional
cadre of experts who were in his office and under his control. With them,
he no longer was reluctant to engage in open debate on matters with
technical and financial detail. He could expect to be well prepared by

his people for Question Period, debate on legislation, major speeches and media scrums and interviews. He was a quick study for MacNichol's impressive briefing books and notes. The two men were the same kind of policy tag team Klein and Cornish had become.

Klein faced a political choice between resource developers and anti-resource activists. When he chose to stand with the professionals around him in the department he avoided public conflict in a way that was consistent with his dislike of conflict in his office and in his private life. He kept his head down and avoided serious media scrutiny. He evaded attempts by environmentalists to pin him down or corner him on the substance, the scientific content and the ecological implications of various conflicts. He ended up with better press and a better reputation than his impact on the major issues involving his department merited. Style won out over substance.

As the troubled government of Don Getty lurched past its mid-term, Conservatives were quietly engaged in a fierce debate about the party's future. There was a very strong "Getty has to go" faction convinced that survival depended on new leadership. Klein stayed well away from the talk, leaving his strategy on that matter pretty much in the hands of Rod Love.

When Klein first came to Edmonton, it was soon evident to the caucus that Rod Love was not the political brain behind Ralph Klein. The cabinet and caucus saw that Klein was plenty smart enough all by himself. It was equally clear that Love was the most powerful member of the Klein team, a close friend as well as a political confidant to the environment minister.

Love had liabilities that had not been so conspicuous in a mayor's bureau but that showed up in a cabinet minister's office. He guarded his position as gatekeeper and personal minder more jealously and zealously than necessary. He obtained a reputation among the MLAs in the Conservative caucus for being lazy. He partied and vacationed with the minister, and he was cavalier with caucus. He developed a terrible habit of not returning calls from MLAs.

Love, the political strategist and man behind every previous Klein campaign, was also a constant reminder to others of Klein's potency as a leadership candidate. With Love in the field, Klein was astutely able to distance himself from the jockeying for position around Getty, which got progressively more unseemly. Love was nurturing the flame, quietly keeping the ship in shape, monitoring the struggle for future power. He kept the option for Klein's leadership bid open, often in spite of his boss. Other contenders knew it and resented it.

Surprisingly, to those who had known him for a long time and knew his once casual attitude to the nuances of party politics, Klein's partisan passion intensified. Bob Blair, then chairman and chief executive officer of Nova Corporation, the natural gas pipeline and petrochemical giant, and a well-established Liberal, found himself, one evening, the target of a belligerent attack by the environment minister.

The two men, along with Colleen and Blair's date, were seated together at a community dinner in Chinatown. As the evening wore on and the booze flowed, Klein berated Blair for his Liberal connections. He questioned Blair's allegiance to Alberta's interests, implying that only Conservatives could speak for the province. Klein's attitude, and his attack, stung. Blair considered himself above partisanship, in spite of the cost to his credentials with other Liberals. A former collegiate boxer, Bob Blair does not usually back away from a good political scrap, but the minister's belligerence seemed to be the bottle talking as much as the politician, so he bit his tongue.

Klein's belligerence embarrassed the others at the table; his language became saltier and his wife soon coaxed him out the door. Later, Blair realized that in spite of the influence of drink, Klein really meant what he had said and would have launched the same attack, perhaps in politer language, completely sober.[6]

Loyal Conservatives around the province had picked up on Klein's combative Toryism. It may have disturbed more objective friends like Bob Blair, but it heartened the loyal troops. Here was a guy who wasn't ashamed to be a Conservative and to rub it in your face if you weren't. Here was a leader.

As Getty's final months in office dragged on, with their bickering and scandal, Klein distanced himself from the centre of power and the ill-concealed battle for the succession. He spent more and more time on the road, accepting every invitation to put a positive spin on the government and to explain his maturing conservative vision. He talked about the face-to-face accountability of governments that listen and respond and about the citizen's personal responsibility. You should not expect government to do for you what you could do for yourself. Families, churches, volunteer organizations and communities have responsibilities to care for their members; you just couldn't throw the whole burden on government.

The kid from Tuxedo Park with no advantages had made something of himself. Now he was in your corner, cheering for you while you made something of yourself, but you should not expect him to give you the borrowed and mortgaged resources of an indebted government; you should be relying on yourself.

In many ways, Klein's rambling speeches came to resemble the long talks he had in 1978 and 1979 with Grant Howard and other friends, during which he defined his personal political message. In 1992, the message resonated with the audience, but the messenger procrastinated. Much as he had done in the two years before entering the 1980 mayoralty race, Klein now wavered, as his closest friends and supporters began to talk of a run for the leadership.

I I
The Hijack

*Which was the less dangerous
course—to reprieve him or let him
hang?*

—JOHN W. DAFOE, *LAURIER: A
STUDY IN CANADIAN POLITICS*

When Premier Don Getty announced his resignation on September 8, 1992, the Alberta Conservative Party was dead and waiting to be buried. The level of public anger and repudiation was high. Reading the polls and media commentary and listening to the café and cocktail chatter led to the single conclusion that Getty simply could not lead the party to another victory. But not only had Getty and his party been rejected, people were saying, "Enough is enough," and preparing to end "the old politics." There was a consensus that the Tories would never clean their own house.

The Principal affair, concerning the collapse of the Principal Group, a trust and financial conglomerate managing the investments of thousands of Albertans, irreparably destroyed the trust that the party had enjoyed for twenty years. The issue, from the government's point of view, was a narrow one: Had regulators been too lenient in supervising the investment and trust side of Principal's business? Had the government allowed friends to play by a different set of rules?

Although the company and its owners, officers and directors may have had the legal liability, the government and the Conservative Party carried a huge political liability. The finances of retired Albertans of modest means had been ruined and the plans for the final years of their lives destroyed. The Tories may have just been sideswiped, but the damage was extensive.

Just as damaging was the loss, eventually pegged at over $600 million, of provincial investment in NovAtel, a cellular phone company start-up that was part of the government's economic diversification plan. For sheer cabinet incompetence, in the failure to supervise a public investment closely and respond to the warning signals of problems, this case probably has no parallel in Canadian history.

The epitaph for Getty's short career as premier comes from a cruel jest coined in the press gallery. When an aide, Peter Tadman, wrote an as-yet-unpublished authorized biography, he argued that his boss had been one of the greatest contemporary provincial leaders and that he was just badly misunderstood. Journalists in the basement of the legislative building, who disagreed with the greatest premier thesis, held a contest to help Tadman name the biography. The winner was *Don Getty, Canada's Tallest Premier*.

Several candidates were chaffing to start the race. Ralph Klein was not one of them. If he had private ambition, it was no more than the thought most successful ministers have, that it would be intoxicating to sit at the head of the cabinet table. The widespread impression among Klein's friends and in the media that Getty had promised Ralph an inside track to the leadership in order to recruit him in 1989 was wrong. Now the premier had lost patience with Klein's freewheeling style and his indulgence in liquor. It appeared that Getty was, in fact, impeding Klein's leadership prospects. He said he would not retire before the next election, and Klein believed him.

No one believed that Getty could win another election. He appeared to have lost interest in both the broad direction of the government and the details of the daily agenda. MLAs who wanted to see him typically had to ambush him at the urinals during caucus recesses. He usually deflected their requests, suggesting that they get answers from the civil service. He was also unprepared to surrender the reins or to allow the party to debate its future or prepare itself for a transition. Some caucus members thought he was biding his time, to improve his pension, or to ensure the completion of projects in his riding, to which he felt intensely loyal.

For whatever reason, he stayed just long enough for the poison to infect all of the campaigns of the leadership hopefuls. The party was torn by dissent and disaffection. Membership had plummeted; campaign volunteers were hard to find, and those that stepped forward lacked experience and skill. The money they needed was flowing into Liberal coffers. The only constructive thing that took place, in the vacuum Getty created, was that the party executive prepared the process for its first one membership/one vote leadership convocation.

When Getty threw in the towel, in July 1992, the relief created by his departure energized the party and the major candidates. But the leadership contest revealed the bitter divisions in the Conservative party that played out in the shattered remains of Getty's cabinet. The split was between the aggressive young comers—Jim Dinning, Rick Orman and Nancy Betkowski, who were grounded in the cities and mostly in the south—and an old entrenched guard like Ken Kowalski, Peter Trynchy, Ernie Isley and Peter Elzinga, who had rural roots in the north.

Eventually, there were nine candidates—six, including Klein, from within the Getty cabinet. Health Minister Nancy Betkowski, Energy Minister Rick Orman and Klein quickly emerged as the first tier. Multiculturalism Minister Doug Main was the second-tier candidate from Edmonton, counterpointed by Labour Minister Elaine McCoy of Calgary. Lethbridge MLA John Oldring, who ran Social Services under Getty, and a former Lougheed cabinet minister, Dave King, were in the bottom tier. The campaign also drew two wannabes, self-described futurist Reuben Nelson and Lloyd Quantz, a dean from Olds College, an agricultural school in central Alberta. Education Minister Jim Dinning, regarded for many months as a tenth contender, never entered the race.

The younger cabinet and caucus members believed that the way to overcome the rot of the Getty years was to show a young, trendy face with a slick, urban, liberal leaning. The cure was to restore the style and the politics of the Peter Lougheed years. They were a brash, confident lot who thought that the techniques of politics could turn things around. They believed themselves to be the guardians of the Lougheed legacy, a mythical blend of policy analysis and partisanship.

The young Turks had the open support of Lougheed's wife and children, if not the retired premier himself. They were socially and politically correct, and they were backed by the federal Progressive Conservative establishment in the province. They rejected Klein's politics, feared his power and held him in personal contempt. They thought that the province didn't need and wouldn't elect Klein as its premier; he was a part-time political dilettante who drank too much and, at least from their point of view, acted like the 1990s were the 1970s.

The older caucus members had been sitting in the legislature since the early Lougheed years, while the young Turks were still in school, and, later, while they were running around the legislature as self-important executive assistants. They had a much better understanding of the party's peril. If they ever thought about themselves as a political establishment, they never let it show. They had a more immediate concern: survival on two counts. First, the party had the narrowest chance to hold onto power. Second, if the party retained the government, these MLAs would be on the outside if someone like Betkowski or Orman became the premier.

Two key members of the old guard toyed briefly with the idea of entering the race: Peter Elzinga had been a Member of Parliament and president of the federal Conservative Party. He was on the outside during the Mulroney years, however; he was little recognized across the province and had no base of support in provincial constituency organizations. Ken Kowalski pondered the prospect but decided he was young and could wait; he knew his liabilities as an aggressive politician who would be a natural media target.

When it came time to ante up, there was no uncertainty in the remedy recognized by the party's old guard. Ralph Klein had become hugely popular across the province while holding the base of support he had built in Calgary during the mayoralty years. He had been giving his stump speeches up and down the province for three years, and these astute and calculating men had heard the reviews come back: Klein was a winner.

In the hours after Getty's resignation, a kitchen cabinet to recruit Klein formed and moved from meeting to meeting between the various Edmonton condos and apartments of its members. The players included Kowalski, Trynchy, Elzinga and Isley. They commanded a list of more than thirty-four prospective supporters in the caucus.

When they had their ducks in line, they rounded up Klein; he protested that he had no money and no organization. "Go ahead," they urged him, "the money and the organization will follow."[1] If this was a bit vague, Klein knew that the resources for each one of his past campaigns had materialized after he declared, rather than being marshalled ahead of time. He was already under pressure from the Klein Gang in Calgary to run. On September 17, nine days after Getty announced his departure from public life, Klein launched his campaign.

From the moment of his announcement, the necessary support was there for the asking. Yet it almost got away from him. If politicians were marked as students are in school, on the basis of some objective test, it probably should have gotten away from him. You have to be good to be lucky and lucky to be good, they say in sports. In 1992, Klein was lucky. It was this simple: his key people were relatively inexperienced, and they didn't realize, initially, that to win this thing you had to sell more memberships than the other candidates.

Klein regarded the province-wide open ballot leadership, with all members eligible to vote at polling stations in their own ridings, as the key to his success. He told his father that he wouldn't have run had he faced a convention with delegates picked in riding meetings. "The old guard would simply have put in one of their own," he said to Philip. "But with an open vote, I have a chance." Nevertheless, the open ballot seemed to lull key Klein staffers, particularly because it had been designed by a man sympathetic to Klein's candidacy, Thompson MacDonald. Since leaving CFCN News, in the late 1980s, MacDonald had been a political consultant and Tory party insider. While he had been supporting Energy Minister Rick Orman's leadership ambitions for several years, he was very close to Klein and was torn when his former employee entered the race. When he had been the key member of the committee designing the open leadership vote, MacDonald certainly knew that the end result would be fresh, new leadership—he would be very happy with either Klein or Orman because both represented a break with the past.

In spite of the obvious advantage that the selection process gave Klein, at first it was a hindrance because it gave his organizers the notion that they simply had to put their man's name on the ballot and the common sense of the membership would do the rest.

"It was there for the asking, but Klein's people forgot to go out and ask. There were thousands of Albertans prepared to step forward, buy a membership and vote for the guy. Hell, for the first few weeks, hardly anybody in the Klein organization had a membership book, and when you asked for one, it took a while to find one," recounted MLA Gord Shrake, who joined the campaign early.

More experienced hands, however, knew that this was no different from the nominating conventions that in local ridings pick candidates for provincial elections. The winner sells more memberships than the loser and then takes the prize only by following up to ensure that the buyers vote. These old hands started to sell memberships themselves and to press campaign organizers to do the same. They met unexpected resistance; too many key players wanted to discuss brochure design and advertising strategy. Too few seemed willing to stick a membership book in their pocket and carry it around all day, pulling it out at every opportunity that a potential member endorsed Klein.

In spite of reasssurances given by Kowalski, Trynchy, Isley and Elzinga, there was little money and less organization; these did not follow as automatically as everyone had believed they would. And this time, the media were in Klein's face from day one. They began, for the first time, to give his personal life serious scrutiny. They were willingly fed information by the Klein's opponents, who were scathing in their contempt and beside themselves with concern that the environment minister might work his political magic and beat them. The whispers turned into open questions about his drinking. The old rumours that Colleen was an abused wife were reprised, with Klein cast as the abuser. Angrily, the Kleins denounced the faceless sources of the gossip but would not unveil their private life to reveal that the grain of truth in the innuendoes came from Colleen's first, unhappy marriage.

The limping campaign now cashed in on the political dividend of the three years during which Klein had rarely said no to an invitation from a fellow MLA to travel Alberta for constituency meetings, wedding anniversaries, ribbon cuttings, fund-raisers and the hundreds of other small events that are the glue of riding politics between elections. Everywhere he went, he had exuded enthusiasm, optimism and the kind of acceptable partisanship that gave Conservatives hope in spite of the scandals and the bungles of the Getty years.

He distanced and detached himself from these scandals, urging Tories to keep their eyes on longer horizons; hinting that some day all the miscreants would be gone and the party could renew itself. The longer Getty held onto power, the more Klein became the symbol of the party's future.

He had driven himself to exhaustion and illness, creating the image of a man who would not spare himself for the party. Once he flew from Edmonton to Calgary to attend the annual meeting of the Forest Lawn constituency association. He spoke, raspy throated, for close to an hour. Finally his host, Gord Shrake, gently interjected to bring the speech to a close, both to spare Klein's voice and on behalf of the one hundred thirsty members who were aching to open the bar. Klein stayed for a single drink and then caught a late flight back to Edmonton.

A few days later, Shrake climbed off another flight to Edmonton and met Klein, who had also taken the flight after another political meeting. They went for a drink at a nearby Holiday Inn. Shrake was taken aback at the number of people who recognized Klein. After a time, their table was crowded with folks who wanted to listen and talk to this approachable cabinet minister. After a while, to escape, the two men went downtown to a Chinese restaurant favoured by MLAs. Although it was past closing time, the proprietor willingly stayed to prepare a meal. "I don't think he was doing it for me," Shrake said later. At 2:30 A.M., Klein excused himself; he needed some sleep before catching a 6:00 A.M. jaunt on a government jet to a negotiating meeting for a pulp mill in northern Alberta.

That same day, at the afternoon caucus, Shrake met Klein and asked him if he had made it north for the meeting. "Yes. I did, Gordie; and my God it was a short night," Klein replied. Within a few days, Klein was in bed with pneumonia and didn't make it into the office for a week.

When Shrake joined the campaign, he was dismayed by the lack of organization and the apparent dearth of resources. He shortly realized, however, that Klein had an enormous competitive edge; you just had to ask the people who had met Klein over the past three years, and they would buy a membership. It wasn't just the broad base of support in local constituencies, it was the callow arrogance of other candidates that gave Klein a commanding, if generally unperceived, edge.

Klein's closest advisers were cocky. They thought they knew better than the candidate the advantages he enjoyed. They assumed very early in the campaign that their candidate had locked up a win on the first ballot. They built their strategy on a first-ballot victory. They believed that on a second ballot Klein would be destroyed when everyone else in caucus, the insiders, ganged up to exile the outsider.

To make the next election easier to win, Liberal leader Laurence Decore knew from the word *go* who he supported. He felt, intuitively, that he could beat Nancy Betkowski. Behind the scenes he put the word out, and Liberals purchased memberships to cast votes for Betkowski, in the hope that they could hijack the result. Liberal women especially were persuaded that a female premier would be a good thing. Nancy Betkowski's strongest showings were in ridings with Liberal MLAs or strong Liberal riding organizations well positioned to win against Getty.

On the last Saturday in November, all over the province Conservatives went to polling booths set up in each constituency. On the first ballot, Betkowski led, but only by a single vote; she had 16,393 of the 52,725 ballots cast; Klein had 16,392. The outcome of the second ballot was decided forty-eight hours after the first vote. Klein's people were shocked that they had not pulled off the coup; it was like a splash of ice water in the face. Klein got on the phone and started cashing in his dividends. The rules, however, allowed memberships to be sold in the week between the first and second ballot. All the arguments about selling memberships ended; the troops went to work.

Peter Trynchy gathered the thirty-four MLAs supporting Klein at his Edmonton condominium for a pep talk, to open the second front. The effort was so intense that later the provincial auditor general laconically noted the one-week escalation in long distance bills for Ken Kowalski's office.

Meanwhile, Betkowski's people assumed victory was within easy grasp. They expected the "anybody but Klein" movement to coalesce; the establishment would repel this no-account pretender. Supporters of other candidates, especially Orman, would rally round, preserving the party for its elite.

So Betkowski spent Monday and Tuesday working on the selection of her new cabinet. Then, sometime late Tuesday or early Wednesday, the Klein campaign hit a trip wire; Betkowski's supporters realized what was happening and tried to fashion a response. They were, however, on the defensive; they were too late.

Klein's people finally popped the question Tories had been waiting to hear: "Will you support Ralph?" People would, and Klein picked up 30,000 votes on the second ballot to gain 46,245 votes, easily blowing past Betkowski, who polled 31,722 . Once again, the outsider had kicked in the door.

Klein made the obligatory gestures of rapprochement to the defeated candidates. They were asked whether they wanted to run again, and if they did, what they wanted. Orman elected to leave politics, returning to the oil patch just in time for the brief natural gas boom of 1993. Dinning, who had pulled out before the race really started, stayed around and became treasurer, fuelling speculation—never confirmed by either man—of a deal. Klein genuinely wanted Betkowski in his cabinet. In the hours after the leadership victory, such representations were made on the new premier's behalf. There was an obstacle, however. During the campaign, Betkowski had repeatedly sought to engage Klein in a debate and he had sidestepped her.

She baited him just once too often on this issue for his patience, and in a media scrum he shot back, "Yeah, let's get it on, Nancy." The sexual innuendo was deliberate and direct. She was furious and wanted an apology in writing. An appropriate letter was drafted, and she was given it. It is said that Klein handed it to her and repeated his regret that once again he had spoken in haste. Betkowski took the letter and prepared to depart. Startled, Klein asked about the cabinet. She replied bitterly, no, never. Then she left for a prolonged period of public sulking.[2]

Betkowski, like a good many other young, established Tories, could never accept Klein as leader. They said his leadership was an interregnum that would end, in 1993, when the voters threw him out. They were wrong but found themselves cut off from the party after the Conservative reelection of 1993. Klein, they discovered, keeps score. Those who weren't with him faced a lonely, prolonged and, in many cases, permanent political exile.

Betkowski had strong, covert Liberal support during her leadership bid. Early in 1994, the opportunistic Grits began to court her. They found the irony delicious that whereas they had failed to capture Klein as a leader in 1988, they might pick up Nancy Betkowski in 1994.

She publicly declared her interest after Laurence Decore resigned. Her support came from the predictable "anybody but" faction in the Liberal Party who opposed the campaign's front runner and eventual winner, Grant Mitchell. She withdrew, however, almost as quickly when it was discovered that she didn't have a membership and the required eligibility date had passed for a candidate to obtain one. Betkowski had been badly advised, and the Liberals had made the first of many blunders in their attempt to find a suitable rival to Ralph Klein.

After Betkowski's departure, Klein quickly created the impression that he had wiped the slate of the Getty years clean by firing the villains. Of the main players in Getty's cabinet who had opposed him, only Jim Dinning, who had prudently backed out of the challenge to Klein, went into the cabinet, though he was on a short leash: "He was put there to carry out company policy, not to think for himself," a snubbed caucus colleague remarked, with some glee.[3]

No defeated candidate has since run for office. David King, Reuben Nelson and Lloyd Quantz went back to private life; Elaine McCoy returned to the practice of law; Rick Orman, like Betkowski, entered the twilight zone of private consulting. Doug Main joined a radio station as a talk show host. John Oldring picked up government work as a NAFTA consultant with Alberta Economic Development and stayed under the protection of Ken Kowalski, until Kowalski was fired in 1994. Shortly after that, Oldring was dismissed as well.

There are no smooth or seamless changes in Alberta's jerky, disordered political pilgrimage. Every upheaval, every sea change, is abrupt and unequivocal. There are no long transitions, there are cleavages. There are no slow, imperceptible geological erosions; there are earthquakes and cataclysms, after which it is never possible to reclaim the landscape as it once was. The past is rubble, the future an unformed horizon.

"I will not let you down," Klein promised his exuberant followers from the victor's podium.[4] Now he had to deliver on his promise; he had to restore the Conservatives to their accustomed unassailable place before the impending provincial election.

12

The Restoration

*Alberta ... the volcano of
extraordinary remedy.*

—BRUCE HUTCHISON, *THE
INCREDIBLE CANADIAN*

R alph Klein moved at warp speed. The Conservatives were governing on borrowed time. They considered the pending election
already lost because of the scandals and controversies of the Getty
years. It would have to be won back long before the writ was dropped.
The polls showed the party 15 per cent behind the front-running Liberals, and Klein's instincts, honed during the leadership campaign, told
him that he had only a few weeks, perhaps no more than a couple of
months, to turn it around. He had to create a new Klein government,
which could seek a mandate on its own merits.

The immediate issues were unambiguous. He had to establish his
authority over a balky party with a surplus of defeated candidates whose
animosity towards him was naked. He had to stop the spree of misspend-
ing and waste widely perceived as the Getty signet on Alberta politics.

Klein's political intelligence indicated that fiscal responsibility was
the Liberals' issue of choice in the next election. He had to restore the
kind of government that would resonate with the values he had heard
expressed throughout the province during the leadership campaign and
in the three years before that, attending constituency barbecues and listening to the folks in the bars and coffee shops. It would be a government
that lived within its means, ended deficit financing and paid off its debts.

Klein had to go to the polls before summer. Even waiting until the
autumn would be an admission of weakness, an indication that he could
not fix the government. The only break he got from the calendar was
the Christmas season. With the leadership decided, voters were focussed
elsewhere.

To keep the Liberals off balance, however, Klein said that he would

treat the 78,251 votes cast on the second leadership ballot as a wide test
of opinion and treat that as a mandate for a year. It was a successful
ploy to the extent that it reinforced the contempt with which he was
held by the Grits and lulled them into staying with the election strategy
they had devised to face Getty. Clearly, in their minds, Klein could only
be a change for the worse.

On December 14, 1992, the day he was sworn in as Alberta's twelfth
premier, Klein danced on the steps of the legislative building to the throb
of aboriginal drumbeats, as the sweet grass burned. Then he got down
to work; breaking only for a quick fishing vacation after he had indelibly
put his mark on the hothouse world under the legislature's magnificent
dome—the feature of the building that gave the place its nickname, the
Dome.

He started with the biggest, bloodiest purge in Alberta's political
history. He reduced the size of cabinet from twenty-six to seventeen ministers, and in doing so he unceremoniously dismissed sixteen Getty ministers, including the five who had opposed him in the leadership race
and all but two of the holdovers from the Lougheed period.

Among the portfolios he wiped out was the Ministry of Technology,
Research and Science, which had managed the $600 million collapse of
NovAtel—a political scandal that ranked second only to the Principal
Group case as a symbol of the Getty administration's incompetence.
There was no mistaking his message. He was not distancing himself
from the past; he was confronting it and eliminating its root causes: the
people in cabinet who had allowed it to happen.

Next Klein knocked down the bunker into which the premier's office had retreated in Don Getty's final months. He met every MLA within
a week of his victory and appointed four backbenchers to head the new
standing policy committees that replaced several dozen legislative review
bodies. This was a marked contrast to Getty, who had stopped returning
their calls and had refused to answer their questions in caucus.

Meanwhile, on his first day at work as premier, he ordered the door
to his office suite propped open, and visitors to the legislature became
accustomed to seeing him working in his shirtsleeves. He delivered his
own press releases to the basement quarters of the press gallery. He
worked long hours and made himself conspicuously available for media
interviews and drop-in guests who arrived unannounced and without
appointments. The corridors of the legislature took on the air of a medieval court in which supplicants lined up in the morning and the ruler's
day wasn't done until he had seen them all.

Somehow he crammed into his schedule a round of speaking en-
gagements across the province; these were to continue until the end of

the June election campaign. He started plans to be the chief salesman of what he called the Alberta Advantage. He prepared to go on the road to persuade businesses and investors to put their enterprise and money into the province, promising that conditions would be right for growth and expansion.

Nothing could be clearer than the message he decided almost at once to send to investors on the $5 an hour minimum wage. It would be the lowest in Canada. By the end of 1994, only Newfoundland and Prince Edward Island, at $4.75 an hour, were lower. Alberta had a $2 an hour advantage over next door British Columbia. Business responded by creating plenty of low-paying jobs: in the early winter of 1994–95, 90 per cent of new job listings were at minimum wage.

Before Christmas, the new premier promised that there would be no more secret and costly deals for private business. The government would no longer try to pick the winners in Alberta's diversifying economy, he said. Almost immediately, he had to participate with other western provinces in short-term financing for Canadian Airlines International (CAI). Alberta advanced $50 million as its part of a deal that allowed the airline to consummate its life-saving alliance with American Airlines. CAI had been acquired, as Pacific Western Airlines, by the province during the Lougheed administration and was a political symbol as well as an important piece of Western Canada's economic infrastructure. The airline deal became a political statement that Alberta could compete with the often overpowering Canadian centre.

The premier understood visceral symbols like a regionally based international airline and the tribal memories on which they were based. Alberta's political culture is deeply imbued with what Social Credit chronicler John Barr, in his 1974 book *The Dynasty*, called the folklore of protest.

In his three years as the Conservative Party's advocate in every small town across the province, Klein absorbed through his skin the political, economic and intellectual alienation Barr described as the basis of the Social Credit hegemony created by William Aberhart and perpetuated by Ernest Manning. Now he began to restore the governance trim and true that Manning shaped to turn Aberhart's social conscience into something constructive and successful.

For a few weeks, no one close to government seemed to notice what the premier was doing. No one detected the pattern, and perhaps at first there wasn't a pattern; perhaps he was shaping things intuitively. The issue was the province's debt and deficit. Within a few days of his swearing in, Klein announced that he would attack and control the province's ballooning deficit, without increasing taxes, by cutting spending. He told

Alberta Report, "We finally realized we had to catch up to the voters. People wanted to get back to the basics. They were tired of Getty's style. They were tired of politicians who spent all their time under the [legislature] Dome, telling them things were under control when they weren't."[1]

Klein worked through December and January to assemble a financial plan for review by his treasury that would retire about $14 billion in debt and $6 billion in unfunded pension liabilities over four or five years. He set two ground rules: no provincial sales tax and no liquidation of the $9 billion Alberta Heritage Fund. The government would service the debt, making an annual payment on the principal, like a mortgage, and its remaining revenues would be all that it had for its programs and services.

While he developed the plan, his treasurer, Jim Dinning, went through the books and told his boss the deficit for the year would be $2.8 billion, about $400 million higher than the autumn forecast. So the cuts started even before the May budget. Ministerial salaries were reduced by 5 per cent; eighteen hundred civil servants were laid off. The Conservative majority passed the Deficit Elimination Act, which mandated a balanced budget by the fiscal year 1996–97.

At the end of January, Dinning created the nine-member, $350,0000 independent Financial Review Commission of business leaders, with George Cornish as its executive director, to open the province's books for two months and issue a report on the state of Alberta's finances that would form the basis of budget planning. His Liberal and New Democrat critics waited for the backlash. There was dismay in the civil service and in the education and medical establishments; it was obvious that these areas would be hit by cuts because they were the big three of operating budgets. Surprisingly, however, Klein got his rough ride, through the winter, from a handful of economists and even a couple of journalists who said he wasn't moving far enough, fast enough.

Beyond the narrow world of politicians, public servants, journalists and academics, an emerging political coalition of rural and small town voters, combined with urban blue-collar workers, small business owners and the corporate and financial elite, understood what he was doing. Klein shot ahead of the Liberals in popular support. The polls showed that he had as good as won the election in rural Alberta and in the smaller cities such as Red Deer, Grande Prairie and Lethbridge; he had also taken the lead in Calgary.

William Aberhart and Ernest Manning held office because they welded together the the same votes of agrarian Alberta with the blue-collar and small business classes of the cities. In a matter of eight weeks, and on a single issue, Klein had regained that coalition and added to it the immensely powerful and influential leadership of the petroleum and financial industries.

By the new year, it was obvious to everyone except the Liberal Party that the political momentum had changed. There was, however, almost no comprehension of what was really going on. Klein's supporters talked about a political revolution, but *Saturday Night* dismissed Klein as "political hustle."[2]

In fact, this was no revolution, it was a restoration every bit as dramatic and far-reaching for Alberta as was the restoration of King Charles II for the English, or as the counterrevolution was for the Catholic Church in the sixteenth century. Klein had, intuitively and accurately, connected to the deepest roots of Alberta politics and one of its oldest and strongest tribal memories: the memory of government indebtedness and insolvency.

Albertans believe instinctively and fiercely in balanced budgets for governments. Those who were over forty and who had resided in the province for all their adult lives had experienced Manning governments that didn't borrow for operations and required modest capital financing.

Manning's fiscal prudence was born of experience. Alberta had been insolvent during the 1930s and 1940s. The bitter story of Alberta's ten-year default on its debt is grounded in the harsher nightmare of the depression.[3] When Aberhart came to power, in 1935, Alberta was $385 million in debt and had no means to repay its obligations, much less meet annual service charges of about $40 million. Aberhart carried no brief for the banks and the bond financiers; Social Credit had proclaimed the financial institutions its sworn enemy. Nor, as it turned out, did he have much regard for the federal government. These two enmities put him on a collision course with bankruptcy.

In his first months in office, Aberhart survived on five million dollars in loans from the federal government, which by this time was backstopping all provincial financing in the country. The first Social Credit budgets cut costs and increased taxes, instituting the province's first and only sales tax, later repealed, which became another hated symbol of the hard years of the 1930s.

When the federal government created the Dominion Provincial Loan Council to regulate its financing of provincial governments, Aberhart refused to join. The mandate of Social Credit was to gain control over the province's financial destiny, not to join the monetary establishment. In response, Prime Minister Mackenzie King refused to lend Alberta $3.25 million dollars to redeem a bond issue. On April 1, 1936, Alberta defaulted on the bond when it came due.

Meanwhile, Ernest Manning, the new minister of Trade and Indus-

try, was endeavouring to renegotiate Alberta's commercial bonds—a task
that was to occupy him for nine years. He was stymied almost at once
when the legislature passed a bill attempting to legalize unilateral, self-
declared interest rate reductions on its borrowings.

In May, the cabinet reduced the rate on its bonds to 2.5 per cent.
The bond holders, a blue-ribbon list of banks, insurance and trust companies and pension funds, were enraged, and the province's securities
were barred from trading on the London Stock Exchange. Manning did
not get a single reply to his letters requesting a refinancing. In October,
the province defaulted on a second bond issue of $1.25 million.

The conflict between Aberhart and King over fiscal control of the
province escalated. Ottawa began to disallow legislation that created the
Social Credit system of finance that was intended to displace the banks
and end the depression. Through 1937, Aberhart tried repeatedly to gain
control over the banking system. Each bill was struck down by the federal government.

Having refused to participate in federal financing for its obligations
and having failed to legislate its own extraordinary remedies, the Aberhart government was forced to resort to self-declared interest moratoria
and to default on its bonds. For the remainder of the depression, the
province maintained draconian budget austerity, and remained in default, disgraced in the eyes of the world financial community.

When Aberhart died, unexpectedly, in 1943, Ernest Manning, his
protégé and successor, was finally free to deal with the debt and rectify
the default. But he had to bury the past. According to historian Ernest
Watkins, Manning viewed his chief tasks as, first, restoring the financial
integrity and reputation of the province, and second, bringing back to
the premier's office control of the economic decisions of the government.

The parallels between Manning's situation and Ralph Klein's in December of 1992 are uncanny. Both succeeded unpopular, discredited premiers who faced near certain electoral defeat. Both were initially written
off by the political establishment as good men facing impossible tasks.
Both selected as their first priority the same problem, the disease ravaging
the government's central nervous system—finance. Both men laid the
issues on the table and then sought a mandate, crushing their opponents
by reenlisting the province's business leadership as a fresh source of support and consolidating it with the old Social Credit coalition of agrarian,
rural, blue-collar and small merchant voters.

As the war ended, Alberta owed $59 million on the principal of its
defaulted bonds and accumulated interest. Rejecting a federal proposal
for both terms of settlement and assistance in reaching it, Manning negotiated directly with representatives of the bond holders. With a $29

million new bond issue raised in New York and a $9.4 million contribution from the federal treasury, Manning paid off the bond holders and refinanced the province's $113 million accumulated operating debt with a thirty-five-year sinking fund.

Never again, determined Manning, would the province live beyond its means. For twenty-five years he balanced his books, improved and expanded education and health care facilities, and built a frugal system of social welfare that provided basic care to the needy.

The man who defeated Social Credit, Peter Edgar Lougheed, marched to a different, more Liberal beat. He obtained power partly through Social Credit's negligence and partly because he was an electronic man—through television, he generated a sense of excitement, of possibilities, that tapped into the impatience of younger Albertans who had grown up with affluence. They were impatient to create uses for the enormous public wealth that had accumulated during the sleek, fat years of the oil industry's growth.

Lougheed's political culture was interventionist. He wanted to do things that Manning had felt were none of government's business. He craved the public approval that Manning disdained. Lougheed loosened the purse strings; once the treasury was opened a crack, he found it difficult to stem the flow of public largesse, even when he wanted to do so. Slowly, imperceptibly, Lougheed created the commitments and the expectations that would trigger bloated deficits when, in the mid-1980s, petroleum revenues collapsed. Lougheed departed a political winner, at the peak of his power and reputation. He also departed ahead of the reckoning for his mistakes.

Meanwhile, Ernest Manning's voters had not forgotten the lessons of prudence and prosperity the old man had taught. What first drew them back together, in the 1980s, was Preston Manning and the Reform Party. The young Manning took the fundamentals of his father's governance and reshaped them into a suitably contemporary framework.

Preston Manning put his father's ideas back into the political conversation of Alberta's agrarian, blue-collar and small merchant Conservatives. When Klein began to travel the province, in 1989, he heard these ideas about balanced budgets and the need for government to live within its means and not do what it couldn't afford to do. When he seized on these ideas during the leadership campaign, it was obvious to old Social Creditors and new Reformers where he was coming from and why.

As Klein focussed his government's energy on fiscal reform and deficit cutting in the first months of 1993, he struck an immediate, positive chord, reflected both in opinion polls and in his many social encounters across the province. Klein was on a course that a substantial block of voters recognized and welcomed as a familar, proven way of governing. Happily, it also suited his values, and the more deeply he analyzed it and discussed it with the people whose opinions he trusted, the more common sense he saw in it.

Those first months in the premier's office, however, were not all history and policy. Klein was elated to have captured the leadership and the premier's office, and he wanted to have some fun as well as do some good. The high-spirited, boyish mood recalled the seemingy endless party in his first months as Calgary's mayor twelve years earlier. Often, when he and Love got up to their pranks, he seemed to be miscast in the role of the establishment man that was pressed on him, as the conservative business and political elite began to take the importance of his fiscal agenda ever more seriously.

Brian Mulroney, then prime minister, came to Calgary for a party fund-raiser in early 1993. The event was the usual set piece: hotel reception, dinner, speech and tax receipt for the $150 ticket, with highly visible corporate tables organized by company/government relations hacks. Mulroney regarded Klein as a new Conservative asset needed to shore up support for Alberta's beleaguered federal MPs, withering as the Reform Party hit its preelection stride.

Through the reception and dinner, Mulroney turned on the blarney and later ushered Klein and Love upstairs to his hospitality rooms. The prime minister never entertained cautiously and had opened two penthouse-style executive suites for entertaining on the floor reserved for his entourage. As the evening wore on, the large Tory crowd ebbed and flowed, and Mulroney did his best to impress upon the premier that he, too, was connected and popular in Alberta. Several times, Klein found himself being introduced to his own friends and supporters by the prime minister.

After midnight, there was a lull. Klein and Love found themselves alone in one of the suites. They had another drink and waited a while. Finally, it became obvious that the party was over but that the prime minister had neglected to say good night. This called into question the sincerity of Mulroney's lavish and overweening treatment of the man he had been introducing all evening as Alberta's Conservative star. Rod and Ralph together on a night off are as dangerous a pair of pranksters as has ever been found in politics. In a matter of minutes, they had emptied the contents of the suite's minibars, overstocked for the occasion, into their pockets and were clanking their way uproariously down the elevator and into the night.[4]

13

Miracle on the Prairies

The big thing now is to make it happen.

—PETER C. NEWMAN, *HOME COUNTRY*

Like so many elections, this one was won before it was called, although even Klein's most uncritical devotees could not believe the result until it was over. The victory started with a warning, a klaxon that bolstered Klein's increasingly aggressive attack on his government's spending.

When provincial treasurer Jim Dinning's independent Financial Review Commission reported, ahead of its March deadline, it warned the government that indebtedness was worse than expected. The provincial net assets of $12 billion had melted away to a net debt of $5 billion in only seven years. The per capita debt of more than $1,000 was the highest of any province and only slightly behind the federal level of about $1,250. Alberta, the commission concluded, would inevitably hit a brick wall.

The report put the price tag on the past economic diversification. Some $2.1 billion had been lost on loans and guarantees to business, and a staggering $12 billion was still at high risk because the businesses that had been financed were shaky—for a total of almost half again the $29 billion operating debt. The government knew that unfunded pensions represented another open-ended liability of at least $6 billion.

Klein immediately terminated new loan guarantees and froze grants to hospitals, municipalities and school boards. He rolled back MLA salaries by 5 per cent and ordered more cuts in the civil service. These were small, symbolic acts, but symbols are potent political tools. Oddly, there was no backlash. Then Jim Dinning brought down his budget, which included spending cuts of $700 million, a 22 per cent drop in the first year of a four-year deficit elimination program, and no new taxes.

The cuts dismayed Albertans in the public service unions and the health and medical professions. When they attacked, however, the polls showed that the attacks simply strengthened the premier's support; the oxen he had gored had few friends within Klein's coalition of voters. Not only did the attacks, as weak as they were, confirm to Klein's supporters that he had to do what he was doing, they came from people who were most likely to vote Liberal or New Democrat. Thus, the budget lost the Conservatives very little electoral support.

The only issue that ever threatened the premier's reelection came in April, shortly before the election call. Klein got into trouble because he was not harsh enough in a pension reform bill that would scale back MLA retirement benefits, the richest benefit plan for politicians in the country. The flaw in Klein's bill was that it would come into effect only after the pending election. Opponents of the bill estimated that departing Conservatives, dumped by Klein in the shakedown after he took power, were eligible for $40 million in lifetime benefits. Klein went onto the radio talk shows and found he simply could not win the argument. Campaigning Tory candidates were having doors slammed in their faces.

On April 20, the newly formed Alberta Taxpayers Association released thirty thousand letters that supported immediate and retroactive pension rollbacks. For ten days, Klein resisted, even when his pension bill ran into opposition from within his caucus on the floor of the legislature. He did not think it was fair to renege on a pension plan, no matter who the recipient, and he did not think it was a sound precedent for other troubled public pension funds.

The Liberals were ecstatic. Klein had done what they expected: he had blundered, he had failed the test, and he could not save the Tories. They had the issue that Ralph couldn't bury. Day after day through the spring sitting of the legislature, Decore clobbered the new premier. He focussed on the pensions of Tory MLAs and cabinet ministers who were not seeking reelection. The number that became the symbol of the unacceptable privilege of these self-awarded pensions was the $80,000 per annum income that former transportation minister Allen "Boomer" Adair was to collect. Adair was one of the old-style politicians, and Klein had dropped him from the cabinet.

Klein knew he was on the defensive. The polls showed that the issue had shifted the political momentum back to the Liberals. His underfunded and understaffed election campaign faced mass desertions by party members who were unwilling to defend the pensions. He came out of his office one afternoon, found some reporters and said that he had changed his mind; he acknowledged that people did not accept his proposed bill, or his defence of it. He would amend it.

His decision split the caucus. Outgoing cabinet ministers, suddenly faced with substantial loss of benefits, took advantage of the situation for a little get-even. Klein had disposed of them; now they made his life miserable by threatening to break cabinet solidarity and even bring down his government if he didn't leave their pensions alone. Klein told them there was no middle ground for those who wanted to be reelected. Without warning, he suggested that he would terminate the pension plan for elected politicians who were not yet qualified by their length of service.

The caucus debate went on for two bruising days—perhaps the biggest showdown under the Dome since a rebel faction in Aberhart's caucus unsuccessfully tried to dump him in 1937. In the end, the first-term MLAs backed the premier and won over most of the retiring politicians by giving up all their benefits. It was impossible for anyone to oppose Klein.

He emerged to claim victory; not only would there be retroactive cuts—eventually they amounted to between 10 and 30 per cent—there was no more pension plan. "No *ifs*, no *ands*, no *buts*, no pensions."[1] Klein had hijacked his winning issue from the Liberals and Laurence Decore.

In a single, dramatic act, the novice premier had closed the book on the Getty years, wiping the Tory slate clean and ensuring his own personal credibility and popularity. Meanwhile, a final piece was falling into place that would determine the outcome of the election. Although the oil patch had thrown most of its financial support behind the Liberals, it was reconsidering the Tories because of the new leader. Thus, a cadre of powerful Calgary businesspeople, including rich, powerful and very senior financial and corporate leaders from the petroleum sector, joined Klein's coalition of rural and blue-collar urban voters.

Three books were helping to shape Klein's reelection strategy. Jim Gray, the ecclectic, energetic cofounder of Canadian Hunter Exploration, a wildly successful independent oil company, was giving out cartons of *Tyranny of the Status Quo*, coauthored in 1984 by American economist Milton Friedman and his wife, Rose. The book offers an explanation of how conservative governments could go about reducing the size and cost of government. The Friedmans use the first years of Ronald Reagan's U.S. presidency (a failure in their eyes) and Margaret Thatcher's governments in the United Kingdom (a success) as their prime examples. They also cite, admiringly, the example of British Columbia's Social Credit premier William Bennett, who at the beginning of his third term in office, in the early 1980s, initiated a program to cut the public service by 25 per cent and reduce spending.[2]

The Friedmans had one idea that, said Gray, was seminal for Alberta politics: "You have six to nine months to put your mark on the direction of a new government; so you'd better hit the ground running and do it quick and strong." Gray sent a copy of the book to every Alberta cabinet minister with two paragraphs highlighted in yellow that summarized

Reagan's failed attempt to attack the U.S. deficit.[3] The Friedmans concluded that if a newly elected government did not move decisively in the early months, "it will not have another such opportunity. Further changes come slowly or not at all, and counter attacks develop against the initial changes. The temporarily routed political forces regroup, and they tend to mobilize everyone who was adversely affected by the changes, while the proponents of the changes tend to relax after their initial victories."[4]

Klein was very taken by the Friedmans' thesis, and Dinning was also enthusiasic. And Gray was one of several opinion leaders, including cabinet ministers Dick Johnston and Elaine McCoy, who circulated a second book that had captured Ralph's intuitive and unpredictable politics in a neat, tidy package. The work is called *Reinventing Government*. Gray passed out paperback copies by the boxful. "This is a very important book. Hope you find time to read it," he inscribed inside the cover.[5]

The authors, David Osborne and Ted Gaebler, are public sector management consultants. Osborne is a prolific author; Gaebler, a former California city manager. *Reinventing Government* is about what to do with governments that are broke and are struggling to find their place in the post-industrial, knowledge-based global economy. The authors take government apart piece by piece to debate not what governments do but how they do it. They conclude that the answer to the fiscal crisis at all levels in the system is not to chose between fewer services or higher taxes but to choose better government. Do government differently so that it uses public resources differently, more efficiently and effectively, more entrepreneurially. They conclude that you have to reinvent government so that it does more with less.[6]

A third, less influential book also supported the new doctrines that Klein was developing. Sir Roger Douglas, a former New Zealand finance minister, had written a book called *Unfinished Business* about his deficit-reduction program. This agenda was triggered in 1984 after a run on the New Zealand dollar, when international lenders demanded that the country clamp down on its out-of-control public debt. Douglas went beyond spending cuts to reorganize government and the country's financial institutions. He floated the dollar, deregulated finance, privatized many state operations and eliminated lavish agricultural subsidies.

Douglas came to Alberta as part of a high-profile Canadian tour. He met the new Klein caucus and accumulated a great deal of credit for his influence on Alberta's strategies, although he had no consulting role. He was simply trying to sell books.

Klein adopted one of the book's sound bites: "Don't blink." Douglas's persuasive writing also helped explain the Tory agenda to some important opinion leaders, and he was the toast of the Conservative party's annual policy convention, held in the mountain resort of Banff, at a cocktail reception that featured mugs of Kleineken draft beer hoisted to acknowledge Sir Roger's contribution to the debate in Alberta.

When the premier finally called the election for June 15, 1993, he had prepared a remarkable campaign, even by the standards of his previous election experiences. There was relatively little money and less organization. There wasn't even a firm schedule for the premier's personal campaign. Ralph and Colleen climbed into a borrowed motor home and started driving, accompanied, most of the time, only by Rod Love and one or two others. Throughout the campaign, the pace appeared leisurely. That was deceptive, however, because Klein worked long days, but the tone was easygoing.

Events were lined up in a precarious chain across the province, usually confirmed only a day or two ahead. The candidate was often late because he tended to stay at each function until the last person who wanted to bend his ear had done so and the last reporter had asked the last question. He was never spellbinding in his often rambling remarks. Instead, he showed a great patience for listening and a skill in creating the impression that each person's point of view or problem was the most important thing he had dealt with that day.

In 1933, in the great tradition of mendicant prairie rainmakers, two men in a dusty car travelled across the province's dry face of depression and drought preaching a political gospel of hope to desperate people in a desperate time. Children were hungry, families were thrown off the farms and fathers were committing suicide. William Aberhart—high school principal, Bible scholar and religious visionary—was preaching the politics of deliverance.[7]

Through long, hot days Aberhart and his protégé, Ernest C. Manning, attended picnics, sat in the front parlours of remote farmhouses and spoke from the stages of theatres and school gymnasiums, the pulpits of tiny churches and the cavernous reaches of ice hockey arenas. The format was simple. They assembled a platform full of local personages and sang hymns rewritten into political songs; a soloist entertained; Manning warmed up the audience; Aberhart talked for two hours without notes. He used flip charts and jokes with equal ease; he switched from homily to satire to anecdote. He was a spellbinder, and he converted an entire generation to the politics of personal responsibility.

In that meandering summer pilgrimage, Aberhart spawned a political following that he nurtured through the long, cold winter from his electronic pulpit on CFCN Radio. Every Sunday afternoon thousands of Albertans on isolated rural homesteads or in the tiny homes of the urban poor gathered around the radio to listen. He added to this ragtag coalition the modest middle class: small business owners, teachers, managers and clergy.

A political and social outsider, Aberhart pitted himself against the vested interests of his time. He earned the scorn and contempt of the comfortable, the professional and the respectable. "We recognize this small army of exhorters traveling around the country, holding meetings as an omunum gatherum [sic] of political odds and ends, business failures, social misfits and imitating parrots reciting political speeches that they do not understand," railed an Economic Safety League pamphlet. "We realize what it would mean to turn Alberta over to this heterogeneous aggregation of incompetents."

Although his foes could not imagine how this "mountainous, glistening" spellbinder could deceive so many voters, on August 22, 1935, Aberhart's Social Credit League swept fifty-six of the sixty-three seats in the legislature, with 54 per cent of the popular vote.[8]

In the summer of 1993, fifty-eight years after Aberhart hijacked power, Klein, another outsider and anti-politician, was taking back the province for people who intuitively trusted him. What Klein said, the way he campaigned and how his foes responded was an uncanny echo of Aberhart's style, substance and experience.

Aberhart had created the great continuities of Alberta politics. Aberhart hammered out the template for the province's political eccentricity and anti-politics. In 1993, thousands of Albertans saw in Klein the restoration of Alberta's best-governed years.

The Conservative campaign message was clear: Ralph. The billboards, featuring a black and white photo of the premier with his suit jacket off, his sleeves rolled up and his hands in his pockets, conveyed accurately enough that the Conservatives, contrite for past misdeeds, had only one thing to offer: hard work under new leadership. The copy for the ads, "He Listens, He Cares," was a kind of code for a plebiscite. Klein was saying, "If you think that in the budget, in the cuts since December and in the Deficit Reduction Act, I've got the message you've been sending right, then vote for me. What you see is what you get, and I'm not going to get down off this issue so long as I'm premier."

The casual, late-running tour was, for all its loose ends, single-minded. Klein was renewing and reinforcing the thousands of contacts he had made travelling the province since 1989. He made little effort to court the major media but talked to every small town newspaper or radio reporter who approached him. And he spent hour after tireless hour face to face with people, until those who had been given his time numbered in the thousands. He knew when he went through a town and met a hundred people that in a couple of days, after they had recounted the event to their family and friends, a thousand people would feel that they too had met the premier.

The Conservatives were counting on the New Democrats, the official Opposition, to self-destruct, and they did. They ran a catastrophic campaign. Their leader, Ray Martin, was a bland, colourless ideologue who, by 1993, had been tried and found wanting by Albertans. Martin's voter base was in Edmonton, and Laurence Decore had been eroding it for a long time. Martin promised to increase taxes in order to preserve education, health and social services without fuelling the deficit. The message was completely out of tune with the mood of the electorate, which wanted less government, not more taxes.

What the Conservatives had not counted on was that Laurence Decore and his slick, lavish campaign would go off the rails. The Liberals were better funded and had a larger organization than the Tories. During the Lougheed years people made fun of the struggling Grit rump, saying the party could hold its meetings in a phone booth. Now the wheel had turned; the red juggernaut was poised for what seemed like certain victory.

Decore made a major strategic error at the outset that by itself would have ensured the Liberals' defeat. He had prepared for the election on the assumption that Getty would lead the Tories one last time. The detail of the campaign was incredible and inflexible; before Klein dropped the writ, Decore's staff had scheduled virtually every day of the campaign and the way in which all issues would be managed and all planks of the platform released. The Liberals made no adjustments for Klein and altered no day-to-day detail to respond to changing circumstances in the field. They resembled the bright red coats of the colonial British troops marching into a guerrilla ambush, drums beating and pipes skirling.

The mistake was not obvious in the opening days of the campaign. Liberal preparations were elaborate; the brash yuppies running the show had laid on an impressive array of computer and communications technology to support the leader. A satellite uplink truck travelled with Decore so that television reporters could file film. A deficit clock had been built that recorded the steadily rising provincial debt as Decore gave a set speech about reducing spending.

The long years in the wilderness, however, had left the Liberals without the competitive edge that experience brings. Some of the preparations started to backfire. There was a furor over the party's paying for the television uplink costs and thereby compromising the media. Some journalists refused to use it; others insisted that they pay the cost. The deficit clock struck many as childish.

The Liberals had already blurred their liberal image, before the campaign opened, by courting candidates from the ranks of the Reform movement. This was sheer opportunism that confused and compromised the party's core of centre left support. It made Decore look sweaty, ready to do anything to win. As it turned out, it did not much confuse the voter, who when faced with the choice between two conservative parties, chose the real thing.

In a matter of days the overprepared and overanxious Decore, a Ukrainian Catholic, contradicted himself on the issue of access to and funding for abortion clinics, appearing to oppose abortion one day and trying the next to clarify his position so that he could support public policy while preserving his personal convictions. The vital support of women within his own party was lost; he was publicly chastised on the issue by some of his candidates. The mismanagement of the issue, which blindsided Decore, also revealed that his campaign had ossified and could not respond well to unscripted developments.

As the campaign progressed, Decore's message about fiscal responsibility had became a tinny echo of Klein's better-thought-out and better-expressed theme. The reduction of the deficit started out as a nominal part of the Klein plan during the leadership campaign the previous year, borrowing more from the federal Reform Party than from any Conservative thinking. He also stole some of it from Decore, who had made fiscal responsibility an issue in the 1989 campaign. Klein had not forgotten the image of Decore waving his own wallet above his head as he spoke, dramatically connecting the arcane debate about deficits and spending to people's lives. On his rambling tours of the province that spring, the response Klein got when he talked about money made him realize he had grabbed the winning issue.

In Calgary on a cold, rainy election night after the polls closed, Klein joined a large throng of partisan volunteers, journalists and election night hangers-on, crammed into a cavernous, draughty tent on the grounds of the city's Heritage Park before flying to Edmonton to meet supporters there in a hotel ballroom. They had all come to bear witness to the Miracle on the Prairies and to savour their victory. Ralph, the premier with no last name, the rumpled, boyish home-towner with little formal education and no inclination for buttoned-down professional campaigning, had rewritten Alberta's political textbook again.

The scenario of six short months before had called for him to pilot the Progressive Conservatives to a stunning but expected defeat. Instead, as the returns rolled in, Klein buried the New Democratic Official Opposition and bulldozed the Liberals' vaunting ambitions, and Laurence Decore's career, into rubble. By the end of the evening, the Conservatives held fifty-one of the eighty-three seats in the legislature, the Liberals had thirty-two, and the New Democrats were wiped out.

While the tension of the vote count quickly gave way to euphoria and pandemonium, the man who was at the centre of the victory sat with his wife, Colleen, unruffled and apparently imperturbable, as the beer started to flow and the band pumped its tinny, distorted rhythms into the dark, wet night. Only his eyes betrayed the constant vigilance, the tough-mindedness, the ruthlessness and the moments of bitterness and betrayal that mark every political career, this one more so because of all he had accomplished.

14

Extraordinary Remedies

*The major advances in civilization
are processes that all but wreck the
societies in which they occur.*

—A. N. WHITEHEAD, *PROCESS
AND REALITY*

Premier Ralph Klein returned to power in June with an unequivocal mandate to continue what he had started during the winter
and spring. He began to prepare his fiscal 1996–97 budget, looking
for spending cuts of $3.2 billion, because there would be no new taxes.
To reach his goal, he and his cabinet would have to redefine, restructure
and reinvent government. Alberta was patently overgoverned, with 90
provincial and municipal employees per 1,000, more than any other province and 20 per cent higher than the national average.

His diagnosis and his prescription were based on a sweeping philosophy. Government "had overpromised and underdelivered; it had tried
to be a provider of things it should not provide and could not afford."
It seemed to surprise him that so many people regarded his solution as
radical. "We are saying that we understand our limits; that we can't
provide some of the things that we used to; that we do not have all the
answers."[1] Eliminating the deficit and redefining government would
stimulate growth as investors recognized the advantages of the economic
climate in Alberta, he claimed.

The premier had at least an intuitive sense of how radical the surgery
would be and how risky. He wanted to reduce government, not im-
poverish society. The cuts were not to remove funds from those who
needed them, so government would have to be done in a new way, by-
passing and dismantling the things that soaked up money un-
productively. In education, administrations would be decimated so that
funds could get to the classroom. In health care, funds would be reor-
ganized into community-based delivery systems with less administrative

and regulatory waste. Social assistance would be cleaned up so that people could use it as a bridge to new skills and a self-reliant life and not become dependent on it. "If you think you have the choice between working and not working, you don't," he said.[2]

He was accused by public service unions and the Liberals of trying to run government like a business. "Well, you sure as hell can't run government like a government any more," he replied.[3] His opponents replied that he was a lunatic.[4]

In promising to restore fiscal responsibility, he was committed to changing the vast, cumbersome and cantankerous bureaucracies that encrusted education, health care and the social welfare system. The cuts were easy; they could be done in pen strokes. Changing government carried the risks of mutiny and sabotage and the possibility that it was broken beyond repair.

There was the matter of doing all this and getting reelected, too. One term could never do it; if resistance to the magnitude of change stiffened, he could be thrown out in four years by someone who would undo the good. So Klein, Love, Jim Dinning and Vance MacNichol—whom the Premier had elevated to deputy minister of the executive council, making him the province's senior civil servant—and an inner circle of trusted policy architects that included Klein's version of a minister of everything, Steve West, Deputy Premier Ken Kowalski and, from outside the government, former MP and MLA Peter Elzinga, put their heads down through the summer.

His opponents assumed that Klein depended entirely on his brains trust. In the same way that they credited Rod Love for his electoral success, they considered Jim Dinning the real deficit cutter because he had his hands on the budget. No so, according to caucus members who watched the extraordinary remedies unfold.

Under Getty, Dinning had concluded that it was not wise to be spending all the money that the government was spending. But it took him some time to get to that position. He was a reluctantly born-again cutter. He was not the philosopher or the architect of the debt and deficit strategy; he was the detail man. A familiar image was of the lanky treasurer banging away on his pocket calculator while burrowing through binders of departmental expenditures.

The initial results of the spring budget were encouraging. The government was meeting its bottom line target, although forecast income tax revenues were short by a quarter of a billion dollars and unplanned costs had reached $100 million. Fortunately, the cuts had been more successful. Voluntary retirement incentives and direct staff cuts, plus the reduced payroll when liquor stores and registries for land and automobiles were privatized, had reduced the civil service by 15 per cent. Social

Services Minister Mike Cardinal reduced the monthly allowance for single, able-bodied welfare recipients and saved $150 million when some 25,000 of his clients, 28 per cent of those on social services, dropped off the rolls. "Don't underestimate this man; there is absolutely no doubt he will balance the budget," retired MLA Gord Shrake told his friends.

In late autumn, the first wave of public anger surged against Klein. Students from elementary and secondary schools cut classes and massed with picket signs and bullhorns at the legislature in Edmonton and Government House South, a renovated sandstone school in downtown Calgary. The students were rowdy, stopping traffic and making so much noise that workers in adjacent office buildings found it distracting. The signs were also rude: "Klein A Drop Out Not A Role Model," one read.[5]

The ostensible motive for the rallies was cuts to extracurricular activities made so that school boards could absorb grant reductions. But the students had help in coordinating the rallies from public service union members. Although teachers were circumspect, if not terribly unaggressive about enforcing discipline against truancy, off-duty nurses attended the Calgary rally with their own signs, encouraged the students, gave advice and directed traffic. Klein complained that teachers and students were giving his grandchildren a rough ride at their schools.

Not all the protests to the cuts were coming from Alberta. In British Columbia, Premier Mike Harcourt attacked Klein as a bad neighbour. He claimed that Alberta was buying one-way bus tickets for welfare recipients who wanted to go to British Columbia, where the welfare benefits were suddenly richer. And Harcourt said it wasn't fair for Klein to be luring business and investment east to "socialist free" Alberta. A trade war almost erupted when Harcourt mooted that he had prevented Alberta companies from bidding on his government's contracts; Klein threatened to retaliate by asking Alberta vacationers to stay away from British Columbia.

On November 22, privately disconcerted but publicly unmoved by the taunts of his opponents, which now included obscene calls to his listed phone number, Klein announced a one-time, 5 per cent cut in all public sector wages and benefits. It would save the province $300 million in the fiscal year 1994–95, a gain that would not have to be replaced. He deferred ninety-one school construction projects and recouped $20 million in capital finance savings. And he proposed user fees for non-essential medical services, where charges could be imposed without violating the Canada Health Act and jeopardizing federal transfer payments.

Klein had left the door open for local hospital, school and post-secondary boards to find the equivalent savings in other ways if they did not want to bite the bullet on wages. Some local officials accused him of downloading his problems to the municipalities. But Klein wanted local institutions to decide how to spend what the provincial government could afford to give them.

Local school boards were furious; they were saddled with implementing pay cuts that they couldn't agree with, and they might be forced to reopen Alberta Teachers' Association contracts. The Alberta Health Care Association, a hospital body, demanded that Klein legislate rollbacks if he wanted to make them. Health care unions accused the premier of breaking Alberta's fair labour practices code by interfering with existing contracts. David Inkster, the president of the Alberta Colleges and Institutes Faculty Association, said the province was going to destroy its post-secondary education system. Alberta Union of Public Employees president Carol Ann Dean said the only reason Klein appeared to be getting away unscathed was that he did not have the courage to meet with her.[6]

The cabinet and caucus braced for a rough winter; then almost overnight the steam went out of the Opposition, and by year end it had disappeared. On December 1, the ten-thousand-member Canadian Union of Public Employees cut a deal with the Alberta Health Care Association to reduce members' incomes by the equivalent of 5 per cent in a complex compensation adjustment package. Although United Nurses Association president Heather Smith bitterly accused the government of practising terrorism to divide employees and scare them into settling, in due course the contract adjustments were ratified. By Christmas, all of the province's seven professional health care associations— optometrists, dentists, denturists, opticians, podiatrists, chiropractors and pharmacists—had accepted the 5 per cent fee cut, and doctors were preparing to do the same.

Then Klein confronted teachers. They could agree to the cuts in their contracts or he would legislate it, he warned. And he accused them of masterminding the autumn's student protests. Reluctantly, the teachers capitulated.

Klein had implemented the Deficit Elimination Act's first budget, with its $700 million in cuts, and had laid the groundwork for the second $700 million reduction in February 1994 without disturbing the political equilibrium. He had not lost any support and had confined the dissent to people who had voted against him in June 1993. Opinion was shifting his way; his approval rating and support for his party were growing.

Klein's opponents counselled him to slow down; the health care and education systems could not sustain two years in a row of 20 per cent hits. His response was wait and see, and he repeated that when the budget came down he would be publishing business plans for his departments that would show performance measures, policy objectives and strategies to make the government successful with less money.

Klein met with reporters on his final day in Edmonton before heading to the First Ministers' Conference and then going on the Christmas break. "Just watch, we ain't gonna blink," he said.[7] The government barely took time for a holiday; by now it was clear that speed was as essential as determination if the premier's extraordinary remedies were to pass the political test of reelection.

Klein came back from his vacation and prepared for a television and radio broadcast so that he could put all his cards on the table in front of the widest audience possible before facing the legislature, where the Opposition could narrow the agenda and he would not be able to speak over the head of the Press Gallery directly to Albertans. Before going into the studio on January 17, he told reporters, "The good news is that we are jumping from the frying pan into the future."[8]

In front of the camera, the master of the medium was suitably sombre and stern. He wore the kind of suit you saved for family funerals. He put on his best frank and earnest face, looked straight into the lens, told his audience exactly where he was coming from, and then triggered the earthquake. At the end of the half hour, a viewer did not have to be a genius to know that what Klein said had to be done meant job cuts, hospital closures, lower welfare cheques and three more years of tough slogging to wipe out the deficit. Delivering the bad news, Ralph put the onus on the electorate. "You told me you wanted change. You wanted your government to put its financial house in order, to cut waste while protecting services."[9]

He planned to impose a combined 16 per cent cut on the biggest four items in his budgets—advanced education (universities and colleges), education, health and social services—over three years. He would do his best to cushion education. The targets there would be 12.4 per cent for school boards and 14.2 per cent for higher education; to make up, social services would take a hit of 18.3 per cent and health care would lose 17.6 per cent. All other departments faced an average of 30 per cent reductions.

He offered some reassurance: "People say to me, 'Ralph, am I going to get the services I need when I need them? And are you going to make sure my kids get the education they need to make it in the world of tomorrow?' Essential programs like health and education will be there. We are not going to let you down."

He had a great deal more to say, and it was not about money. His government would rebuild the way it delivered its most important services. He planned to consolidate the 140 school boards in the province to 60. He planned to take away their direct taxing power. He planned to have a single, province-wide union contract with the Alberta Teachers' Association. He planned to consolidate hospital administrations, eliminating 183 boards in the process. He planned to shift fiscal resources from expensive, full-service hospitals to community health care clinics. He planned to cull the welfare rolls by shifting assistance from passive maintenance to proactive financing of education and training to get people off social assistance.

He concluded his broadcast with a bald, cold statement: "There it is, folks. No hidden agenda. We will stay on track to balance our budget in four years."

The unions, which had just settled down after the 5 per cent pay cut, went ballistic. "Thousands of public sector workers are about to lose their jobs—it's insulting to think the deficit will be cleared up in three years without a dramatic effect," Carol Ann Dean, president of the Alberta Union of Public Employees, told the *Calgary Sun*'s Rick Bell.[10]

Advocates for the poor were also stunned by the implications of Klein's speech. "He [Klein] is staying the course on the deficit because we're picking up the tab," Gloria Goldson of the Calgary Interfaith Food Bank told *Calgary Sun* reporter Bill Kaufmann. Goldson predicted the food bank's clientele would jump 30 per cent before the end of winter because, as Kaufmann summarizes, "Klein has abandoned Alberta's underprivileged in his determination to slay the deficit."[11]

The medical and educational leadership in the province were more careful in their choice of words, but equally plain. They just did not see how what Klein proposed could be done. Several economists and most media opinion makers implored the premier to look at taxes, possibly even the heretical sales tax, before rushing blindly ahead with the cuts and the disruptive overhauls he planned in education and health care administration.

Liberal leader Laurence Decore's response was surprisingly spiritless: the words were tough, but the speaker was subdued and did not seem to feel the defiance of his message that Klein's television speech was damage control for a government in trouble. At his party's annual convention a week later, Decore said Alberta's future under a Conservative government would be "apocalyptic" and that Klein had a "dark side," which was now emerging and sapping the province of its optimism. "His hidden agenda isn't deficit cutting—it is the dismantling of Alberta as we know it," Decore said.[12]

In response, Klein upped the ante in the 1994 budget, brought down on February 24. Jim Dinning announced that the cuts for the fiscal year would be $918 million, $200 million more than expected. There were no new taxes, but there were forty new levies and user fees. The three-year departmental business plans outlined another $1.7 billion in cuts that would give the province a surplus of $212 million in the fiscal year 1996–97, better than the break-even target of the Deficit Elimination Act and on deadline.

Individual measures were extremely tough. Half the extreme-care beds in Alberta's hospitals were to be slashed. A proposal for year-round universities and colleges was put up for discussion. Privatization was proposed for a broad range of services, as was more decentralization in the management of others. Nonrepayable student grants were terminated. Tourism funding was decimated; oil royalty tax credits were squeezed. Klein left no ox ungored.

The critics, however, were muted by the louder paeans of praise from business and the conservative media, whose voice was growing in strength. In the month between Klein's popularly received television address and the budget, the wind seemed to have gone out of the sails of the Opposition.

For the next six weeks, as the legislature worked through a blizzard of implementing legislation, Klein looked worn and distracted at times. He told friends and sometimes admitted publicly that he found the bitter, angry and even vicious criticism—accusations that he was psychotic or a white racist or part of a Jewish world financial conspiracy—frightening at times. He was especially upset about the calls that came to his listed phone number. People cursed him, threatened him and threatened his family. He installed a call recognition device on his line that allowed him to dial back to people who left messages, and he often did, especially to those that were most threatening.

In July, he was to be Marshall of the Calgary Stampede Parade. This was both an honour from his home town and an opportunity. He turned it down, and his office cited security concerns. There had been threats, but there was also the possibility that Klein would be booed and jeered. It did not fit his communications strategy to have television news clips showing the one-time mayor and now the premier of all the people attending the city's major festival and being assailed by the crowd. Instead, he went for a bicycle ride and watched the parade on television at his home in Calgary.

And yet as early as April the polls were telling the Conservatives that they had struck the mother lode. An Angus Reid poll showed that Klein had 57 per cent support, up ten points from his standing just before the 1993 election. A poll taken by COMPAS ten days after the budget showed that he was seven points ahead of his rating when he had taken office in 1992. The momentum was building and by November 1994, he was a full sixteen percentage points ahead of his standing in the 1993 election, with an approval rating topping 60 per cent.

He was also winning the deficit battle. Shortly after the Legislature adjourned in November for a prolonged mid-winter break, Jim Dinning gave a speech to federal party loyalists at a Macdonald Cartier Club luncheon. He told the faithful that by the end of the fiscal year his government expected to have cut real spending by $1.9 billion—much better than the scheduled $1.5 billion. This meant the Tories had achieved 60 per cent of their deficit reduction target in only two years, with $1.3 billion remaining to be chopped.

Within a few days, the news improved. Dinning released a financial report forecasting that program spending would be $30 million underbudget and capital spending $40 million underbudget. Moreover, a package of revenue windfalls—from resources, lotteries, corporate taxes and Worker's Compensation premiums—had contributed an unexpected $800 million to the treasury. The 1994–95 deficit might come in under $1 billion. If the revenue pattern held up for fiscal 1995–96, then the budget might balance before it ended, a year ahead of schedule.

Dinning was cautious about declaring that the battle was over; Klein was animated by the news and used the opportunity to brag about his polls. Both, however, stood firm that they were not going to relent but that deficit reduction and the reinvention of government would continue until the objectives were secured and enduring. This was no time to blink. Revenues and expenditures can turn both ways; all the government had earned was breathing space until the 1995 budget.

There was now a cushion, and Klein began to probe beneath the surface, measuring the results of what his government had done. Klein has a very old friend, Andy Philip, who is a retired newscaster. When both were at city hall, Klein had a lot of time for the older man, and they kept in touch after Philip's retirement. As mayor, Klein had spoken at the fiftieth wedding anniversary of Andy and his wife, Catherine.

In early 1994, Philip had surgery. He was taken aback when he was told that he would be home much earlier than he had expected. The nursing administrator was quite frank; with budget cuts and reductions in the number of beds, she could not afford to have him on the ward any longer than absolutely necessary. Reluctantly, Philip went home.

A mutual friend called Klein before Philip checked out and suggested that this was a shabby way to treat a patient. The premier promptly telephoned the hospital and reached his old friend. "I don't think it's wise to come and see you, because I'm not very popular where you're staying," Klein said wryly. "But I want you to tell me exactly what's going on with your hospital care."

A long and detailed conversation ensued. Klein was sympathetic but not apologetic and did not make any offer or attempt to pull rank and get Philip's situation changed. Nevertheless, he listened and seemed to care. Mused Philip, "That was the 1993 campaign slogan, and Ralph is a man to keep a his word."[13]

15

The Rivals

*Politics ... is a clash of greedy
interests ... with supreme power as
the prize.*

—BRUCE HUTCHISON, MR.
PRIME MINISTER

A s Premier Klein fought the highly visible battle for public acceptance of his fiscal program and its administrative implementation
during the first eighteen months of his term, a bloody little private war was raging around him for power and influence over the
premier's office. On one side was his ambitious deputy premier, Ken
Kowalski, whose career plan included being Klein's successor at the helm
of government. On the other side was the Klein Gang. In the middle of
the dispute was the referee, Klein's political alter ego, Rod Love, whose
own ambitions were cloudy but seemed to include a hazy notion of someday holding elective office.

No one in this guerilla action trusted anyone else; because Klein
hated conflict and wanted everyone to get along, they shielded the premier from the intense rivaly that swirled around him. Like siblings with
a powerful father, they fought most intensely when he was out of the
room.

The Klein Gang, a group of approximately eighty Calgarians, had
prior claim to the premier—to access, influence, repayment for services
rendered in helping him win elections and in furthering his career, and
to his loyalty when the chips were down and the tough choices had to
be made. The half dozen or so charter members of the gang came from
the vagabonds and beautiful people who joined in August 1980 for the
first of Klein's campaigns. The rest had taken the oath at each subsequent stage of his political career, and in the gang's closely guarded roll
call, one could read the stratigraphy of the premier's political progress.
The gang was now the most exclusive club in town.

Like every political alliance—for that is what the Klein Gang is; it
behaves like a family—members come and go on the periphery, but an
essential core holds it together. The then federal energy minister Bobbie

Sparrow was an influential member during his leadership drive and re-election, as were Klein's own energy minister, Patricia Black, then Amoco Canada Petroleum senior vice-president Sherrold Moore and Rob Peters, president of Peters & Co., an independent brokerage firm that led the financing of junior independent oil companies. Klein's constituency president, Hal Walker, a resort developer, and Klein's personal lawyer, Jack Donahue, were part of the gang's inner sanctum.

Former University of Calgary president Norm Wagner, chairman of Alberta Natural Gas Co. until June 1995, and George Cornish, retired from city hall and teaching in the university's management faculty, were the intellectual powers of the group. James Gray, the president of Canadian Hunter Exploration, was a dynamo who constantly brought forth ideas and recommended books. Powerful lawyers such as Web MacDonald Jr., Bruce Green and Paul Rondeau had travelled with the gang since its city hall days. Conspicuously, no powerful media baron was seen with this group, nor were there many Calgary Olympic organizers, although old boyhood friends like Tom Minhinnett, now a registered nurse, and Klein's original 1980 campaign managers, Webster MacDonald Sr. and Ted Takacs, connected the gang to Tuxedo Park and the original vagabonds and beautiful people of his political past.

On the surface, the gang was an eclectic, pragmatic bunch of people from across the spectrum of partisan politics with a common loyalty to the fortunes of the man—if not the man himself—they now regarded as arguably the most powerful, and certainly the most dynamic, provincial leader in Canada. Often bemused but always captivated by the charm and integrity of the man, this varied lot of monied land developers, oilmen and professionals, city employees, old neighbours, school chums, political junkies and groupies had witnessed his trials by fire in the vicious infights of municipal land development politics and the meaner world of international Olympic rivalries. The gang was part fan club, part political machine, part excuse to party once in a while.

A layer below the surface, the Klein Gang was a cadre of the most powerful and wealthy in the Calgary establishment. Almost without exception they were men in high positions in business, and they had a great deal to gain in personal wealth from the success of fiscal reform: reduced corporate and personal taxes, lower minimum wages than in other provinces, a cap on employee medicare premiums, the ability to attract investment from international bankers and financiers around the world and the energetic services of a premier who was willing to travel exhaustively to promote the Alberta Advantage to customers and investors around the world. The loyalty of the gang matched its collective influence and the strength that members' opinions carried in business, in academe, with the media, with the federal Conservative and Reform

Parties, in the most powerful forces in the city, and in the unions, churches and service organizations of ordinary folk.

The focal point of the gang—its unofficial general secretary—was Rod Love; he maintained the connection with Klein, he welded together the diverse interests and mixed motives, and he kept the morale up and the doors opened. He brought in and removed members. He kept the gang in shape as a well-oiled fighting force and a powerful network of opinions and wisdom and advice that his boss trusted and relied upon constantly.

Klein Gang members had walked on point with him across the minefields of the provincial environment portfolio that his enemies gambled would destroy him. They had provided the dollars and the horsepower for the *coup d'état* in which he had seized the Conservative Party from its own establishment. They had been the elite troops of his summer election victory. Now they were defining their role in his new government, and they considered Kowalski a rival for the affection Klein had reserved for them.

Following the 1993 provincial election, Klein revealed a new political order. It had its own ranking of insiders and outsiders. The Klein Gang was at the centre of power and they brought to the premier's political machine a decidedly conservative overtone. Corporate executives, well-to-do small business owners, lawyers and academics from fields such as economics and political science were in. Activist union leaders, artists, writers, teachers, nurses and gays were out. Some of the people on the outside bore a striking resemblance to the vagabonds and beautiful people who were with Klein when he won his first election in 1980. Yet there was still the gang, and Klein still pretended to be the same old guy.

At times, hard choices between Klein's public duty and his allegiances demonstrated that there were limits to the gang's influence and power. One such occasion arose when Amoco Canada Petroleum lost a fight with environmentalists over an application to drill for natural gas at a place called the Whaleback, in the southwestern Alberta foothills. The arena for the dispute was the Energy Resources Conservation Board (ERCB), which refused the drilling permit. Amoco's vice-president of government relations, Sherrold Moore, a senior member of the Klein Gang, and environmentalists, who were dismayed by the connection, waited for the inevitable cabinet decision to reverse the ERCB.

Klein and his energy minister, Patricia Black, however, immediately smothered the issue. Cabinet would not even consider questioning the ERCB ruling. Amoco could take its chances with a second application if it wished, but there would be no special deals. The ripples spread even farther. Klein had all but announced a decision to appointment Moore as chairman of the Alberta Energy and Utilities Board (AEUB), to be created by a merger of the ERCB and the Public Utilities Board. In the summer of 1994 Moore had been hinting to his friends that this was the job he would have after his long-postponed retirement from Amoco. Klein decided not to put Moore in the position, however, and left the position in the hands of an acting chairman.

In spite of decisions like the tabling of Moore's appointment to chair the AEUB, the elected members of the Tory cabinet and caucus could see that unelected Klein Gang members—often unidentifiable to people on the outside—rivalled the cabinet for power and influence. The potential impact on the present power and future careers of MLAs like Kowalski, who coveted their current authority and aspired to higher office after Klein moved on, as they were sure he would, was great.

Ken Kowalski was a high school teacher in Barrhead, a rural community in east central Alberta, when Dr. Hugh Horner, then Premier Peter Lougheed's deputy premier, brought him to Edmonton as a parliamentary assistant. Horner groomed Kowalski as his political successor, teaching him, among other things, the fine skills of patronage in the operation of lottery and rural economic development funds. When Horner retired from politics in 1979, Kowalski easily won the seat.

Horner had fallen out of favour with Lougheed, so Kowalski was not appointed to the cabinet until Don Getty became premier in 1985. Then he served as a minister of environment, public safety, career development and employment, public works, public affairs, and supply and services and as the minister responsible for lotteries, the Wild Rose Foundation, major exhibitions and fairs, the gaming commission and the racing commission. When he was appointed to cabinet in 1986 by Premier Getty, Kowalski quickly established that he was the stronger of the two men; Getty never controlled his political excesses, and the MLA from Barrhead was always in the vortex of controversy.

When Klein arrived on the scene, Kowalski was shrewd enough to see a comer; he postponed his own ambition to lead the party, and he became part of the old guard of MLAs and cabinet ministers who worked to get Klein selected as the leader. He made sure that he got maximum credit, as well, and nurtured the impression that he had been the king maker. In fact, there were several others with an equal claim, but Kowalski was more intimidating and the most skilful at getting the recognition.

Whatever the detail of his contribution to Klein's successful hijacking of the party, by the end of the campaign he and Kowalski were friends as well as cabinet colleagues, and the premier, coping with the crushing burden of the self-imposed fast pace of his fiscal agenda, came to rely heavily on the deputy premier to manage the day-to-day business

of the legislature and carry out myriad other assignments and small fa-
vours. Kowalski was always willing to oblige and was unfailingly cheerful; with each assignment he completed, his power and his favour with
the premier grew.

As Klein's minister of everything with the same autocratic style as
C. D. Howe, Kowalski amassed a kind of absolute power that those
under him resented absolutely. To those who were more detached,
Kowalski, with his disregard for decorum, dignity and taste, was a constant reminder that if Klein were vulnerable at all, it was because of
people around him. Kowalski was a charmer, however—handsome, gregarious, well tailored, smoothly shaved. He loved to organize golf tour-
naments, evenings out for dinner and charity fund-raisers. Even people
who suspected his motives and were uneasy with his power found it
hard not to like Ken Kowalski.

Kowalski and Klein were two different styles of politician. The premier had no Edmonton experience before he entered cabinet, lived modestly, made no attempt to exploit his position for the possible perks and
marched in the dead of night whenever he did have to award a patronage
plum. Kowalski was smug, high-living and arrogant, and made no pre-
tense of his ruthless use of patronage. During Klein's leadership campaign, the Liberals accused Kowalski of threatening to pull lottery grants
from Tory ridings where MLAs did not deliver blocks of votes. He was
always close to sources of largesse; lottery funds and half a dozen granting agencies reported to him at one time or another in his high-flying
career through several portfolios. Kowalski never left a portfolio; he
would move on but would be back to interfere and get under the skin
of the new minister.

Kowalski was not a convinced deficit cutter; he accepted Klein's
change of direction only as an expedient. And he put his own political
interests ahead of the Klein agenda. On the eve of cuts to capital spending
for medical facilities, he manipulated to get approval for construction of
the Immacula Hospital in his riding of Barrhead.

Klein wanted to get out of the business of supporting business, but
Kowalski was able to go against the flow and maintain support for the
Swan Hills waste disposal facility. He arranged the extension of a $100
million loan guarantee while Klein was travelling, shortly before
Kowalski's demise. The government was on the hook, in any event, to
continue the financing pending a more satisfactory way to reverse operating losses, make the plant profitable and dispose of it. In fact, when
Klein was environment minister, he loved to boast about the plant and
worked hard on semi-secret plans to make Swan Hills an effective waste
management monopoly for Western Canada and to crush rival enter-
prises such as Laidlaw and Browning Ferries Industries. Nevertheless,

Kowalski had been minister of the environment in 1987 when the guarantee was first written, and renewing it when Klein's back was turned seemed an act of defiance.

These incidents made it seem that Klein and Kowalski were not on the same page and that it was Kowalski calling the shots. People called Kowalski's style the old politics and thought it contradictory that Klein, the new politician, tolerated it. They waited for the alliance to tumble.

The fact of the matter was that Klein thought he was very much in control, and Ken Kowalski was operating under a deliberate guise that had been carefully orchestrated. Kowalski was the lightning rod. His tactical role was to create controversy and draw the anger directed against the government. He would say or do something outrageous and the furor would soak up the energies of the government's foes and the attention of the public.

While the editorialists and opposition critics were fuming about one of Kowalski's indiscretions, Klein could get on with the more important things on his agenda out of the limelight and therefore with relatively little fuss. The idea was to avoid the heat by sending Kowalski into the kitchen to entertain while Klein barbecued dinner in the cool of the back yard. Rod Love described this casting of Klein, himself and Kowalski as, "God [Klein], Vice-God [Love] and Lightning Rod [Kowalski]."[1]

After the election, it was inevitable that a politician so blunt in his use of power and so close to the premier would clash with the Calgary loyalists who were seeking to enhance their position in the new regime. Klein knew that there was animosity between Kowalski and the gang. On October 28, 1993, the premier brought his controversial deputy home to Calgary to meet his political family.

Hugh Dunn, the director of the premier's southern Alberta office, had called the gang in, that chill late autumn Thursday afternoon, to meet Kowalski face to face for the first time. The cavernous third-floor reception room of the McDougall Centre, a renovated sandstone school in downtown Calgary, gleamed with the light of the late slanting sun. The splendid oil paintings, the heavy curtains, the dark wall panels and polished wood floor created an ambiance of affluence and self-satisfaction. A large table in the centre of the room was spread with a sumptuous array of hors d'oeuvres, wine and beer were served by white-coated waiters at a mahogany bar, and large vases of flowers were placed on oversized sideboards. The conversation was easygoing, confident, well lubricated.

Well past the appointed hour, Klein strode in from his office down the hall, dressed in an expensive charcoal wool suit, hair carefully styled and blow-dried, pumped a few arms and then stood up at the portable podium, wired for sound. In a rambling circumlocution, the premier

endeavoured to persuade the Klein Gang to understand and accept the
deputy premier as an asset to the team. "He is my friend; he's a good
soldier in the field," Klein said, and the gang listened with the politeness
of good breeding.[2]

Kowalski, with all the charm and deference he could muster, gave
a self-effacing little soliloquy, the gist of which was that he had no ambition and that he had always devoted himself to "Ralph's best interests."
Kowalski even hinted that he was finding the burden Klein had given
him an onerous one and that he looked forward to life after politics. "I
don't want power, I'd rather be golfing."

The gang warmed to him—he is a very engaging man—but they
were still unconvinced of his motives and more certain than ever that
he impeded their access to and uses for the premier.

"Ralph had better watch that guy," they thought. Many who had
been in the gang over the years said that you could depend on Klein but
you had to watch the people he brought in around him. Klein was capable of very poor judgement regarding people he liked, and his undoing
someday would be someone he trusted. Of course the members of the
gang always meant someone else—particularly Love, Kowalski or Steve
West; they never meant themselves. They especially worried about
Kowalski. For the rest of the evening, however, loyalty to Klein over-
came suspicion, and the party continued, rather sedately, long past the
supper hour.

Kowalski feared the influence of the gang as much as they feared
his, and the reception did nothing to reassure him. The deputy premier
believed that Klein was allowing the caucus and the party to come apart
at the seam joining its rural and urban components. Without representation in Edmonton, which was locked up by the Liberals, almost a third
of Klein's cabinet came from Calgary. The remainder were from the
province's smaller cities and its rural districts. The influence the business
elite in the Klein gang was gaining over the premier was coming at the
expense of Kowalski's personal power.

Kowalski saw signs that Klein was losing touch with the farming
and resource-producing regions. He suspected that the premier's occasional lapses into the bucolic—his blue jean trips around rural Alberta
in the motor home and his hayseed drop-ins to the Legions, weddings
and birthday parties—were affected.

The man in the gang Kowalski most feared and hated was Rod
Love. But the man who would be Kowalski's undoing, in the end, was
the Klein Gang's dean, Art Smith, chairman of engineering firm SNC
Lavalin's Calgary-based petroleum and chemicals division. A former
Conservative MP in the Diefenbaker years, Smith was the senior member
of the group working the oil patch that brought Klein crucial support

for his June 1993 election victory. The two had a previous working relationship, when Klein was mayor, making a success of the Calgary Economic Development Authority, which became the template for the Alberta Economic Development Authority—the issue in the conflict that forced Klein to choose between Kowalski and the Klein Gang.

16

The Duel

*There are those who find benefit in
confusion
and make it a labor of delight*

—Carl Sandburg, "Under the
Capital Dome"

The conflict that fatally divided Klein and Kowalski was the creation of an Alberta Economic Development Authority (AEDA) in April 1994. Klein wanted the AEDA to be a joint business and government initiative that would create a powerful team to sell the Alberta Advantage to business and investors outside the province. It was at the core of Klein's fiscal strategy. The public dividend from deficit, debt and tax cuts was to be economic growth, but the province had to initiate the sales pitch that would catalyze the investment and job-creating decisions of the corporate sector. Klein was persuaded that such an effort would succeed only if the province drafted the business establishment to participate on the sales team.

In 1994 Premier Klein brought Art Smith to Edmonton to set up the AEDA and iron out the details of the partnership between business and government. It was modelled on the Calgary Economic Development Authority, a jointly funded chamber of commerce and city hall institution that had successfully been used to attract investment to Calgary when Klein was mayor, in part because of the efforts of Smith. Klein wanted the AEDA to provide a board of businesspeople, essentially, to direct the $138 million Department of Economic Development and Tourism—a reinvention of government that would see modestly compensated business "volunteers" do what deputy ministers once did. The seventy-five-year-old Smith was not terribly busy in his day job as chairman of SNC Lavalin's petroleum and chemicals division in Calgary and had been hanging around the premier's office since he had helped write the Throne Speech in February 1994.

Kowalski, who carried the Economic Development and Tourism portfolio in addition to his responsibility as deputy premier, balked. He did not want to erode the power of his ministry by empowering the

AEDA to meddle in its policy or operations. He knew that senior bureaucrats in many departments were fearful that Klein would allow businesspeople on the AEDA to dicate the government's economic policies in many spheres, such as energy and agriculture. He rejected several proposals that would have given business significant responsibility for the authority. Meanwhile, without consulting the premier, he engaged John Oldring, a defeated leadership candidate and former minister of social development, for a $125,000, eighteen-month stint as Mexican trade consultant.

By September it was apparent that Klein was having difficulty persuading Kowalski to get with the program and get the authority launched the way the premier wanted it running. Klein started his road tour to promote the Alberta Advantage—the idea that the province was a good place for business investment—without the AEDA in place to follow through. The premier may have been trying to avoid a confrontation, but his point man on the file—Smith—was beginning to be seriously concerned about the entire project.

During the autumn, as the inevitable showdown between Smith and Klein over the AEDA approached, Kowalski weakened his position by making some powerful enemies. The more time Klein spent on the road, promoting the province, the more liberties Kowalski took in interfering with the premier's office. He began to kick around Klein's staff members when he did not get what he wanted. They became angry; not only was he exceeding his authority over them, but he was also usurping the premier's responsibilities during Klein's absence. The more Kowalski insisted that he was in charge, the more the premier's staff resisted and resented him.

A strong bloc in caucus, as well, wanted Kowalski dealt with, and soon. When the deputy premier took a lavish trip to Mexico for the tenuous reason that he was promoting economic development, and came back with little to show for it, the knives came out. A right-wing group of Calgary MLAs who called themselves the Six Pack and gave Klein his strongest backbench support on fiscal policy were openly hostile. Kowalski had become an ideological liability.

But the caucus was divided and the deputy premier had support from members of the old guard, such as Peter Trynchy. There was a north-versus-south and rural-versus-urban split between the pro- and anti-Kowalski forces that was a fault line along which Klein's entire political coalition could easily fracture. It is in the nature of things for caucuses to reflect the outside political reality.

If politics were less guarded, voters would realize that capital cities are closer to reality than they are given credit for, in spite of their out-of-touch, hothouse reputation. If politicians were able to be more open, and felt freer to speak, cabinets, bureaucrats and even premiers would lose much of their power. So the deep political reasons behind splits like those between Klein and Kowalski go mostly unreported and are consequently not understood as part of the checks and balances of a democratic government. If Klein held off longer than he should have in dealing with Kowalski's increasingly rebellious behaviour, it was, in part, because he was doing his best to make cabinet and caucus reflect the real world.

The confrontation came at a 2 ½-hour meeting of the Alberta Economic Development Authority to resolve the delays in its start-up. The session was convened by Art Smith at 2:00 P.M. on Thursday, October 20, at Government House in Edmonton. It was just eight days short of a year since Kowalski had met the Klein Gang at the Calgary reception. The AEDA meeting, ironically, took place at the former residence of Alberta's first premier, Alexander Cameron Rutherford. The building is now used as a formal centre for the lieutenant-governor and premier, making it a northern Alberta equivalent of McDougall School in Calgary, where Klein had tried to make peace between Kowalski and the gang. Rutherford House is part of a magnificent park high above the North Saskatchewan River that also houses the provincial museum and archives.

As the meeting wore on, Kowalski once again tried to beat back proposals from Smith that would get the authority moving, at the expense of what the deputy premier regarded as his turf. The temperature in the room rose, along with the tempers of the participants. Smith insisted that the AEDA be a joint business and government venture; Kowalski was adamant that it should only advise him, and he wanted to be between the AEDA and the premier. The meeting broke up at an impasse, and Smith reported to the premier, who was also in the building, that the logjam had not been broken.

At 4:30 P.M., Kowalski was summoned to meet Klein. The premier summarily told him he was gone and gave him three choices: retire and get out of Edmonton, go to the back benches or take the chair of the newly formed Alberta Energy and Utilities Board, a deficit-cutting amalgamation of the Public Utilities Board and the Energy Resources Conservation Board. Given almost no time to make up his mind, Kowalski accepted the offer of the $110,000 a year patronage post. It was a cabinet minister's version of a golden parachute. It would also ease the blow to Kowalski's credibility and ego.

The news travelled across the city like a prairie fire. When some deputy ministers received the news, they stood up behind their desks and cheered. A resource lobbiest in Edmonton called a colleague in Calgary to say, "They're dancing in the street. Klein will be premier forever.

The bureaucrats are happy, and, my God, the guys in the real world are super-happy."[1]

At 10:00 P.M., Klein met the full cabinet to tell them of Kowalski's resignation and to adjust the cabinet. There would no longer be a deputy premier, and the premier would also be the minister of economic development and tourism. To those who defended Kowalski, Klein said, in so many words, "It's him or me."[2]

In spite of the near unanimous endorsement he got for the decision, the premier was anything but jovial. He viewed Kowalski with a characteristic sentimental loyalty as a dear and trusted friend. Klein fired Kowalski reluctantly, and only after he had crossed too many lines, too many times, and behaved once too often as if he were the real premier and Klein just a figurehead. The two men did their best to close ranks in the hours after the demotion. They agreed that for public consumption Kowalski had resigned and was to become chairman of the Alberta Energy and Utilities Board.

The next morning Klein made the announcement to the media with Colleen by his side, a rare occurrence that betrayed just how difficult, emotionally, it had been to let the deputy premier go from the cabinet. He had his heart on his sleeve; it was a tough moment because Klein is loyal, even when he has been let down. He does not like to think of himself as a man who uses people. "He's not being shown the door, he's being offered, and has decided to accept, an exciting new challenge," Klein said.[3] When the questions became too probing, he nearly walked out and struggled to restrain himself and complete the news conference.

In a characteristic gesture Kowalski, ever the trooper, went golfing Friday morning, leaving his staff to box up his personal files and move him to the humble quarters of an MLA. Then he returned to his constituency for the weekend to reassure his riding executive that he had not been pushed out and that he and Klein were still close. Yet it was an open secret that there had been a showdown with Art Smith and that he had lost. For his part, Smith prepared to take a temporary office in the economic development department, with no pay and no formal authority, to get the AEDA on the road.

In spite of the emotional roller coaster he was on that Friday morning, Klein had won three ways. First, he had tightened his grip on the party and strengthened his power; the power he shared with Kowalski, as deputy premier, he never shared again. It was said by his rural MLAs that he no longer needed an advance man to deal with their ridings.

Second, he had done what Ernest Manning had done: disposed of a minister who played fast and loose with standards for cabinet ministers. He had created a villain, a man to blame for the Swan Hills loan guarantees, for the Paddle River dam controversy and for the old abuses of patronage. As if to confirm this view, media commentators on the Friday evening news were blaming Kowalski for everything, including the weather, the Oldman Dam and the quality of the premier's suits. Klein was depicted as a guy taking control, no longer needing a rural lieutenant or a lightning rod to protect himself. That also made Klein the guy who should wear the goat's horns when the government erred in future. Ironically, however, Kowalski could continue to be used as a retroactive lightning rod for blame, just as blame had been deflected away from Klein to Getty and his ministers, months after they were gone and Klein was in charge.

Third, Klein had readied himself to kick off the good news part of his agenda, without fear of contradiction from a senior minister on his fiscal polices and with the Alberta Economic Development Authority in the field to start delivering results on the Alberta Advantage. The positioning for the next election campaign began the moment Kowalski left Government House without a portfolio to his name. Now Klein was free to construct the future, without being saddled by the past.

Treasurer Jim Dinning was also a winner. With Kowalski out of the way, the cabinet was now clearly hard line on spending and would no longer have its highest-ranking minister violating the spirit of restraint.

The file wasn't quite closed. The following week, Klein faced a deluge of objections from the oil patch about Kowalski's appointment to the Alberta Energy and Utilities Board. The province's energy regulators have a long-standing reputation for impartiality and independence from politics. There had never been a partisan appointment to such an important position before; the industry—indeed the entire business community—let Klein know that the patronage he had provided Kowalski with was inappropriate. The Liberals kicked the stuffing out of him in Question Period.

The legislature's ethics commissioner, Robert Clark, was asked for an opinion and warned in a public report that Klein and Kowalski could be fined $20,000 each for violating stipulations that ministers wait for a six-month cooling-off period after leaving cabinet before taking government jobs that relate to their former responsibilities. At the end of the week, Klein pulled the appointment. He confessed he had not thought the thing out. Later he told Peter Gzowski, in a CBC *Morningside* interview, the decision was probably the dumbest thing he had done all year. It was done for a dear friend, and it was the kind of thing that comes from doing things in politics with friends, but it was also a mistake. He changed course when the oil industry made it clear that the decision was objectionable.

At first, Kowalski was furious that Klein had reneged. The issue went to the Tory caucus on October 31, and Kowalski relented. He emerged to tell journalists that he loved Ralph Klein and respected him and was prepared to take the bullet. He took the ethics commissioner's advice and went to the back benches to go through the six-month decommissioning. It was widely assumed that he would either get a senior appointment or leave the legislature and start a government relations consulting practice. Those closer to him knew that Kowalski considered himself a potential leadership candidate for the future and that the future might come sooner than expected if Klein decided to move on to federal politics after winning reelection in Alberta in 1997.

It had been battering experience for Klein. He took heat because he procrastinated for some time before his showdown with Kowalski; it was a mistake he would not make again. Then he stumbled a second time with the Alberta Energy and Utilities Board appointment. When Ethics Commissioner Clark and the oil industry gave him compelling reasons to reverse himself, he did so with dispatch, taking an issue away from his opponents in the Liberal caucus and the media. He demonstrated that he was still the forthright guy people could trust, and he saved himself a great deal of political fallout by dealing with the problem quickly and cleanly.

In the aftermath of the Kowalski affair, his cabinet ministers were put on notice that the ethics commissioner was no figurehead and that Klein would not protect anyone who made a mistake. There was no grumbling because the ministers already knew they could trust him to stick up for them when they were under unfair attack.

The warning was too late for Transportation and Utilities Minister Peter Trynchy, however. On December 15, just eight weeks after Kowalski left the cabinet, Klein unceremoniously dumped Trynchy after Ethics Commissioner Clark said the minister had demonstrated poor judgement and inappropriate behaviour in hiring a company with a provincial road contract to pave his driveway.

There was more to Trynchy's dismissal than a paving job on his long, sweeping country estate driveway; he had been aggressive in capturing patronage for his riding and had written an indiscreet letter to Kowalski proposing that they split the political allocation of the contracts and benefits for the Paddle River Dam. The correspondence may have been a practical discussion of the routine political task—every cabinet has a process to divide the legitimate spoils of power. When the letter leaked to the media, however, it did not read well for public consumption, partly because it was drafted like a contract to be countersigned by Kowalski (he did not do so) and partly because Trynchy wanted the giant share (75 per cent) of the spoils.

Klein let Trynchy go with a one-sentence dismissal letter, even though Clark said there had been no breach of the Conflict of Interest Act. Trynchy was Alberta's longest-serving cabinet minister, with twenty-three years in various portfolios under Lougheed, Getty and Klein. "It is with regret that I must advise you I am relieving you of your duties as Minister of Transportation and Utilities," Klein wrote. No parachute, no press conference and no warm words, even though Trynchy had been an important supporter in the premier's leadership campaign.[4]

Klein knew that his maverick politics relied on people's confidence more than their partisan allegiances. He knew that many people would agree with only part of what he was doing, and most acknowledged that he was so unusual that they would never understand him. But as long as people trusted him, he would have a secure grip on power. His popularity as mayor of Calgary had often reached well over 80 per cent in the polls. After the Kowalski affair, his popularity rose above 60 per cent and kept rising after he fired Trynchy. Through the rest of the winter, the approval rating continued climbing into the mid-70s, and Klein knew that the strength of his popularity was an indication that people took him at his word.

Calgary writer Gillian Steward, in an opinion piece for the *Calgary Herald* written shortly after the 1993 election, said that people voted for Klein "because they liked and trusted him. He made government seem accessible and simple. He was easy to approach and had no difficulty talking about complex subjects in direct, uncomplicated language."[5] Kowalski and Trynchy were the antithesis of that style. They became liabilities to the public trust upon which Klein relied because they became the symbols of trust betrayed. They had to go. It was an incidental benefit for the Klein Gang and Rod Love that Kowalski had removed himself from the inner circle—and the bitter rivalry around Klein. Trynchy was a bonus. He was not as powerful as Kowalski or as troublesome to the interests of the Klein Gang, but he was one of the old guard of ministers with a strong rural base who had prospered in the Getty years when ethical discipline was lax.

In the end, the young Turks of the unelected Klein Gang had vanquished the old guard of the elected Tory caucus, in the bloodiest episode of Klein's reinvention of government. The comfortable environs of the gang, however, created a certain dramatic irony, a paradox, for a politician who was more accustomed to the company of mavericks. Indeed, by the time the twenty-third session of the Alberta legislature ended on November 10, 1994, Klein could scarcely be recognized as, or legitimately claim to be, the outsider. His challenge to the status quo had become the measure of the Conservative counterreformation in Canada and the restoration of government practised before the 1960s.

The hijacker of office and usurper of power was now the respected and respectable enforcer of the Conservative agenda. He was the prince of less government, of reinventing government, of doing government differently. Although other politicians in other parties were tinkering with the same solutions, what made Klein different was the sweep, scope and persistence of his changes. He was publicly committed to cutting the deficit entirely by reducing spending and without increasing taxes. While he quietly raised user rates for elective services such as parks and downloaded other costs onto the municipalities, he had maintained the "all cuts, no taxes" myth. He captured the Conservative agenda, reducing the deficit and reducing government—reinventing it and restoring its accountability.

Liberal-minded Albertans were still disappointed that Klein acted like a doctrinaire political conservative. The premier seemed not to object when people called him Red-Neck Ralph. When he was an outsider, Liberals had thought Klein was with them; now he was an insider, and he had left them behind. To the premier, his programs were necessary and showed basic common sense; to his philosophical adversaries, these programs were ideology and formed the basis for a new elite in society. Meanwhile, Klein was spending more of his time with corporate and financial decision makers who would bring investment to the province to take advantage of the Alberta Advantage he was creating for business.

The Klein Gang now met for beer in the elegance of the premier's reception room at the McDougall Centre, not in a frigid campaign head-quarters with no toilets, no hot water and stolen electric power. As his power became more entrenched, his friends found him harder to define and to reach, and his foes found him more difficult to pin down. He was everything he seemed to be and yet nothing about him was as it appeared to be.

17

The Failure of Opposition

*It was an era when politics could
not be combed out of people's lives;
every trifle became a badge of party
defiantly worn.*

—LOUIS KRONENBERGER, *KINGS
AND DESPERATE MEN*

By the end of the spring session in 1995, Klein dominated the Alberta landscape because, in addition to his direct popular support, he had no rivals. There had been three possible challengers: the Liberal Party, the media and what Rod Love sardonically labelled MUSH: the municipal, university, school and public health care professionals and interests, including elected officials, unions, managers and executives whose status quo was destroyed. For different reasons, each rival foundered in its attack on Klein. The most difficult to explain was the default of the education, health and municipal establishments, which claimed to see harm being done but were unable to mount, focus and sustain an alternative vision.

Harold Millican, a Calgary chamber of commerce past president, boyhood friend and sometime political aide to former Premier Peter Lougheed and, paradoxically, a Liberal, was a governor of Mount Royal College. He watched as the college was buried under the paperwork of budget cuts, business plans, round table public consultations and white papers, as the college reinvented itself. "The fallout is still to come; there are people in positions of responsibility who just can't cope with the level of adjustment that has to go on, and we're just through the first phase of this," he told friends in the spring of 1995.[1]

"Look, there are questions for the education system that will take time to deal with," Millican said. "You can't run a college like a company; it just won't work." Millican was also baffled that the formerly moderate

Ralph Klein was doing this. "Is it all too much for him; has it gotten ahead of him? Does he know what's going on down the line?"

In spite of the grave worries of community leaders like Millican, no element of MUSH mounted an effective, sustained attack or proposed alternatives that gained a broad base of support. No common front developed to link these interests. Instead, Klein turned the attack back on the attackers, positioning them as members of a hostile establishment who were protecting their privileged lives at the expense of the taxpayers.

He called his opponents irresponsible for spreading doom and gloom. "No politician is deliberately going to go out and try and hurt someone. We are trying to streamline the system and create efficiencies," Klein told Anthony Johnson of the *Calgary Herald*'s legislative bureau.[2] When the Alberta Teachers' Association resisted his request for a voluntary mid-contract wage rollback, he said they would be forced to do it at the bargaining table for the next contract. One way or the other, the teachers would join other government sector employees who had already agreed to take less money. It became a matter of numbers. When the polls were taken, or the unions decided on contract changes, Klein had more votes.

Meanwhile, Liberal leader Laurence Decore had hoed a long row during his tenure as Liberal leader. First, he had fought off cancer. There had been several deaths in his family, and now his father was ailing. The June election had been a personal defeat; he had fully expected to beat Klein and was taken completely off guard by his loss. His message of fiscal responsibility was reduced to a faint echo of Klein's more dramatic call to action. "Little Larry Me Too," snickered the wags in the Conservative machine.[3]

As Budget Day approached, Decore's future was a matter of open speculation and his mediocre response to the budget finished off his career. His attack was unspirited and vague. He repeated again and again that Klein had a hidden agenda but never produced evidence of a scheme. He accused the premier of destroying the hopes of Albertans, but Klein's popularity contradicted that attack. Worse, Decore had no compelling alternative to offer. He was leaving Klein a clear field on which to operate. The knives were out.

On Sunday, March 20, Lethbridge MLA Ken Nicol gathered the caucus dissidents in his Edmonton apartment to assess the situation. Decore faced a scheduled leadership review at a party policy convention later in the year. Should he be persuaded to go without the embarrassment of a vote? Were there candidates for his job who could defeat Klein? Little thought was given to whether the party should run from the centre, the left or the right of the political spectrum. One Grit MLA who had been recruited for his Reform Party, right-leaning politics, Paul Langevin, had deserted the caucus to sit as an independent. Instead of looking like an alternative, the Grits looked like opportunists. Nicol knew that Klein's budget cuts had support in southern Alberta, so why fight that issue?

Then Decore was involved in an embarrassing incident that should have been minor but became the lever for antagonists within the caucus. After a Friday lunch with a woman on his staff, he agreed to take a spin around the legislature grounds in her new four-wheel drive. She raced the vehicle up an embankment and slid out of control on the icy snow, slamming into a truck owned by Nick Taylor, the MLA from Westlock who had been leader before Decore deposed him in 1988. There were difficult questions about just how much wine had been consumed over the lunch, two glasses or a bottle, and who would pay for the torn-up lawn, Decore or the woman's insurance company.

The rebellion against Decore was out in the open. It festered and Klein rolled on, unimpeded, to the end of the session. Finally, in mid-July, after his brother, John, was killed in a motorcyle accident, Decore resigned, catching the party off guard and ill prepared to put strong, credible candidates into the field. A date for a leadership convention was set for November.

Decore deserved a more graceful exit than he got, but politics is a brutal game; the leadership convocation, at his insistence, did not include the customary tribute to a retiring leader. In any event, his father, John N. Decore, died on the eve of the vote, and the family gathered to prepare for the funeral while the party picked Decore's successor.

As the leadership race opened, Edmonton MLA Grant Mitchell was considered the only serious contender. He had placed second to Decore in the 1988 leadership contest and had spent the past six years getting ready to finish first. Within hours of Decore's resignation, Mitchell hit the ground running, with money in the bank, offices operating, posters printed and a schedule laid out.

He faced three problems, however. First, he was a former vice-president of the notorious Principal Group, the financial empire that collapsed in disgrace during the Getty administration. Older Liberals who had seen the impact on the thousands of fixed-income seniors who lost their life savings worked hard to defeat him. Second, Mitchell was dogged by the province's north-south rivalry, in which he was the "Edmonton" candidate. Mitchell's third problem was the open membership of the Liberal Party—anyone can join and there is no fee. That gave millionaire candidate Sine Chadi, also an Edmonton MLA, a huge opening to recruit widely and aggressively. Allegations of a bought campaign sullied the race nearly from its outset. They were first aimed at Chadi, but if you throw mud, some sticks to you, and the well-funded Mitchell soon faced the same charge.

Calgary Liberals worked so hard to produce an "anybody but Edmonton" candidate that they ended up with two. These were earnest and listless Gary Dickson, a civil rights lawyer, and the perennial candidate for anything, Tom Sindlinger, a former MLA whose claim to fame was to have been tossed out of the Tory caucus more than a decade earlier.

The final candidate, Fort MacMurray MLA Adam Germaine, entered the race partly on the encouragement of a "none of the above candidates" group of lawyers. Germaine was a Ralph look-alike who thought that would enable him to preempt Klein's other qualities and who entered the race because a Mitchell-Chadi split might lead to an opportunity to be the compromise.

The forgettable candidates ran an invisible campaign. When the legislature resumed sitting in October, Ralph had a 61 per cent approval rating in the polls, 16 points higher than on election day 1993. In the final days before the November 12 vote, ugly allegations of membership improprieties were made. There was an internal party investigation, but it found no evidence of dirty tricks to sign up registered voters. Despite the party's best efforts to fudge the fact, the charges had been aimed at Chadi, who had emerged as a serious threat to Mitchell. Chadi was a third-generation Lebanese who grew up in a single-parent family in Fort MacMurray and had made a fortune in real estate and land development.

Chadi was an easy target for innuendoes that he was block-buying ethnic votes. During the 1970s and 1980s, the organization and delivery of blocks of ethnically based votes became an established practice, especially in battles to win Conservative nominations for the largely safe provincial and federal seats. It is the unpleasant truth that in Alberta's predominantly white Liberal Party, it was all too easy to smear a man from the Middle East by whispering that he was brokering votes. Powerful Liberal insiders went in determined to keep him out of the leadership, regardless of the number of votes he had, because they believed a non-white could not become the premier of Alberta. And they wanted to win. "You can't have a man like that running our party," said one highly placed Liberal to justify the manipulation of the leadership ballot.[4]

With the Chadi affair poorly resolved, on voting day the telephone and computer technology that were to record the vote failed. The leader was to be selected by a province-wide telephone ballot. Using personal identification numbers, eligible voters were to dial their vote into a computer. Rules were drawn up to control the sale of $10 PIN numbers and to allow fax balloting and proxy voting for those who had to vote in advance.

The computers crashed an hour before the first ballot was to close at 10:00 A.M. It took another seven hours to get through the second ballot. After the first ballot, Mitchell had 4,799 votes, Chadi 3,772, Germaine 1,663, Dickson 706 and Sindlinger 64. Mitchell won the second ballot, which incorporated a preferential voting option that allowed electors to name first and second choices. Mitchell was the first choice of 4,934, Chadi the first choice of 3,794.

Then controversy erupted because the Liberal machine had found the lever with which to dump Chadi. After the first ballot, Chadi protested that the returning officer had accepted only 1,528 of the 3,600 proxy votes he had delivered. Had they all been counted, he would have won on the first ballot. Chadi felt he had been robbed. The technical foul-up overrode the significance of his protest, and Chadi swallowed his anger and joined all candidates on the platform to endorse Grant Mitchell's second-ballot victory. Even this gesture was almost frustrated by organizers who tried to get all-candidate support for Mitchell without Chadi, forcing the humilated MLA to sprint to the platform.

The party closed ranks, and an investigation of the handling of proxies and possible voting irregularities exonerated the returning officer and party officials. The inference was left hanging that some of the proxies Chadi had tendered were irregular, although no evidence was offered. Organizers claimed that they could not investigate because Chadi supporters did not speak English.

Then Klein claimed that before the Liberal leadership, Chadi put out feelers that he was interested in crossing the floor to the Conservatives if a cabinet post were possible. The premier had spurned the overture, telling his caucus, "You can't have a man like that in cabinet," without saying why not.[5] The Liberals used Klein's information as retroactive justification for the shabby treatment they had given Chadi.

In all the confusion and infighting, Mitchell, the new leader, had not made a single substantive statement about where he was taking the party or would take Albertans. A poll released during the final week of the Liberal campaign showed that Klein had 57 per cent of the popular vote, the Liberals only 38 per cent. As the weeks passed, following Mitchell's election, he was unable to find a platform for his views, as the Opposition continued to falter in Question Period.

The collapse of resistance from special-interest groups and the failed Liberal attack meant that the strongest voices opposing Klein were in the media. The legislative Press Gallery was the centre of gravity for media antagonism, which extended to the Edmonton-based CBC *Alberta News* and the editorial boards of the *Calgary Herald* and *Edmonton Journal*, the Southam papers in Alberta.

Klein enjoyed the always qualified support of *Alberta Report*, which has its strongest roots in the Klein coalition of rural and blue-collar Albertans, as well as the business community, and understands his

THE FAILURE OF OPPOSITION

anti-political style because it runs against the mainstream in journalism. Nevertheless, the magazine, particularly its founder and keystone columnist, Ted Byfield, constantly scolded Klein for deviations from the true conservative faith. He received more unconditional endorsement from the *Sun* tabloids, but they were too contrary to hand him a blank cheque of approval.

Unexpectedly, Klein found unqualified support from Canadian business and financial editors and columnists, who were almost without exception anchors for a new conservative voice in Canadian public life. From the beginning of his administration in 1993, he was venerated in column after column by leading right-wing journalists like Diane Francis of the *Financial Post*, who called Klein "Canada's best economic manager by a long shot."[6]

After Dinning's February 1994 budget, the *Globe and Mail*, in a lead editorial entitled "Hope from Alberta," said, "It's hard to over state the importance of what's happening in Alberta. It is important not only for what it means for the province, but for the nation, and not merely for what it says about our economic prospects, but about the ability of governments to govern in this country. The hope and seeming paradox in Alberta's experiment is this: that as the size of government shrinks, faith in government rises."[7]

Paul Martin brought down the federal budget on February 22, 1994, two days before Dinning's. When the *Globe*'s columnist Kenneth Whyte compared the two in his Saturday column "The West," he called Klein's government "a moral example to the nation." Martin, he said, just talked, insincerely, about doing the things that Alberta was getting on with.[8]

Something in Klein's nature, or in his experience as a politically powerful broadcast journalist, resulted in a compulsion for media management. He followed his coverage assiduously, went down to the basement Press Gallery office personally with copies of news releases and invited two or three favorites, such as Rick Bell and Neil Waugh of the *Sun* newspapers, for drinks after work.

At city hall, Klein had mastered control of the media through intellectual seduction. He never broke his connection and nurtured the "he is one of us" sentiment that made reporters reluctant to criticize or report on his excessive partying.[9] Klein led late night drinking sessions with reporters, always picking up the tab, always creating an obligation. In provincial politics, more sophisticated management was required.

Following the Kowalski affair, Klein tightened his grip around the throat of the Press Gallery. Through his handlers, he imposed complete control over physical contact with reporters and journalists assigned to the Press Gallery. Scrums became carefully managed set pieces. His cabinet ministers took on, almost exclusively, the role of detailing policy.

His office and the adjacent corridor were physically cordoned off and, from behind the fortress wall, he withheld and granted audiences with a regal disdain for his former craft.

Klein created a competition for his imprimatur and for access. Some journalists and broadcasters were willingly complicit because they were entranced by his unreformed Press Club persona and by the sheer audacity of one of their own capturing and holding high office. Klein's is the type of success, comparable to that of another broadcaster cum premier, Québec's Réne Lévesque, that turns journalists into power junkies.

The price of access for journalists was to assent to his terms, and Rod Love's, for the agenda and for focus, tone and slant. Klein continually humiliated local correspondents by aggressively bragging about the trickle of U.S. journalists who came to see his brand of fiscal conservatism in action after the Republicans took control of the U.S. Congress in the 1994 November midterm elections, since there were some strong similarities between the Alberta fiscal strategy and that of the Contract with America.

Klein was accessible to major Canadian business journalists such as Peter C. Newman, who dined in Vancouver with the Kleins and Rod Love early in 1995 and then wrote a mildly approving column for *Maclean's*.[10] Newman said, after the dinner, that he found Klein compelling and credible and Colleen a treasure, possibly the best political wife in the country, but that Rod Love was disturbing and in the long run would not be an asset to Klein.[11] Love's foreboding presence was, undoubtedly, linked to his discomfort that Newman was a journalist he could not control. Meanwhile, the access Newman enjoyed was salt in the wound to Alberta reporters, who got the message that the premier valued access to his home-town media less than access to the superstars of the larger media stage—unless, of course, the Press Gallery regulars cared to accept his terms for coverage. As a tool for suppressing critical inquiry, this was unparalleled.

In a news economy in which their editors and news directors demanded that they all have the same story every day, the ink-stained wretches of the Press Gallery idled away countless hours, waiting around all day because the premier would appear once or twice to throw out a bone—a sound bite—that they could file. Then, if some hapless scribe put a spin on the story that was frowned on by the inner sanctum, Rod Love would make an appearance to enforce the correct version of the story. Love also aggressively worked the telephone, constantly calling to berate reporters, editorial writers and columnists outside the Press Gallery when they were critical of Klein. He was described by reporters as "intimidating" and "harassing." The result, however, was "brilliant" media management, producing broadly positive coverage for Klein.

LEFT: Klein's hard rock aide Rod Love calls himself Ralph's vice-god and air traffic controller; the two have a sibling relationship in which Love is the over-awed younger brother. ALBERTA REPORT

BELOW: The warm relationship between Klein, wearing his mayoral chain, and IOC chairman Juan Antonio Samaranch contributed to the success of the Calgary games. THE CITY OF CALGARY ARCHIVES

RIGHT: Klein and the Olympic flag and torch, with the Bow River and city skyline to the south. The Games were an opportunity for this feel-good politician to lead a home-town party. ALBERTA REPORT

RIGHT: When Klein turned the Olympic flag over to IOC chairman Juan Antonio Samaranch and the mayor of Albertville, France at the Games' close, his mayoral years effectively ended. THE CITY OF CALGARY ARCHIVES

LEFT: As Alberta's environment minister, Klein emerged as a process politician and policy wonk, absorbed in reports, field inspections, commissions and the legislative process. ALBERTA REPORT

BELOW: On September 17, 1992, Klein, flanked by MLA Pat Black (*rear*) and then-deputy premier Peter Elzinga, announced he would seek the leadership of the Alberta Conservative Party. ALBERTA REPORT/ PAT PRICE

Top: Klein's organization was chagrined that Nancy Betkowski led by a single vote after the first leadership ballot, on November 28, 1992, and Klein was exhausted. ALBERTA REPORT/KEN MCCURDY

ABOVE: Klein, flanked by three of the people he loves most, his father, Phil (*left*), Rod Love (*rear*) and Colleen, hears that he has won an upset on the second leadership ballot, December 5, 1992. ALBERTA REPORT/AL POPIL

RIGHT: After being sworn in as premier on December 15, 1992, Klein, with his eagle feather in hand, danced with Chief Lloyd Sutton and John Chief Moon Sr. in the entrance to the Alberta legislature. EDMONTON JOURNAL/JIM COCHRANE

RIGHT: The premier and
his wife arrive in Edmonton,
during the 1992 Christmas
break, for his traditional
year-end with his father,
prior to launching his
extraordinary fiscal
reforms. ALBERTA REPORT/
STEVE SANFORD

RIGHT: In a media scrum
confrontation with Jason
Kenny (*right*) of the Alberta
Taxpayers Association,
Klein faces the issue of
MLAs' pensions, the key to
the 1993 election. ALBERTA
REPORT/CFRN-TV

Top: The premier, Colleen and Rod Love were ecstatic when his landslide victory in the June 1993 election became apparent just moments after the polls closed. ALBERTA REPORT/KEN MCCURDY

ABOVE LEFT: Rarely able to hide their emotions, both Colleen and Premier Klein were near tears as they met the media together on the night of the Miracle on the Prairies election victory. ALBERTA REPORT/KEN MCCURDY

ABOVE RIGHT: Ralph's father, Phil Klein, a lifelong political junkie, helped his son in all his campaigns, including the 1993 Miracle on the Prairies. EDMONTON JOURNAL/LARRY WONG

Top: Klein with Ontario Tory leader Mike Harris at the National Citizens' Coalition awards in November 1994, when Klein was given the Colin M. Brown Freedom Medal for his fiscal reforms. ALBERTA REPORT

Above left: On his annual accountability presentation, "Talking with Albertans," in January 1995, Klein said he would hold the course on fiscal restraint; his popularity soared in subsequent polls. ALBERTA REPORT

Above right: In a formal portrait for an *Alberta Report* front cover in April 1995, Klein betrayed the weariness and worry of the hardest year in his political life. ALBERTA REPORT/STEVE SANFORD

The late night drinking sessions of Klein's mayoralty days resumed, with members of the *Sun* newspapers' legislative bureau as the principal guests. "The attitude at the *Sun* newspapers was that someone has to sacrifice his liver to go on the Klein beat," former *Calgary Sun* city hall reporter Peter Miller said. The renewed sessions, however, led to questions by the deposed Ken Kowalski as to whether they were the venue for leaks of the 1995 budget.

So unproductive had the Press Gallery become that *Alberta Report* did not bother to keep a regular reporter on the legislative grounds. The magazine pulled its reporters because, as Ted Byfield said, "The legislative gallery doesn't cover either the legislature or the government, and the government won't give them the time of day. So journalists in the gallery end up covering the gallery; they drink their own bathwater." A few reporters perceived the problem, but their editors and managers, who worked away from the legislature, were Klein wannabes who were not prepared to back critical inquiry.

When he could not overpower a journalist, Love turned to his relationship with the journalist's editor or publisher. He once confronted Jim Cunningham, *Calgary Herald* legislative reporter and host of a Friday television show, *Fair Comment*, which follows the government, on the *Herald*'s "negative" editorial page. Love singled out then editorial page editor Catherine Ford for her "unreasonableness." Then he added, "Well, Jim, I like some things about your paper. I'm going out to play golf with your [managing] editor next week." An independent columnist who witnessed the clash, Gillian Steward, said, "They [Klein's handlers] squeeze you from both the top and bottom."

What Aberhart had tried but failed to do, through the 1938 Press Gag Act and his bid in 1935 to purchase the *Albertan* newspaper and turn it into a Social Credit house organ, Klein accomplished with the apparently effortless ease that has always marked his manipulation of the media. Aberhart's press bill would have given Aberhart's cabinet the power to terminate the publication of any newspaper and required newspapers to disclose sources for all stories and comment about the government and to publish statements corrected by the chairman of the Social Credit Board or to amplify their political coverage. The Supreme Court of Canada overturned the bill, and the *Edmonton Journal* won a Pulitzer Prize for leading the fight against it.

As the result of the media failure, Albertans were hearing mostly what Klein wanted them to hear. Catherine Ford, for example, was shuffled out of Klein's way to write a national column for Southam, although there were no fingerprints on the decision to link it to Love's intensive pressure. There were exceptions. Mark Lisac, political columnist for the *Edmonton Journal*, produced a rambling polemic, *The Klein Revolution*, based on his columns and published in the winter of 1995. Otherwise, the toughest liberal assessments of Klein policy came from a cadre of academic writers and media commentators, such as the University of Alberta's Allan Tupper and the University of Calgary's Roger Gibbins, and from newsletter publishers, such as Richard Vivone, of *Insight into Government*, and Gillian Steward, cofounder of a short-lived public affairs newsletter called *The New Albertan*.

Ironically, given the anti-Klein passion of the liberal media, it was the conservative writers and editors of *Alberta Report* who provided consistent questioning of Klein's policies and legislation. They remained out of reach of his manipulation, challenging him for his failure to extend his conservatism beyond the fiscal arena to include social policy.

18

The Long Haul

The infusion of a new spirit into Industry ... demands above all else a fine discernment between economic and human values; between the ends which Wealth and the ends which Life were meant to serve.

—WILLIAM LYON MACKENZIE KING, *INDUSTRY AND HUMANITY*

On a late November day in 1994, the National Citizens' Coalition, an advocacy organization for politics to the right of conservative, packed four hundred people into a Toronto hotel luncheon to award Ralph Klein the Colin M. Brown Freedom Medal. The event became a right-wing love-in, which wasn't surprising given that the coalition's motto is "More freedom through less government,"[1] and its president, David Somerville, moved from Ontario after the election of the Rae NDP government in 1990 to live in what he regarded as Alberta's more hospitable environment.

The event confirmed Klein as the national touchstone for the special interests who were the enemies of the liberal agenda and who wanted to seize the next century for a new brand of government that welcomes its limits, lives within its means, takes less from national economies and leaves society open, mostly to the imagination of its corporate sector. There were plenty of conservatives, from *Financial Post* editor Diane Francis to Ontario Tory boss Michael Harris, who grabbed Klein's coat-tails that afternoon. "I'm humbled and honoured to be sitting at the same table," said Harris,[2] who introduced Klein to the gathering as a politician of courage, vision and leadership.[3]

The occasion also provided an opportunity for detractors to revile him; anti-politics, it had turned out, was the stuff of a polarized world. "It's not something to be proud of," sniffed Alberta Federation of Labour president Linda Karpowich about the deficit cutting that brought the award. "I think it's only the actions of a lunatic who could continue in this vein and not think it's causing human suffering."[4] In her report on the luncheon, the resolutely liberal *Toronto Star*'s Sandra Contenta acidly commented that Klein was honoured as "the undisputed leader of Canada's debt-obsessed conservatives."[5]

The crowd at the Colin M. Brown luncheon, however, had come to praise not scorn him; they wanted to hear how he had launched the task of putting Alberta's fiscal house in order. He gave them seven steps. It was so much like an Alcoholics Anonymous testimonial that it was as if he had stood up and said: "Hi, my name's Ralph. I'm a Premier. I have a debt problem, but I've had two budgets in a row that cut the deficit. One day at a time, I'm going to balance the budget and start paying down the accumulated debt."

The speech had the ring of self-help slogans:

First, be prepared to start at the top. Ask nothing of others you would not do yourself. Second, go fast; the longer the program, the later the payoff; you can't leap a canyon in two jumps. Third, there are no sacred cows; those who consume the lion's share of the money must assume the lion's share of the solution; if that means health, education and social services, then so be it.

Fourth, be honest; don't sugarcoat; if it requires sacrifice, say so. Fifth, keep it simple: the solutions to the problems we face in this country are not necessarily complex. Sixth, there is no such thing as too much information; change must be communicated, and it must be done by the senior people in an organization.

And seventh, be prepared to take the heat; enormous change is never accomplished with ease in silence. The critics don't like it; they say, "You can't run government like a business." But to that I respond, "Well, we can't run government like a government any more. It wasn't working."[6]

The ebullient Klein said politicians should stop pandering to special interests; he extolled the silent majority. This was leadership by sound bite—Winston Churchill come to late night motivational television. It revealed the premier's shamelessly sentimental side. It also had its calculated purpose: Klein was on the road to bring investment into his province because he couldn't deliver his political dividend unless the economy grew. "We believe eliminating the deficit and redefining government are the two most effective actions government can take to foster economic growth," he said in his speech. He was talking directly to Bay Street.

This was his prospectus; he was asking the audience to bring their business to Alberta.

Klein barnstormed the country through the autumn and travelled to China with Prime Minister Jean Chrétien's business opportunities tour for premiers and business leaders. He took advantage of every opportunity. He spoke at a real estate seminar in Toronto, to business students in St. John's and on a radio talk show in Vancouver. He went to Ottawa for a round of photo opportunities. Halifax and Sherbrooke shared the itinerary with the flashier centres. He schmoozed with chief executives; he talked to investment analysts and gave media interviews.

The message was always the same: lower taxes, less government, great lifestyle. High-income migrants, the kind of people who decide to move big investments and big companies, would put an extra $25,000 to $30,000 in their pockets just on reduced personal income tax, he boasted. The subtext was invest in Alberta, move your company, get with the program.

Like any good huckster, he accentuated the positive and left the impression that he had fixed it all up in Alberta, that there were no more problems to get in the way of those who had come to his business haven. The money could flow two ways; he hinted at energy development in Newfoundland and he kept alive the impression in Nova Scotia that he might reduce interest rates on Heritage Fund loans made by Alberta to that province in the 1970s.

Back home, however, he was less expansive and less generous. He was reluctant to say what could be done with budget surpluses once they occurred. He would not commit himself to personal and corporate tax cuts. He was dedicated to a policy of the most competitive tax regime in Canada, and the treasury board was debating tax cuts. But, he speculated, first the government might have to shore up its aging infrastructure: "At some point you have to reinvest in the community. You can't let roads fall apart, you can't let bridges fall apart, you can't let universities and the fine institutions that have been built just disintegrate."[7]

His restoration had passed its first quantitative test; the budget numbers were working. The ground rules were simple: a balanced budget by 1997; orderly repayment, "like a home mortgage," of the $32 billion accumulated debt; no new taxes. As the year drew to a close, he was ahead of schedule; prodigious oil and gas revenues were feeding a surplus for the 1994–95 budget.

The task was unfinished, however, because it had not been tested for its qualitative results: the development of better government for less money and a vaguely defined dividend called the Alberta Advantage—the tax reduction, elimination of red tape and reduction in the regulatory role of government that would attract investment and create new jobs. The advantage would trigger the march into a political future no longer to be feared, led by this unconventional pied piper.

The investment had been made, but the dividend had yet to be paid. Surprisingly, there were no effective voices asking who would benefit or exactly what the advantages would be. The physics of politics usually dictates that for every winner there will be an equal and opposite loser. Now that Klein had shown that Alberta could enforce its tough prescription, there were thoughtful, tougher questions to answer. When governments cut costs in the 1960s to recapture balanced budgets, they called it austerity. Would the new Alberta be an austere place in which the schools had no books, the hospitals no beds and the helpless, however they were defined, no hope?

At the beginning of 1995, Klein came back from his Christmas break and resumed the breakneck pace that had characterized the first six months of 1994. On January 18, 1995, he appeared in a carefully prepared television broadcast, *Talking with Albertans*, designed to reinforce his support, maintain the initiative and blunt the attacks he now faced. The pretaped show, which aired midweek in the heart of prime time, had none of the intensity and spontaneity of the previous year. He narrated some of the script from the cramped cabinet room, standing beside the table and empty chairs framed by dark panelled walls. The balance of the talking was done from his office, seated near his broad, impeccably tidy desk with most of the personal items fuzzy and out of focus in the background.[8]

The production was tense and choppy, edited into segments like an overripe grapefruit divided by tough membranes. Many of the cuts showed the marks of a long taping session, with retakes in which the hair was never quite the same, and there were subtle shifts in the level of his voice and the lighting on his shirt. Klein's message was illustrated by computer graphics in which the designers had run amok with numbers and bars and squiggly lines that defied the viewer to absorb the detail and the impression before they were jerked away. He used an armoury of clichés: "the Alberta Advantage," "creating the climate for business to generate jobs," "reinventing our province," "this is starting to pay dividends," "the youngest, highly skilled, highly educated, most productive work force" and "it's possible to put our house in order." But somehow, in the blizzard of rhetoric, he conveyed the point that all of this was a renewal of something familiar, a return to basic values, a restoration of the familiar and the comforting.

It was poor, predictably dull television, but he got the message across that what had unfolded since he became premier was just Phase One, and in Phase Two, Albertans who helped him would discover "the most exciting thing about change is the outcome ... the new, deficit-free Alberta ... doing it right this time ... fresh ideas ... all Albertans working together." In spite of himself and his overzealous writers and producers, Klein managed to ignite a spark. This process was like renovating a home, he said, and soon Albertans would be able to put their feet up and enjoy the results. His post-broadcast polls continued to rise steadily.

A month later, Provincial Treasurer Jim Dinning tabled a budget with a $110 million surplus for 1994–95, a result of unexpected revenues of $1.5 billion, and what he predicted would be the last budget deficit for Alberta in 1995–96, of $506 million. There were more cuts ahead, but Dinning depicted the cutting process as a highly rational one, in which business plans for every department and operation of government were ensuring that measurable, politically acceptable results were being achieved.

Meanwhile, health care became the testing ground for the Alberta Advantage as the Liberal federal government stuck its hand into the pot. Since the election of the Chrétien Liberal administration, in October 1993, its abrasive health minister, Diane Marleau, had been conducting a chippy little skirmish with her Alberta counterpart, Shirley McClellan. The issue was whether the combination of cuts to the province's health budget and its encouragement of private clinics for specialized services such as abortion and laser eye surgery had violated Canada Health Act provisions that guarantee equitable care regardless of income. Marleau repeatedly accused Alberta of creating a two-tier medical system, with different standards of care for rich and poor. She threatened so often to penalize the province by deducting penalties from federal transfer payments that Dinning had finally told her to put up or shut up.

The Klein cabinet was certain that it was in compliance with the Canada Health Act and would win a court challenge if Marleau actually had the courage to penalize the transfer payments. They suspected that Marleau was simply conducting a reconnaissance of Alberta's will to engage in a constitutional row over money. Ottawa, they were sure, was motivated to take advantage of Alberta's fiscal health by finding a way to pick the pocket.

There was history to back up the suspicion, dating back to the Rowell Sirois Royal Commission on Dominion Provincial Relations. *The Case for Alberta*, prepared for submission by the Aberhart government, framed the classic thesis that Alberta paid more into the coffers of Confederation than it received back; along with Saskatchewan, it was the province most penalized by national membership.[9] Characteristically, the document never made it to the Royal Commission; Aberhart feuded bitterly with Prime Minister Mackenzie King because there was no commissioner from the West and withdrew Alberta's participation.

More recently, when oil prices were rising in 1974, then finance minister John Turner tried to circumvent the province's control of resource taxation by eliminating a tax break that allowed oil companies to deduct as a cost of business royalties paid to Alberta before they calculated their federal income tax. Alberta believed that Turner was just trying to tap into the oil price windfall. He backed off under pressure from the financial community, which showed him that the measure would impair Canadian investment in its own petroleum industry.

The federal government finally got its pound of flesh, however, through the Petroleum and Gas Revenue Tax (PGRT), in the National Energy Program. That tax was imposed on production revenues at the wellhead. In other words, it was calculated on sales revenues before royalties or business expenses. The damage that tax did to the economics of oil and gas production and the industry's development is a story for another time and place. But it left Albertans with a deep and abiding suspicion of the lengths a federal Liberal government would go to suck money out of the province.

Marleau's threat to reduce health care transfer payments was thought by many in the Alberta cabinet and Tory caucus to have nothing to do with health care and everything to do with Ottawa's desperate search through a bare cupboard for any nest egg, however small, that would allow it to avoid spending cuts. In fact, by the autumn of 1994, Klein was being urged to slow the pace of deficit and debt reduction because it created a temptation for Ottawa to find ways to steal from Alberta's renewed economy.

When Finance Minister Paul Martin, in his 1995–96 budget, set down the federal plan to reduce deficits and, eventually, balance its budget, the bottom line for the provinces was reduced federal contributions for provincial health care, education and social services. So the Klein government asked the federal government to set a national standard for the inevitable reduction of health care that would correspond to reduced spending. Marleau and Chrétien evaded the question, saying that by asking the question the Klein government proved it was planning a two-tier health care system, with a limited list of insured services for those of modest means and full services only for those with the means to purchase private insurance.

By now, the Liberals had inserted Marleau, Chrétien and health care into the first by-election the Klein government faced. Klein had called an April 20 vote to fill the vacancy created by the death of Tory MLA Harry Sohol, who represented the riding of Calgary McCall. Chrétien came to Calgary early in April, ostensibly for a fund-raising dinner, but he also met the premier to discuss health care, thus injecting himself into the campaign.

By this time, Klein was getting the "slow down" message from the entire medical establishment—not just the medical service unions, but the doctors, the prestigious specialists and even Bud McCaig, the blue-chip chairman of the Calgary Regional Health Authority. McCaig, the chairman of Trimac Limited, represented the cream of Alberta's business community, and his appointment in 1994 to head the hospital superboard was a powerful symbol of change. It implied that only business produced people capable of overseeing government services, reducing their costs and making them efficient. When McCaig said, on the eve of the by-election vote in Calgary McCall, that the medical system needed some time to absorb the change before a fresh round of cuts, Klein was caught between the ambitious schedule for deficit and debt reduction and the realities of making reduced government a successful provider of services.

The Liberals poured their resources into the by-election and, as voting day approached, talked openly of the "miracle in McCall." Grant Mitchell visited the riding again and again, and in Question Period, back in Edmonton, his caucus made "two-tier health care" the issue of the day every day. The Conservatives responded to the threat by committing their best political talent to the election organization, and Klein toured the riding frequently as the April 20 polling day neared.

In the confrontation, only 30 per cent of eligible voters turned out. Shiraz Shariff, the Tory candidate, a social worker and teacher, won with 43.6 per cent of the popular vote. Although that was far less that Klein's 73 per cent approval rating in the polls, the Tories had won the seat in the 1993 election with a 44.8 per cent plurality, so the party could claim that it was holding its ground through the bad news years of its agenda. The Liberals, however, with circuitous logic, proclaimed that they had won because they lost much less badly than they should have. If Klein was doing the right thing, he should have blown them away, said their candidate, Jeet Shergill. The outcome was a message of voter dissatisfaction; the premier had better get the message and mend his ways on health care. Whatever the spin, the Liberals came out of the by-election committed to making health care the opening issue of the election expected in 1997.

On another front, Klein was dealing with the unresolved future of the Heritage Savings Trust Fund, the capital pool created in 1976 from surplus oil and gas royalties when petroleum commodities were going through the roof. The fund's ostensible purpose was to create a provincial nest egg. Premier Peter Lougheed had always talked about an apocryphal rainy day when the fund would come in handy. As the province weathered storm after storm, Lougheed and later Don Getty had always said it wasn't stormy enough, so Klein had inherited the perennial headache of how to manage the thing. Income from the fund had help pay operating costs, and $3.4 billion had been invested in capital projects, but most of the capital was preserved, although much was in investments that were not very liquid. Deciding the future of the fund was an unavoidable part of deficit elimination and debt repayment.

The fund had assumed the mythical proportions of a sunken Spanish galleon or a buried pirate's treasure. In reality, it was a portfolio of investments valued by the government at $11.9 billion and independently at $8.5 billion. The fund's managers believed they could only recover $7.1 billion in cash, and that would take time. The recoveries could be made from $6 billion in Canada and provincial bonds and mortgages, $725 million from corporate securities and $310 million in Hydro Québec. The balance of $4.8 billion was lent internally to Alberta and its agencies, and to the Atlantic provinces, whose loans represented $1.1 billion of the assets.

Shortly before the Parti Québécois came to power, Premier Klein offered the opinion that if Jacques Parizeau formed the government, the prospect of Québec sovereignty would force Alberta to review its investment in Hydro Québec. The threat drew the predictable angry response from Parizeau, and in Alberta Klein got a lot of advice that he had to avoid inflaming the situation and keep out of the election. Chastened, he said he had shot from the lip, again, and appointed an advisory board of academics to counsel him on relations with Parizeau. He continued, however, to quietly court refugee business and capital from Montréal.

Klein did not think liquidating the fund was wise; it would be a powerful economic tool at some future time when there were also budget surpluses and the accumulated debt was reduced to nominal levels. His opinion was shared by Dinning. The two faced intensifying political pressure to speed up debt repayment by using some of its assets, however, and a great deal of that pressure was coming from within Klein's caucus and his cabinet.

On December 5, Klein moved to defuse the issue, launching public consultations to determine the fate of the fund. He appointed a bipartisan committee of backbenchers to manage the review. He gave the committee $250,000 and instructed it to distribute an information kit to every household in the province as part of the process. When the Liberals suggested a plebiscite in conjunction with province-wide municipal elections in October 1995, the premier found the idea intriguing and asked the MLAs' committee to give him a recommendation. Thus, the Heritage Fund issue, a matter in which the government would find it all but impossible to find a compromise, was successfully stalled until it could be dealt with in an atmosphere less charged by the bigger controversies resulting from the budget cuts.

To keep the Heritage Fund in what he regarded as its proper context, however, Klein also announced that he was drafting the Debt Elimination Act, patterned after the Deficit Elimination Act. The new act would legislate repayment of the accumulated debt with annual payments over a prescribed term. The bill became law during the spring legislative session.

As the session ended, Klein stood at the pinnacle of popularity. His unconventional politics had worked. Or so it seemed, if you looked at the province through the narrow window of fiscal responsibility.

19

The One-Issue Government

As long as Klein has a winning fiscal agenda, he wants no part of a real right-wing revolution.

—"DON'T CALL ME RADICAL,"
ALBERTA REPORT,
APRIL 3, 1995

When Alberta's Conservatives gathered, on the last weekend in March 1995, for their annual convention, there was a predictable contentment in the air, a self-satisfaction based on their success. The party's prospects for the long haul seemed good. "There's a lot of light at the end of the tunnel," Klein told delegates; the convocation was replete with the assurance of power that would not be lost on the road ahead for a long time.[1]

But a powerful segment of the party did not share Klein's often repeated sentiment that he would like to finish the fiscal home renovation and put his feet up for a while. This segment was composed of the social conservatives, and they had a broad political agenda that extended the reach of Klein's central themes of political responsibility and the restoration of old values. The closest they had ever been to a distinctive political movement was Ernest C. Manning's failed attempt, in 1967, to meld Social Credit and western Progressive Conservatives into a national political force, which he advocated in a book called *Political Realignment*, a short, pithy paperback that foreshadowed both the Reform Party and Ralph Klein's hijack of the Conservative Party.[2]

The strong social conservative wing of Klein's Tory party was a coalition of rural families and their young suburban cousins. The alliance notably Christian, but it had grown to embrace Jews, Chinese Buddhists or Confucians, and Muslims. These Conservatives had a vision beyond Klein's fiscal agenda, which they thoroughly endorsed.

"They [the social conservatives] see our schools in chaos, our streets unsafe, our prison system ineffective, our families disintegrating, our children neglected, our work ethic gone, and our treasury bankrupt—all through the misuse and misdirection of government," *Alberta Report*'s Ted Byfield wrote of what he saw on the convention floor. "The problem, in other words, goes a long way beyond the fiscal, which is a mere symptom. Trying to cure it without excising the ideological root causes behind it, they believe, is a waste of time."[3]

In contrast, Klein, Byfield believed, was the product and the captive of what his daughter-in-law, Joanne, wife of *Alberta Report* publisher Link Byfield, called "the wine and cheese conservatives," the urban business men and women who were interested only in the restoration of conservative, fiscally responsible government.

An outside observer, Anglican theologian, lecturer and writer Herbert O'Driscoll, who lives in Victoria, British Columbia, and travels to Alberta regularly, told a Calgary seminar that the prairie populists of the 1930s, Aberhart and Manning of the Social Credit and the CCF's James Woodsworth and M. J. Coldwell, were Christian preachers who believed in a Holy City, a New Jerusalem, and whose faith persuaded them that here on earth they ought not to wait for the future but had an obligation to move things a little closer to perfection, even though it would not be achieved until heaven.[4]

Klein's own private religious practice of Blackfoot prayers and meditations and his own personal ceremonies, while fervent, dealt with personal spiritual relationships in the here and now and did not bring him an accompanying zeal to reform society on a moral template borrowed from religious hope. Prairie aboriginal religion produces tolerance, individuality and belief in responsible individual behaviour.

At the convention, the social conservatives were led by a group of backbenchers that included both urban and rural MLAs and had the backing of one visible cabinet member, Stockwell Day, and a handful of other, more timid junior ministers. They presented a twenty-thousand-name petition and poll results showing 71 per cent support in Alberta for the disqualification of abortion from medicare funding. Thus, they tied abortion to the fiscal agenda and to Klein's own persistent efforts to get the federal government to define essential medical services. The argument was that "if eye examinations, circumcision, cosmetic surgery and wart removal weren't covered by medicare, why abortion? Pregnancy isn't a disease." And, by inference, abortion is an elective medical procedure.[5]

Klein had made it clear in the run-up to the convention that he had a maverick fiscal agenda but no desire beyond that to be a trailblazer. "Voters wanted fiscal austerity and we are delivering. I am no more radical than the people who elected me," he told Edmonton businessmen.

The spending cuts, he said, "are a reaffirmation of the values and beliefs that Albertans already hold dear." The premier wanted to be seen as the man people wanted to see. He and his aides believed that abortion, which among themselves they called "the Big A," was not the issue on which he could work his masterful optics of popularity.[6]

So he drew the line on the abortion de-funding resolution. He whipped his cabinet into line and said he would personally speak out "unmistakably." At the convention, Love arranged for delegates to get copies of newspaper clippings about Liberal leader Laurence Decore's fumbling of the abortion issue during the 1993 election campaign. The Grits had tried to be on both sides of the question early in the campaign, and the pounding Decore took, from candidates and women in his party, as well as the voters, had been the start of his defeat.

In a harsh speech to the convention, Klein attacked a "conspiracy of the churches" in his own party for trying to embarrass the party with the issue. He said abortion was a moral question, and the legislature was not the forum in which to debate it. He said he would ignore the will of the convention if it passed the de-funding resolution. With all his muscle out on the floor, he was able to beat back the proposal by only ten votes. He won, but he had made his leadership the issue on a question that obviously divided his own party deeply.

He told reporters at the close of the convention that beyond the deficit he had no agenda—not on tougher law enforcement, the strengthening of the family, giving parents control over education or other issues on the social conservative agenda. It seemed to have been an unnecessary confrontation; one Liberal told Ted Byfield, "When all your worst enemies are delighted and your best friends are furious, maybe you've made a mistake."

Byfield thought there was a simpler explanation, that the issue revealed Klein for what he was: a member of the one-issue, glass-tower conservative club, "though until he won the provincial Tory leadership the club most assuredly did not want to include him." According to Byfield, "they [members of the club] regard themselves as urban; they tend to assume that all city dwellers think as they think. This, however, is a grave misapprehension, for their numbers shrink rapidly as you leave the downtown cocktail circuit ... and head out to the suburbs. Here, where people live in families and have children [the glass-tower conservatives] become less and less relevant and more and more irritating because they do not seem to actually do much."[7]

The seeds of a serious division were planted by the time the convention ended. The split between the fiscal and the social conservatives reinforced the concerns of rural-based cabinet ministers and the now deposed Ken Kowalski that Klein was losing his grip on his rural constituency and was being unduly influenced by a politically limited, urban group of business interests. The almost imperceptible crack was papered over in the Calgary McCall by-election victory less than a month later. It followed an old fault line in Alberta politics, however. Albertans are loyal to ideas, not parties. There was an opening now for ambitious and disaffected conservatives on the right to threaten the formation of a new political movement within or without the Conservative Party if Klein did not respond to their agenda.

Before his party's 1995 annual convention, Klein succesfully kept to a focussed agenda of deficit and debt elimination and fiscal restoration. Forestry, for example, was not on it, although it has been Alberta's fastest-growing resource sector in new investment and was a major headache for him when he was the environment minister. The many problems related to overselling and overcutting of timber Klein left entirely to his current environment minister, Ty Lund.

Unlike Peter Lougheed, who reviewed and frequently revised virtually all ministerial decisions before they were announced, Klein did not try to do it all. Ministers were given broad authority over their portfolios; caucus held considerable power and became the focal point for strong, often strident debate. Klein let caucus wrestle with decisions for a long time, even when they were important, if no consensus was reached. This drew criticism of delay on many matters, but those attacks did not hold much weight against a government that had moved so far, so fast, on its one big issue.

Meanwhile, as Klein used his singular focus to sidestep a change in the status quo on abortion, his silence on other issues had raised questions. For instance, he had created the impression that the conservative restoration included censorship, the repression of homosexuals and the protection only of the rights of the strong and homogeneous. The culling of the welfare rolls had proved to be an inexact surgery; people had fallen through the cracks. Klein admitted this and promised that ways would be found to restore help to those who could not fend for themselves. But he had not defined "fending." How far would he allow people to fall before they found the safety net?

There was a darker undercurrent, barely noticed in the first heady months, to the new freedom and power given his MLAs on side issues because of the single focus in the premier's office. Community Development Minister Dianne Mirosh, a close crony of then deputy premier Ken Kowalski and a former Calgary alderman, was a brash, aggressive politician with a reputation for shooting from the lip. Mirosh represented Calgary's upper-middle-class Glenmore riding, a community of notable affluence and privilege where people believed that food banks were a scam. She regarded the Alberta Human Rights Commission with scathing suspicion and took advantage of her new platform to attack it for giving special treatment to homosexuals.

Klein neither restrained her nor contradicted her, disturbing people who had thought him tolerant and certainly liberal on civil rights issues. At the time, Mirosh was dismissed as a loose cannon; she disappeared from cabinet after the June 1993 election. Later, as relentless parallel campaigns against homosexuals and the commission, driven from Conservative back benches and supported by half a dozen prominent cabinet ministers, gained in velocity and voltage, Klein's silence on the issue was interpreted as tacit support.

When MLAs began to support efforts to ban books in schools, halt the teaching of evolution and advocate other extremist positions on censorship and freedom of expression, especially in the arts, early in 1994, Klein's silence became ominous to those who feared the repression of intellectual freedom. Outspoken critics drew parallels between the Klein cabinet and the anti-Semitism of some Social Credit cabinet ministers during that party's regime. The standard refrain became that Klein kept quiet as a price for rural support; but the issues had the same strength of support in his urban caucus. Eventually, the unavoidable conclusion was that the premier was much less liberal on these issues, personally, than people had thought. Government would be open and accessible, but not for everyone.

What most disturbed those in the arts was his silence on the two issues of gay rights and book banning that emerged in 1994. In March, Red Deer South MLA Victor Doerksen stood up in the legislature and demanded that the government ban John Steinbeck's *Of Mice and Men* from schools because it demeaned God and Jesus Christ and contained 197 instances of profanity. He filed a petition containing 881 names to back up his request and said that he had never read the book and had no intention of doing so. The petition asked the government "not to allow literature in the education system that is intolerant of any religion, including Christianity, and in particular, not to allow any books in the school curriculum that demean or profane the name of God or Jesus Christ."[8]

The Department of Education listed *Of Mice and Men* as suitable for the classroom, but it was not on any required reading list. Doerksen's initiative was chilling to teachers and school librarians engaged in a chronic battle with the religious right over the use and banning of more than a score of titles common to many school libraries that were under attack for being immoral, new age or anti-Christian or for advocating witchcraft; the proscription list was long and growing fast. Censorship had become an important issue for intellectual freedom in Alberta, and any sign that the government condoned or tolerated it was chilling.

Education Minister Havlor Jonson, a former high school principal, was firm that teachers and parents decide such issues, but it was only mildly reassuring that the government would not do any banning itself. There were many communities in which teachers thought that it was just a matter of time before they would have no role in these decisions and that small groups of dedicated religious activists would force the removal of books they didn't like from library shelves and classroom study.

The darker, meaner matter of the civil protections for minorities was indeed chilling, as was Klein's silence on these matters. One cannot reconcile that silence with the young journalist who, in his 1980 *Calgary Magazine* columns, exhibited a social conscience that should now have been enraged by the book-banning behaviour of some of his caucus. His silence on the issue made it impossible to judge whether his values had changed, or he had learned to be expedient. Klein, the civil liberties movement felt, was abdicating his own well-known standards of decency, fair play and moral integrity to remain silent on the book-banning controversy because he had measured the political outcome and self-interest required him to bite his tongue. This analysis seemed the most probable; Klein was dancing with the far right devils in his caucus and, to complete what he regarded as the bigger task of deficit cutting, he was parking his uneasy conscience.

There was a mean-spirited atmosphere, as well, in the legislature when gay political issues and gay rights were raised. Not only would the caucus not support emerging issues such as same-sex benefits, they were endorsing such initiatives as the purging of homosexuals from the teaching staffs of private Christian schools. By the end of 1994, it was clear that gays would be nonpersons in the Klein government; they could count on losing every gay rights issue—from benefits for same-sex couples to inclusion in human rights codes. There was a poisonous, petty atmosphere, however, that made the legislature's treatment of such matters frightening.

One such incident arose when Alberta playwright Brad Fraser, author of *Unidentified Human Remains and True Love* and *Poor Superman*, was nominated in the autumn of 1994 for a Genie Award in recognition of his screenplay adaptation *Love and Human Remains*. When Liberal education critic Michael Henry asked the legislature to pass a motion congratulating Fraser on the nomination, a block of Conservatives refused because Fraser's work deals with homosexual themes. The motion, which needed unanimous consent, died.

Klein let down people who had once expected him to be more liberal. An influential environmental organization, World Wildlife Fund (WWF), mistook his fair-mindedness for support when they went to see him on business. In the late 1980s, when he was environment minister, WWF persuaded Klein and his deputy, Vance MacNichol, to support its endangered spaces campaign by preserving ecological regions in the province. The thrust of the WWF campaign was that 12 per cent of the global land mass, including representatives of all important ecological environments, should be kept in as close to pristine condition as possible. Globally, there is wide, UN-sponsored support for the notion of reserving 12 per cent of the earth's land surface from human intervention; there are sound scientific arguments for this that few dispute, not even resource developers.

In Alberta, a public consultation was launched with appropriate fanfare, and the environment minister, in his best mellifluous tones, expressed soft, fuzzy sentiments about sustainable development. The exercise was called Special Places 2000, and it produced a report of that title, with a plan for setting aside five types of reservations covering Alberta's nineteen ecological regions.

The study was at first commended as a job of public participation well done. Klein endorsed, or at least created the impression that he endorsed, the report, and the WWF thought it had a "gimme."[9] It was important because the recommendations were among the most aggressive that had been endorsed by a Canadian provincial government, and the more satisfying because Alberta's reputation was not progressive on such issues.

Then the Special Places project hit a brick wall. Environmentalists began to brag about the vast preserves of land that would be created, including an imaginative series of protected corridors that would link up the reservations. Some analysts, including staff in the Department of Energy, began to say that more than 35 per cent of the province's surface could face some form of restricted access.

The petroleum industry, which to its peril had ignored the public process, thinking it a piece of fluff, reared up in dismay. The oil and gas rights to much of the land slated for preservation were already leased out. The mining industry, which had just completed a geophysical reconnaissance of the province and was staking more than 70 per cent of its surface for gold and diamond exploration, also started to worry. The forest industry was already embroiled in half a dozen festering confrontations with environmentalists and knew the threat was very real.

Special Places 2000 was off the rails in a matter of weeks; the Department of Energy began to quietly reassure industry that at most a diluted version of the program would be phased in over a painlessly long period of time. Meanwhile, supporters of the plan fought back, saying that it was erroneous to claim implementation would freeze a third of Alberta's land area.

Klein was by now the premier, and the WWF could not believe that he would renege on what they considered a firm commitment from him, as environment minister, to 12 per cent preservation. Now that he had the power of the premier's office, the WWF was sure that he would come through on something he believed in. Klein's environment ministers, Brian Evans and then Ty Lund, ducked for cover. Lund, appointed in the autumn of 1994, is regarded as the environment minister in Alberta's history with the least regard for special-interest groups like the WWF. In April, nearly two years after the government received the recommendations of the public consultation, Special Places was an initiative without a serious cabinet sponsor. Klein had made no commitment to follow through. In April 1995, the WWF gave Alberta a failing grade, its first ever, in its annual ranking for environmental performance of Canada's governments.

Meanwhile, as the fight over Special Places 2000 ground on, Alberta was vigorously fending off proposals kicking around Ottawa for a carbon tax. Such a tax would be more devastating to petroleum production than was the 1980 National Energy Program. It would also cripple electric production, which is tied to coal, and the future development of the oil sands. The tax was an initiative of the Sierra Club, part of the anti-fossil-fuel strategy that federal Environment Minister Sheila Copps was facing in the first years of Prime Minister Jean Chrétien's government. The definitive test of Klein's environmental policies, Special Places 2000 and the carbon tax, defined exactly how far he was prepared to go on protection issues opposed by industry. He was smoother and more po-litically astute on these matters than any previous premier. He knew how to create public processes, how to navigate the political shoals of envi-ronmental review. But he was cheering for industry, not the special-interest groups. He had a knack for nudging the outcome. And he was not the same man who as journalist and mayor took on big interests for environmental causes.

Yet it was hard to peg Klein as a deep blue conservative; he avoided ideology and he proved capable of being unpredictable and wearing a liberal cloak. Klein had supported Social Services Minister Mike Cardinal when the quiet-spoken Cree became a target of the Liberals early in January 1994. When Cardinal was in his thirties, he fathered an illegiti-mate daughter on the Calling Lake Reserve and left the mother two months before the girl was born. The mother went on welfare, and he did not offer to make support payments until he was contacted by the Social Services Department. The Liberals attacked Cardinal when he began to say, as social services minister, that parents should take more responsibility for their actions and for their children. The Grits said his position was two faced, that he had no credibility and that he should resign.

No way, Klein replied. "He has been an exceptional minister. I'm not going to ask him to resign over something that happened 21 years ago."[10] Klein pointed out that Cardinal had, in fact, faced up to his responsibilities and supported the child, once he was asked to do so. The Liberal attack on Cardinal collapsed after it was clear that Klein was adamant and that public sympathy and support were almost entirely behind Cardinal.

The pattern in Klein's avoidance of issues and in the issues that he takes on is hard to discern. The only sense that could be made of it is that he never behaved like a twentieth-century liberal. Only on abortion did he actively risk a confrontation with conservative forces. He knew that many conservative Christians, Catholics and others, did not support the stridency of the pro-life movement but considered abortion a private matter between the woman, or the couple, her doctor and God.

Ever unpredictable, and always grounded in the readings that he took of political opinion, Klein in his first months in the premier's office may have just been a maverick conservative whose remedies for the paradoxes of politics were proving as effective as they were risky and unconventional.

20

The Eclipse of the Populist

*Was I too dark a prophet when I said
To those who went upon the Holy
  Quest
That most of them would follow
  wandering fires,
Lost in the quagmire—lost to me
  and gone?*

—ALFRED, LORD TENNYSON,
THE IYDLLS OF THE KING

Through the contentious winter of 1994–95, the distance between the premier's legislative office and any other place in Alberta came to be measured in light-years. The laid-back prankster of the Mulroney dinner had disappeared under the weight of office. Klein became the prisoner under the Dome; the change that swept Alberta swamped him with the endless detail of power. It all seemed an endless blur—the Kowalski and Trynchy crises, the travel to China, Korea, Hong Kong and across Canada, the budget, the Throne Speech, the Debt Elimination Act, the endless preparations for Question Periods and media scrums. Klein grew weary and grumpy as the days flew by without an opportunity to renew himself, to get out and on the road in Alberta. When he stood in the house to answer a question, eyes would glaze over as he plunged into a level of detail only a few could follow. He answered some questions with prompting from his ministers, but more often that invisible teleprompter in his head would begin to roll, and he would lapse into the arcane trivia of policy and legislation.

In spite of his government's steady rise in the polls, in approval for its decisions and endorsement of Klein's personal popularity, the premier was changing in subtle ways that distanced him from his roots until even sympathetic men and women of affairs began to think of him as "the populist fading from view," as Harold Millican, a Calgary businessman and former president of the Chamber of Commerce, called him.[1] Millican, although a lifelong Liberal, spent six years working for Peter Lougheed as one of the then premier's most trusted aides.

"He's [Klein's] just a mortal human being. At times he looks like he's paying a terrible price. Does he have the time he needs for quiet and reflection?" mused Millican as he saw the pressures of office register on the furrowed brow. "Is he having fun anymore? This isn't him. He's surrounded by this kitchen cabinet of influential, privileged people who don't understand why we need food banks. Ralph, look after people. Slow down, look after yourself."

Millican had dealt with Klein during the mayoral years, understood the inner workings of the premier's office and the pressures coming from the Klein Gang, and was dealing with the impacts of the cuts on Mount Royal College, of which he was a governor. Few Albertans outside the Conservative Party had as complete view of the premier, and none of the other critics were as charitable or detached. To Millican, Klein seemed to be a much changed man from the boyish, open politician of his mayoralty day. He had ventured too far into the realm of the powerful and the privileged. He had become cocky and even arrogant; he had forgotten his connection to the vagabonds and beautiful people of anti-politics.

Especially bothersome was his close connection to Alberta's elites, and as the winter unfolded, it was the kitchen cabinet and his aides, like Love, who seemed to be in control. "Who is using whom, here?" Millican asked himself. "Has Klein become the patsy that his opponents say he has?"

Once, on a Saturday in the autumn, Harold and Donna Millican met Rob Peters and his wife, Donna, at the Millarville Fair, a popular market garden and craft fair that runs at a dirt race track southwest of Calgary. The district around Millarville is stunningly beautiful foothills country, with large, expensive estates of oil and ranching millionaires and lavish stables for the most expensive horses. There are also working farms and the homes of semi-retired executives like the Millicans who don't need to be in the city any longer. Peters was the president of Peters & Co., an independent, Calgary-based underwriting stock brokering firm, and a member of the Klein Gang inner sanctum. One of his volunteer community activities was the Star Ambulance Society, which raised funds to support a paramedic emergency helicopter service based in Calgary.

That morning, Millican had read in the newspaper that the province had decided to award the Star contract to an Edmonton helicopter company. This was a blow in prestige for Calgary and for Peters, who had raised a lot of money from the corporate sector for the project. When

Millican asked him about the story, Peters had not heard of it and was very upset, the more so because Millican needled him a bit. "You've got so much influence with Ralph, get that decision changed, Rob, " said Millican. Peters departed the fair looking like thunder. Sure enough, by Tuesday there was an announcement that the government had reversed itself on the Star Ambulance decision.

Ralph Klein could scarcely be recognized as, or legitimately claim to be, the outsider. His challenge to the status quo had become the measure of the conservative political counterreformation in Canada, and the restoration of government as it had been practised before the failed liberalism of the 1960s. His success in deficit elimination and debt reduction was assumed; his store of credibility gave him room for the unexpected and the setbacks. He could relax and relish his power; he had come a long way from the time when power was not the issue, just the ideas of what he could do with it.

Politics had shown his mettle, and the approval of the social establishment had muffled, if not ended, the gossipy whispers about his self-indulgent lifestyle. Robert Lamond, the founder and chairman of Czar Resources and a Klein supporter, told a story about Klein's drinking: "President Abraham Lincoln was confronted, during the Civil War, by a cabinet secretary who accused Ulysses Grant, the Union's brilliant general, of being a drunk. 'Find out what he drinks and send a barrel of it to the other generals,' ordered Lincoln." That, according to Lamond, should be the end of it. You could not find a premier you would rather have than this one.[2]

The path that Klein had travelled had changed him; he was now part of the establishment. Calgary was ever the domain of single interests—in turn, the North-West Mounted Police, the Canadian Pacific Railway, the cattle barons of the Ranchmen's Club, the flinty oil finders of the Petroleum Club. Calgary always spoke with one voice, moved to one purpose and remained ever the quiet, parochial preserve of a benevolent but unquestioned establishment.

Calgary was now a more eclectic, argumentative, sometimes fractious polyglot, but it was still a place of commercial fiefdoms. The oil patch had diminished, now supplemented by the business of financiers, biotechnology and software firms, transportation giants, coal companies, educators and artists.

Nevertheless, it was still "mercantile."[3] Past, present and future, Calgary's business is business. Politically, it is a city for the self-reliant. It is a city with few liberal instincts; the ruthless practicality of the mercantile mind senses there are few wrongs that can be righted with public largesse. The family, the church, the neighbourhood will rally around the needy; the state should save its energies for other things.

Klein now operated politically in a milieu from which he had been excluded in the past. He was from Tuxedo Park. His business was never that of business.

He had a formidable arsenal of political strategies, however. He knew how to be transparent, to create the impression of accountability and accessibility. He had learned to be prompt in acknowledging mistakes; often that was the only way to repair the damage they had done. He was decisive, and his intuitions functioned with uncanny accuracy. He had learned how to manage his bureaucrats, how to delegate and how to rely on his minders and keepers. He knew how to be underestimated and overestimated and when to chose between the two.

He had also mastered darker arts. He knew the secret passageways of political finance. He knew how to get even, how to bury bodies and when the means justified the end. He knew how to equivocate with silence and how to mask the truth with innuendo and inference. He knew how to maintain the support of people on both sides of an issue. He knew how to politically destroy his more dangerous opponents. He knew how to bully the weak and disarm the strong. He knew how to let others take the blame. He knew when to use a stiletto and when to use a bludgeon. He had learned to distrust, to defend, to strike back. He had learned how to polarize opinion to strengthen his own support and weaken that of his foe. He now knew exactly what it would take to achieve important things in politics, what it would cost and how to judge whether the price was worth it. The open, idealistic populist of 1980 often seemed to be eclipsed by the tougher, cynical requirements of power.

The last Friday in April 1995 was chilly, grey and wet—not uncommon for Alberta's month of spring snows. It was the kind of Calgary noon hour when people scuttle into their favourite restaurant or pub for a hot meal, then linger past one o'clock over coffee, reluctant to face the cold and steady drizzle that cannot make up its mind to be snow or rain.

In the basement of the St. Louis Hotel, where time stopped some years ago with the last paint job, the tiny, terrycloth-covered tables were jammed and damp with spilled beer. The cracked leather-upholstered benches against the walls were sagging with people, sitting two to each chair. At the high steel food counter, high-spirited patrons jostled one another while they waited to be served heaping paper plates of chicken and chips, smokies and cabbage rolls.

The air smelled of hot grease, stale beer and sweat commingled with half the perfumes and colognes advertised in *Vanity Fair* and *Playboy*. Cowboy jeans, leather jackets, thousand-dollar suits on both sexes, earrings, nose rings, lip rings, mechanics' hands covered in grease, carpenters' hands with cracked nails and ground-in dirt, homeless hands with chilblains, street whores' hands with purple nail polish, criminal hands with needle tracks running down from the wrists and accountants' hands too soft for the kind of living people had to do up on 8th Avenue East, removed from paycheques and perquisites in the office towers west of city hall—all were there at the St. Louis Hotel.

The tavern jukebox thumped, and the sound level pushed the decibel needle off the dial. The waitresses carried trays bearing legions of foaming glasses of beer high above their heads while they threaded the invisible pathways through the throng. As more people, the latecomers, came down the stairs, folks made room for them, although a good many ate and drank standing up. It was Rockin' with Ralph Day; the premier had come home for the weekend and the managers were laying on one of their periodic celebrations for their most famous client. And there he was, his face fractured into a thousand creases by a grin that he couldn't stop grinning.

He was exhausted, and the stress of the long legislative session seemed to have pummelled his body nearly into shapelessness, but by God he was happy to be here. He shook hands, and he gave a moving little speech, a fragment of his hopelessly sentimental heart, about how good it was to be out from under the legislature dome and back here with his friends. People held his hand with their two hands, they wanted to hug him, but he was the premier now, so they just beamed at him, and he beamed back until the room was full of silly grins and people felt good for reasons that they couldn't ever talk about. A few people importuned him; the opportunists got a frosty, detached smile and soon read in the steady grey eyes that it was time to move on. Some folks really needed to talk to him, really needed his help, and he bent closer to hear them and to nod reassurance. How he distinguished between the two types of petitioners was a chemical wisdom well hidden by his inscrutability. Mostly, people knew that it was bad manners to talk politics here; this was a family occasion.

Charisma. It's a word Philip Klein, his father, uses about him, although it has been overused in politics and bears the taint, in Alberta, of Pierre Trudeau. Whatever it's called, in an hour the gap that was widening between Klein and these people through the controversies of the winter, closed as seamlessly as a split in the Arctic Ocean's September ice sheet closes after a ship has passed through. Down here, amid the beery bonhomie and the raucous laughter of the first inebriates, as the noon hour trickled into the afternoon, Ralph Klein was the maverick again, living by his own lights and doing things other politicians would not.

As long as he keeps coming back, people will believe they could never find his replacement, no matter how something he said offended, no matter how outrageously he behaved, no matter how vexed you were because his decision cost you something in money, time or principle: "All is forgiven; please come home." And when he was back, off the TV screen and at a table with a beer in his hand that afternoon, frayed trust was restored, and he had the look of a man who knew his limits, loved his people and would be in politics as long as he wanted.

Epilogue

You could read the log of that journey on his face.

—BRUCE HUTCHISON, *THE INCREDIBLE CANADIAN*

Everything Ralph Klein does in his public and private life, he does by his own measure. His private life is a reproach to the timid conventions that sanitize and homogenize civic figures. His public record accurately calibrates the extraordinary anti-politics of Alberta in the twentieth century. His government resonates with the radical new conservatism of the industrial democracies of America, Europe and Asia. He tips his cap to no man. He dances in the jaws of large and powerful forces that threaten to overwhelm troubled government and, as yet, has evaded the bite of the beast.

To his political foes, Ralph Klein is the Chimera of Greek legend—part fire-breathing creature of the underworld, part wild and foolish idea, entirely dangerous and misdirected, who must be destroyed by a virtuous hero, mounted on a white Pegasus. To his supporters, he is the ebullient maverick of the Canadian northwest frontier, a cunning and savvy loner who is reestablishing the private values and public mores of rural self-reliance and urban entrepreneurship.

He is loved or he is hated, liked or disliked; there is no middle ground of indifference. Those who disagree with him believe he is leading his province into a social Armageddon where everything worthy will be destroyed and everything that survives will taste of ashes and blood. Those who agree with him recognize in his decisions their own dreams and desires. For them, he is conducting a restoration, not a revolution. Few in either camp pretend to comprehend him; even fewer have a grasp of the man.

A child of adversity and rootless adolescent whose rite of passage was the wreckage of a sentimental and undisciplined ambition to be a fighter pilot, Klein defined himself as an adult through a career in public service: teaching and charities, broadcast journalism and elective office. He carried an incredible amount of pain into adulthood, and after an exhausting pilgrimage through journalism and public relations, politics became the soothing of his soul.

His two worlds, both egocentric, of private rebellion and civic duty shaped a competitive, assertive man equipped and groomed for power, with no inclination to accept or be governed by the customs of Alberta's self-assured and quiet-spoken old guard. While he is ruthless in pursuit of his policies, he has emerged from his private crucibles as the self-effacing, easygoing life of the party who engenders loyalty and trust that endures the thousand slights that friendship with a busy public figure can deliver. Toughness in tandem with vulnerability is simply one of the paradoxes that defines him.

The unhealed wounds and juvenile slights of his early years as a poor kid outside the world of privilege and power have imbued him with a disregard for the customary rules of engagement in public life. He has been liberated to take risks that other mortals, closer to the earth, do not dare. He has learned to mask his deeper feelings behind a shield of gregarious, laid-back sociability. His alienation kept him close, as journalist and mayor, to the disenfranchised: urban aboriginals, ex-cons, bikers, homeless people, hookers, dirt farmers and the simply poor.

At the same time, he developed a profound need to be approved of and accepted by the wealthy and influential. He first tasted their favour working for the Red Cross and United Appeal. As a politician, he has connected himself to the petroleum executives, lawyers, financiers, cattlemen, grain barons, land developers and innovators of Alberta's upper social landscape. He deliberately and relentlessly courted the favour of those whose prestige, campaign contributions and suasion he needed, but more because he admired them than was motivated to use them.

Thus balanced between the two repelling poles of outcasts and insiders, he navigates the shoals of ordinary politics, headed towards an inchoate ideal: a renovated society that will be better for all the people to whom he has attached himself, both the underclass and the establishment.

Strategically, he wins elections and the thousand lesser confrontations of politics by coming from nowhere and being underestimated; he enters late, runs unorthodox campaigns, does not appear to worry much about the money or the organization. The paradox and the secret is that in fact he works to a very long horizon. He has reflected, analyzed and calculated his major campaigns for months and even years. He introduced the concept of perpetual political fund-raising to city hall, raising funds for the next election as soon as he had won the current campaign.

In his all relationships, he is the centre of gravity. He commands friendship, and he also expects respect. In the same manner that bikers who partied with him did not complain when his news stories exposed their unsavoury aspects, public servants who have had pay cuts, seen their professions redesigned or lost jobs seem capable of separating the man they trust from the painful decisions he has made, and they continue to vote for him. He avoids conflict and confrontation. He deliberately creates the impression that he is winging it. His feet are generally on the ground, however; he has a shrewd sense of what he needs for survival, what his strengths and weaknesses are; he has street smarts.

With Klein very often reality is illusion and illusion is reality. He is paradox, caricature, charade. What you see is what you get, yet he is nothing of what he seems to be. He is inscrutable; in his political strategy, optics are paramount. His micro-managed public persona is the triumph of spin doctoring. Like most successful or enduring Canadian politicians in the twentieth century—from Mackenzie King and Pierre Trudeau to Maurice Duplessis and William Aberhart—he maintains an aura of mystery about himself that brings lasting respect and forgiveness at the ballot box.

Klein is a trick of the light. At a distance he is transparent; he keeps an open book on his drinking, prankish humour, maudlin, affectionate loyalty to family, friends and colleagues, and bucolic civism for the narrowly circumscribed empire that he leads. He is buffered from the normal political consequences of his imperfections because people think of him as "one of us."

Up close, the light changes. Klein is guarded, secretive, insecure, impenetrable. This complex, brilliant, brooding man who is so self-deprecating and gregarious in public is thin-skinned and grudging in private. He trusts only a few, nursing grievances and balancing his own scales of justice for those who cross his path.

He is insecure; he has allowed an environment to be built around him in which there is an atmosphere of intrigue and paranoia. He lives in a world surrounded by enemies. The man hidden behind the fortress wall is attuned to power with a genius for public life that sets him apart from the common herd of politicians.

There is nothing particularly unique or proprietary about the main achievement of the current chapter of his life, in which he appears as the premier of Alberta. Several other Canadian provinces and a score of U.S. states rival, in detail, his attack on public debt and deficit. His name, however, is synonymous in Canada with the conservative fiscal agenda— balanced budgets, debt repayment and the reinvention of government.

Yet Klein is a poor choice for a figurehead. He is his own man. He is self-reliant and unpretentious. He does his own shopping when he is

home in his Calgary residence of Lakeview. He likes to drink at the
Legion, to go to wedding anniversaries of people he scarcely knows and
to stay until it seems he wants to turn off the lights and lock the place
up himself. He is tough, craggy and still relatively unpolished. When he
appears smooth it is just that he is at ease and has never met the person
he could not look in the eye.

He does not have an ideology, although his philosophy of life fits a
conservative agenda. He believes that people have to pull their own
weight. He believes in live and let live. He is positive, a man of enthusiasm and energy. He tempers his conservatism with an understanding
of the human condition; he is decent and fair minded; he is not inclined
to be judgemental. He firmly believes in the politics of responsibility:
You are responsible for your life; with few advantages he did something
with his. There are no free rides; people ought to be self-reliant.

He does not seek to be an icon and stands out among Canadian
fiscal conservatives because he has become their storyteller, the best in
Canadian politics—the wise man at the village well who can explain
what is being done and why, in a way that commands attention and
provides the antidote to the fear that political change invariably brings.
The clarity of his program makes him a national lightning rod; other,
more circumspect first ministers and finance ministers have embarked
on the same fiscal course but with less fanfare and, consequently, less
controversy. Klein's unpredictability and unconventionality further en-
liven his actions.

Klein resonates with Alberta's eccentric past, attuned to the singular
aspirations that have bred political philosophies across the spectrum from
the social democracy of the Canadian Commonwealth Federation to the
social conservatism of Social Credit. The image of Alberta as a province
removed from the mainstream and producing a peculiar breed of politicians is ingrained in the Canadian psyche and is endlessly fascinating
both to Klein's compatriots and to outsiders. His style flaunts and taunts
what the arbitrators of Canadian public life regard as normative. He
makes for good copy.

Ralph Klein is the summing up of Alberta's political conviction, passion, achievement, self-interest and compromise, past and present. He
provides the perfect coda to the century that transformed the province's
wilderness landscapes into an affluent North American urban and industrial economic, social and political culture. Only a politician cut from
Klein's cloth could do it, at times with panache and élan, at other times
with a hangover and in a sweat suit.

As always in politics, there is a darker side. For a time it seemed
that Klein, in his uniqueness, had banished the shadowy, invidious elements in the Progressive Conservative party that had tainted it, in the

1980s, with the reek of scandal and abused public trust. Now it is not so clear. If Klein has a vulnerability it is that as an unbranded political animal, he depends too much on old-style colleagues inside the pack without his detachment and integrity.

The much graver danger—for most of us have learned to live with the veniality of power—is in his policies. Klein has renounced orthodox government without an alternative plan of much detail. There is no comfort in the possibility that all North American governments grappling with fiscal reform and restructuring face, more or less, the same hazard.

The superstructure of Klein policies is as visible as it is simple. Below decks, where educators, physicians, deputy ministers, and the rest of the public service are trying to run the ship, chaos is loose. New wine is bursting old wineskins. To a man who has lived on the outside, whose career is to hijack old establishments and turn them to sometimes whimsical, sometimes outlandish, sometimes quixotic purposes, perhaps the turmoil really does not matter. Or perhaps other things matter more.

Klein's is a province in which ideology is thin soup and the main course is hard work and common sense. The United Farmers of Alberta, who removed government from the hands of Canada's mainline parties in 1921 with the blessing of Andrew Klein, were less adherents to a creed than folks who made a pact to cooperate; the legislative equivalent of raising a neighbour's barn and harvesting one another's wheat. The doctrine of Social Credit for all practical purposes withered in a few months of the 1935 election. The party won seven elections, from 1944 to 1967, because Aberhart and, later, Ernest Manning made sense.

So while Albertans enjoy the company of splinter parties with eccentric, sometimes wacky and even extreme views, they grant the helm to practical hands. Aberhart reached office with ideas that turned politics on its ear; the other great premiers, Manning and Peter Lougheed, were resolutely mainstream.

Ralph Klein has managed to give Alberta something of both; personally a renegade of the dimensions of a Diefenbaker or even larger, he has created a new orthodoxy of common sense in debt and deficit control that Albertans understand and endorse on its practical merits.

Klein has shifted careers twice: from public relations to journalism, and from journalism to politics. He has had two marriages and two families. He is predictably scarred by his experiences, as anyone would be who has lived so active a life. There are changes, yes, but they are subtle, and only those who know him best realize how different he is from the man one might have met earlier in his career.

Yet the essential Klein has changed little. His pleasures are simple, he is frugal to the point of stingy, and his bank account is modest. He is obsessed with his credit rating, having learned some hard lessons on that score as a young man. He bums cigarettes and cadges drinks. He will take the bill in the bar and then turn to a group of apparent strangers and borrow the cash to settle up. He has apparent regrets and no appetite for greed. There is not a covetous bone in his body for material things, although there are personal, emotional deficits that he cannot undo or will never relinquish.

His life is more comfortable because his income has increased with each graduation; but he remains a man of limited means. The fishing is done now for salmon on the coast of British Columbia. As a lad, he fished for suckers in Nose Creek; in journalism days, for trout in the Bow River. The quick, inexpensive weekend junkets to San Francisco are supplemented by flights to the Caribbean hideaway of friend Sam Switzer.

The battered, sometimes garish off-the-rack jackets kept in the news room for on-camera interviews have been replaced by carefully tailored suits. The hair is styled and blow-dried. His wife's better taste has been allowed to intervene and change his former irreverence for fashion.

It is in his face that the inevitable changes are most apparent. The boyish grin, the piercing grey eyes and the deprecating shrug are there for life; he is ever upbeat and cheerful. But in his eyes one catches the hard underside of politics. He is more guarded; there is an indefinable sadness.

The unlined, pudgy visage of his early twenties, with the jug ears, double chin and crisp hair cuts, has evolved into a craggy, battered pottage of jowls, shadows and crinkles. He has a penchant for working himself to the point of exhaustion, of pacing the floor over the impact of his decisions on people's lives, of never managing his time well and wanting to be everywhere, including with the last group at the bar in the wee hours. It shows.

Something else shows: the determination is imprinted on the chin; the confidence of his successes is in the set of the mouth. He hides the discipline, the long hours reading and being briefed, the attention to detail that has come to mark his work. He hides many of his strengths: the faultless memory, the love of the arcane that marks the true policy wonk. For all his sentimentality, he hides his most personal feelings. He is uncomfortable with people close in. He prays in secret, more or less, as a practitioner of the religion and ceremonies of the Blackfoot. He jealously guards the privacy of his first marriage and of Colleen's first marriage as well.

What is most concealed and most underestimated in the man is the inner stability he has developed as a mature adult. In many respects, he is the inventor of his own image as a renegade maverick. The expectation that he will be the iconoclast is frequently self-fulfilling. The stabilizing core of his life is composed of three elements: his closest relationships, his political ideals and his connection to the natural—the splendid, panoramic, eclectic landscapes of Alberta.

The three people who have been constant in his private life are his father, Philip; his wife, Colleen; and his aide, Rod Love. One expects that his ties to these are unseverable, not simply because he is sentimentally loyal to a fault, but because with these three he has been capable of the deep and abiding love reserved for fathers, true soul mates and best friends. There is a wider circle including his children; his brother, Lynn; his uncle, Ralph Harper; and a handful of present and former colleagues to whom he is profoundly attached. But only Philip, Colleen and Rod have moved him, changed him and retained him. And although he is a self-made man in the truest sense of the idiom, without them the outcome would have been much different.

His political idealism, learned in the turbulent and agonizing months of his life from June 1977 to October 1980, as his career in journalism ended and his life in politics began, seems unalterable. The central ideas are relatively clear, but Klein acts them out rather than talking much or writing much about them, so it is difficult to fully capture them. Klein's political science centres on the personal responsibility of all citizens and the public accountability of their governments.

Interventionist government dehumanizes people, reduces liberties, thinks for people, removes the power they should have over their own lives. Klein has a deep and abiding trust in "the people" and a parallel distrust of "the government." Governments are at their best when they constrain themselves from action, when they leave no damaging footprint on the lives of people and do not displace family, church or community. Klein fears government's worst side more obviously than he respects its potential for goodness.

Ralph Klein enters the afternoon of his life as a celebrated man who has achieved, during a few years, more than most premiers aspire to in several terms. He has travelled a very long political road and achieved enormous power for one still so young, as age is measured in Canadian politics. He has performed radical surgery, and his patient requires long and skilful treatment to heal. The journey he is on has just begun.

For all his accomplishments, he is visibly restless and even impatient, as if his race has not yet begun. One experience he has not yet had is that of campaigning against a foe of equal ability and resources. For Klein no such opponent is on the horizon in Alberta. He needs a new horizon, a new frontier for his ideas.

Yet a foreboding holds him back. It comes from the codes and secret stories of politics that warn westerners of the dangers of the quest for the Holy Grail of national power. "Every human society possesses a mythology which is inherited, transmitted and diversified by literature," Northrop Frye said.[1] In Prairie politics, the mythology of power follows the Arthurian legend of medieval Britain. In this mythos, Klein is a powerful, ruthless warrior-king governing a fractured, divided land. He is sure of himself in his own fiefdom but is drawn to be the single, strong hand that would bind his province to a greater whole. In the Prairie variant of the Arthur story, the hand that will hold Excalibur, the mystic sword and symbol of regional strength, will also seek and find the Holy Grail, the prime minister's office, and use it to bridge the fissures that separate the regions and bring Canada to a single harmony and greatness.

When, in legend, Arthur created the Round Table, he left one empty seat—the Siege Perilous that could only be held by one who found the Holy Grail. Tragically, most who went on the Holy Quest were lost. When Galahad found the sacred cup, he was destroyed. But each warrior-king and knight who aspired to power lived in hope that it would be he who laid hands on the Grail and returned it safely to the Round Table, where it belonged.[2]

In their time, the great Western premiers—Duff Roblin, Ross Thatcher, W. A. C. Bennett and Alberta's Manning and Lougheed—achieved Arthurian stature and held the sword of Excalibur, but they waived the greater task of searching for the Holy Grail. Tommy Douglas was lost on the Holy Quest. Four federal politicians from the West, R. B. Bennett, John Diefenbaker, Joe Clark and Kim Campbell, held the Grail and were destroyed.

Some inner wisdom compelled R. B. Bennett to quit the piece and find some dignity in obscurity. Diefenbaker became a living phantom lost in a personal political netherworld that is uncannily described in the quagmires and the wandering fires of Tennyson's account of the Holy Quest. The anguish of Clark's and Campbell's brief encounters with the highest office are still fresh and are particularly gruesome auguries against ambition. There has never been a happy ending to this story—not for Galahad or Arthur and not for the Western Canadians who were instructed by it and defied its lessons.

The maverick of cowboy lore shares one characteristic with the Arthur of political legend: he walks in no one's footsteps and sits by no one else's fire. It is in Klein's nature not to seek political comfort. He has a restless soul that can only be soothed by politics; he may never be able to disappear into the hidden world of private power where Lougheed made his peace with the furies that torment the politician. Klein has a self-assurance denied to Clark, a maturity beyond Campbell's and a gritty realism that R. B. Bennett lacked.

If Klein embarks upon the quest for the Grail of federal politics, "there is one thing you need to know about his prospects," one of his oldest friends and political staffers said. "If he decides to do it, he will succeed."[3]

Klein's third touchstone is the land, Alberta, the wide swath of country from the Milk River to the mighty Peace that embraces the prairies and steps up through the parklands to the foothills and the towering Rockies, the spine of the continent. He knows every inch of it: cactus and tumbleweed of the southeast and subarctic aspen and spruce forests of the north. He has climbed the buffalo rocks. He has fished the secret trout pools of the mountain-born creeks and rivers. He has watched the summer lightning rip apart the wheatland sky and seen the devastation of the hail that levels the promised crop. He knows the sweat of summer fields, the balmy Chinooks of the south and the bone-cold deep frost of winter on the windblown streets of the north. Alberta is a remarkable place of clear skies that canopy an incredible diversity of landscapes, and its singularity marks the man.

Knowing the place, he knows the people and what they do to keep the land; the dotted lights of a summer night that are the combines working until the first dew, and the lights strung up the mast of the drilling rig. Or the dotted lights of winter midnight from the window of an aircraft, when you cannot tell where the diamond shards of stars end and become the diamond shards of street lamps in the towns or the lights of the home place and the barns. He sees the place at a remove—a personal vantage point, inaccessible to others, that he cannot seem to describe. He is ever the maverick, never a part of the main herd. This has not changed, even though he is often, now, crowded around by those who are scrutinizing what he does and studying where it may lead.

Chapter Notes

Chapter 1 Home Country
1. Watkins, Ernest C., *The Golden Province: Political Alberta*, Calgary: Sandstone Publishing Ltd., 1980.
2. Archer, John H., *Saskatchewan: A History*, Saskatoon: Western Producer Prairie Books, 1980.
3. Brennan, J. William, *Regina: An Illustrated History*, Toronto: James Lorimer & Co./Canadian Museum of Civilization, Secretary of State, 1989.

Chapter 2 Rootless Years
1. Interview with Philip Klein, 1995.
2. Interview with Rod Love, 1993.
3. Interview with Philip Klein, 1995.
4. Interview with Philip Klein, 1995.
5. Interview with Ran White, 1995.
6. Milberry, Larry ed., *Sixty Years: The RCAF and CF Air Command*, Toronto: CANAV, 1984.
7. Interview with Philip Klein, 1995.

Chapter 3 The Invention of Ralph Klein
1. Interview with Rod Love, 1993.
2. Interview with Ralph Klein, 1980.
3. United Appeal files, Glenbow Archives, Calgary.
4. United Appeal files, Glenbow Archives, Calgary.
5. United Appeal files, Glenbow Archives, Calgary.

Chapter 4 Epiphany
1. Klein, Hilda May and Klein, Ralph Philip. Records including Memorandum of Agreement (property settlement), Petition for Divorce, Decree Nisi and Decree Absolute. Trial Division of the Supreme Court of Alberta, February 27, 1970 to April 7, 1972.
2. Pinder, Colleen Evelyn and Pinder, Frederick Harry. Records including Restraining Order and Affidavit, Petition for Divorce, Decree Nisi, Decree Absolute and Affidavit (child support). Trial Division of the Supreme Court of Alberta, October 28, 1970 to April 6, 1976.
3. Interviews with Gordon Shrake, 1994, and Peter Millar, 1995.
4. Conversation with Candi McLean, 1995.

Chapter 5 The Miracle in October
1. Klein, Ralph; "Blockbusting—Or What Smacks of It," *Calgary Magazine*, March 1980.
2. Interview with Ralph Klein, 1980.
3. Klein, Ralph, "Blockbusting—Or What Smacks of It," op. cit.
4. Klein, Ralph, "The Filthy Bow," *Calgary Magazine*, June 1980.
5. Klein, Ralph, "The Light at the End of the (Construction) Tunnel," *Calgary Magazine*, January 1980.
6. Klein, Ralph, "Big Money," *Calgary Magazine*, July 1980.
7. Klein, Ralph, "Ears at the Crack in City Hall Doors," *Calgary Magazine*, April 1980.
8. Havel, Vaclav, *Summer Meditations*, Toronto: Alfred A. Knopf, 1992.
9. This account of the campaign is based on interviews with Grant Howard, Rod Love, Philip Klein and campaign workers, 1993 to 1995.
10. Interviews with E. Manny Martin, 1993 to 1995.
11. Ibid.
12. Dabbs, Frank Wesley, "Mayor Microphone," *Calgary Magazine*, December 1980.
13. Interview with Rod Sykes, 1994.

Chapter 6 The Inauguration

1. Dabbs, Frank Wesley, "The Case of Milt the Maverick and Mr. Justice Aza Milton Harradence," *Calgary Magazine*, October 1979.
2. Dabbs, Frank W. "Political Passion," *Calgary Magazine*, November 1980 and interviews with Rod Sykes, 1994 and 1995.
3. Interview with Ralph Klein for a CBC television script, *Klein's Calgary*, 1982.
4. Interview with Rod Love, 1993.
5. Interview with Ralph Klein, 1981.
6. Interview with Rod Sykes, 1995.
7. Dabbs, Frank Wesley, "Mayor Microphone," *Calgary Magazine*, December 1980.

Chapter 7 The Feel-Good Mayor

1. Interviews with Isobel Rainey and other former members of Klein's staff, 1994 and 1995.
2. Interviews with Harold Millican, 1995.
3. Conversation with Roger Francis, 1994.

Chapter 8 The Winter Games

1. Interview with Rod Love, 1993.
2. Interview with Gordon Shrake, 1994.

Chapter 9 Choices

1. Interviews with Rod Sykes, 1994.
2. Interview with Peter Miller, 1995.
3. Details about the Liberal Party and Klein's contact with it have been enhanced by a list of the author's notes, numerous articles and recollections, too lengthy to record here, of a long-standing relationship with the Liberal Party in Alberta.
4. Interviews with Gordon Shrake and other MLAs and former MLAs, 1993 to 1995.

Chapter 10 The Ecotrap

1. Dabbs, Frank Wesley, "Mayor Microphone," *Calgary Magazine*, December 1980.
2. Adair, Al "Boomer," *Boomer: My Life with Peter, Don and Ralph*, Edmonton: Polar Bear Publishing, 1994.
3. Corbella, Licia, "Dam Disgrace," *Calgary Sun*, November 13, 1994.
4. Lisac, Mark, "Waste Gets Special Treatment," *Calgary Herald*, November 27, 1994.
5. Interview with Peter Hutton, 1995.
6. Conversation with Bob Blair, 1994.

Chapter 11 The Hijack

1. Interview with Gordon Shrake, 1994.
2. Interviews with Thompson MacDonald and Rod Love, 1993 to 1994.
3. Adair, op. cit.
4. Author's notes of the event.

Chapter 12 The Restoration

1. Serres, Christoper, "Ralph's Remarkable Rescue," *Alberta Report*, December 20, 1993.
2. Whyte, Kenneth, "Klein of the Times," *Saturday Night*, May 1994.
3. Watkins, op. cit.
4. Interview with Thompson MacDonald, 1994.

Chapter 13 Miracle on the Prairies

1. Interview with Gordon Shrake, 1994.
2. Friedman, Milton and Rose Friedman, *Tyranny of the Status Quo*, San Diego: Harcourt Brace Jovanovich, 1984.
3. Interview with Jim Gray, 1995.
4. Friedman and Friedman, op. cit.
5. Author's personal copy of *Reinventing Government*, given by James Gray.
6. Osborne, David and Ted Gaebler, *Reinventing Government: How the Entrepreneurial Spirit is Transforming the Public Sector*, New York: A Plume Book, 1993.

7. Dabbs, Frank Wesley, *The Summer of 1934: William Aberhart and the Something for Nothing Gang,* CBC Radio (*Ideas*), 1973.
8. Hutchison, Bruce, *The Incredible Canadian*, Toronto: Longmans Green and Company, 1952.

Chapter 14 Extraordinary Remedies

1. Serres, Christopher, "A Nice Problem to Have," *Alberta Report,* December 12, 1994.
2. This was a frequent Klein line in speeches and media scrums in 1994.
3. Francis, Diane, "Klein Has Important Lessons," *Financial Post*, December 1, 1994.
4. Linda Karpowich, President of the Alberta Federation of Labour, in media interviews, November 30, 1994.
5. Author's notes taken at the demonstration.
6. Johnson, Anthony and Jim Cunningham, "Klein Swings the Axe," *Calgary Herald*, November 23, 1993.
7. Bell, Rick, "Deficit Revolution," *Calgary Sun*, December 19, 1993.
8. Bell, Rick, "Premier Targets Biggest Budgets," *Calgary Sun*, January 18, 1994.
9. Klein, Ralph, "Alberta Advantage" (transcript of a television address), *Calgary Herald*, January 18, 1994.
10. Bell, Rick, "More Layoffs Feared," *Calgary Sun*, January 18, 1994.
11. Kauffman, Bill, "Cutbacks Slammed," *Calgary Sun*, January 18, 1994.
12. Johnson, Anthony, "Fighting Words," *Calgary Herald*, January 23, 1994.
13. Interview with Andy Philip, 1994.

Chapter 15 The Rivals

1. Interview with Rod Love, 1993.
2. Author's notes taken at the event.

Chapter 16 The Duel

1. Conversation with Don Currie, Alberta Chamber of Resources, 1994.
2. Interview with Gordon Shrake, 1994.
3. Johnson, Anthony, "Kowalski Reign Over," *Calgary Herald*, October 22, 1994.
4. Sheremata, Dave, "Pavin' Pete Hits the Ditch," *Alberta Report*, December 19, 1994; and Bell, Rick, "Trynchy Tossed by Klein," *Calgary Sun*, December 16, 1994; and Johnson, Anthony, "Trynchy Dumped," *Calgary Herald*, December 16, 1994.
5. Steward, Gillian, "Governments Should Start to Listen," *Calgary Herald*, December 1, 1993.

Chapter 17 The Failure of Opposition

1. Interview Harold Millican, 1995.
2. Johnson, Anthony, "Decore Slams Tories' Hidden Agenda," *Calgary Herald*, January 23, 1994.
3. Interview with Rod Love, 1993.
4. Conversations with senior Liberals, including Richard Pootmans, 1994 and 1995.
5. Conversations and interviews with Conservative MLAs, 1993 to 1995.
6. Francis, Diane, "Klein Is in a League of His Own," *Financial Post*, October 1, 1994.
7. Editorial, "Hope from Alberta," *Globe and Mail*, February 25, 1993.
8. Whyte, Kenneth, "Martin Pays Lips Service to What the Alberta Budget Actually Does," *Globe and Mail*, February 28, 1994.
9. Interview with Peter Miller, 1995.
10. Newman, Peter C., "The Fiscal Gospel According to Klein," *Maclean's*, February 6, 1995.
11. Conversation with Peter C. Newman, 1995.

Chapter 18 The Long Haul

1. Campbell, Murray, "Alberta Premier Receives Medal," *Globe and Mail*, November 22, 1994.
2. Contenta, Sandra, "Klein Hailed for Chopping Deficit," *Toronto Star*, November 22, 1994.

3. Campbell, op. cit.
4. Canadian Press, "Klein Boasts: Axe is Popular," *Calgary Herald*, November 22, 1994.
5. Contenta, op. cit.
6. Francis, Diane, "Klein Has Important Lessons for Politicians Dealing with Debt," *Financial Post*, December 1, 1994.
7. Serres, Christopher, "A Nice Problem to Have," *Alberta Report*, September 12, 1994.
8. Author's notes of the event.
9. The Premier's Office, *The Case for Alberta*, Government of Alberta, 1938.

Chapter 19 The One-Issue Government
1. Author's notes of the event.
2. Manning, Ernest C., *Political Realignment: A Challenge to Thoughtful Canadians*, McClelland and Stewart, 1967.
3. Byfield, Ted, "Westview," *Alberta Report*, April 17, 1995.
4. O'Driscoll, Herbert, "Revelation: A Source of Contemporary Hope," unpublished lecture for the Friends of the Cathedral, Calgary, March 17, 1995.
5. Byfield, Ted, "Pro-Choice Stance Taken by Klein is His Biggest Blunder," *Financial Post*, April 8, 1995.
6. Serres, Christopher, "A One-Dimensional Revolutionary," *Alberta Report*, April 3, 1995.
7. Interview with Ted Byfield, 1995.
8. Johnson, Anthony, "MLA Demands Schools Ban 'Profane' Book," *Calgary Herald*, March 2, 1994.
9. Conversation with Monte Hummel, World Wildlife Fund, 1994.
10. Feischuk, Scott, "Alberta Liberals Exploit Minister's Past Mistakes," *Globe and Mail*, January 11, 1994.

Chapter 20 The Eclipse of the Populist
1. Interview with Harold Millican, 1995.
2. Interview with Robert Lamond, 1994.
3. Dabbs, Frank Wesley, "The New City Has an Old Base," *Calgary Magazine*, October 1979.

Epilogue
1. Frye, Northrop, *The Secular Scripture*, Cambridge: Harvard University Press, 1976.
2. Vinaver, Eugene, ed., *King Arthur and His Knights: Selected Tales, by Sir Thomas Malory*, London: Oxford University Press, 1977.
3. Interview with Isobel Rainey, 1995.

Selected Bibliography

Books

Adair, Al "Boomer," *Boomer: My Life with Peter, Don and Ralph*, Edmonton: Polar Bear Publishing, 1994.

Barr, John J., *The Dynasty: The Rise and Fall of Social Credit in Alberta*, Toronto: McClelland and Stewart, 1974.

Friedman, Milton and Rose Friedman, *Tyranny of the Status Quo*, San Diego: Harcourt Brace Jovanovich, 1984.

Havel, Vaclav, *Disturbing the Peace*, New York: Alfred A. Knopf, 1992.

Havel, Vaclav, *Summer Meditations*, Toronto: Alfred A. Knopf, 1992.

Irving, John A., *The Social Credit Movement in Alberta*, Toronto: University of Toronto Press, 1959.

Kennedy, Fred, *Alberta Was My Beat*, Calgary: The Albertan, 1975.

Lisac, Mark, *The Klein Revolution*, Edmonton: NeWest Press, 1995.

Manning, Ernest C., *Political Realignment: A Challenge to Thoughtful Canadians*, Toronto: McClelland and Stewart, 1967.

Osborne, David and Ted Gaebler, *Reinventing Government: How the Entrepreneurial Spirit is Transforming the Public Sector*, New York: A Plume Book, 1993.

Thomas, L. G. *The Liberal Party in Alberta: A History of Politics in the Province of Alberta 1905–1921*, Toronto: University of Toronto Press, 1959.

Watkins, Ernest C., *The Golden Province: Political Alberta*, Calgary: Sandstone Publishing Ltd., 1980.

Wood, David G., *Lougheed Legacy*, Toronto: Key Porter Books, 1985.

Magazines

Bergman, Brian, "Ralph's Way," *Maclean's*, March 7, 1994.

Bronstein, Richard, "Governing in a Dangerous Time," *Business in Calgary*, March 1994.

Dabbs, Frank Wesley, "The Case of Milt the Maverick and Mr. Justice Aza Milton Harradence," *Calgary Magazine*, October 1979.

Dabbs, Frank Wesley, "Changing Guard in the Newsroom," *Calgary Magazine*, December 1980.

Dabbs, Frank Wesley, "Mayor Microphone," *Calgary Magazine*, December 1980.

Dabbs, Frank Wesley, "The New City Has an Old Base," *Calgary Magazine*, October 1979.

Dabbs, Frank Wesley, "Political Passion," *Calgary Magazine*, November 1980.

Klein, Ralph, "Big Money," *Calgary Magazine*, July 1980.

Klein, Ralph, "Blockbusting—Or What Smacks of It," *Calgary Magazine*, March 1980.

Klein, Ralph, "Co-operation," *Calgary Magazine*, April 1980.

Klein, Ralph, "Ears at the Crack in City Hall Doors," *Calgary Magazine*, April 1980.

Klein, Ralph, "The Filthy Bow," *Calgary Magazine*, June 1980.

Klein, Ralph, "A Fresh Start," *Calgary Magazine*, November 1979.

Klein, Ralph, "The Light at the End of the (Construction) Tunnel," *Calgary Magazine*, January 1980.

Serres, Christopher, "A One-Dimensional Revolutionary," *Alberta Report*, April 3, 1995.

Whyte, Kenneth, "Klein of the Times," *Saturday Night*, May 1994.

Wood, Ron, "Future-Gazing," *Calgary Magazine*, December 1980.

Electronic

Dabbs, Frank Wesley, *The Summer of 1934: William Aberhart and the Something for Nothing Gang*, Fred Diehl, producer, broadcast on CBC Radio (*Ideas*), 1973.

Klein, Ralph, *The Blackfoot: 100 Years*, Ralph Klein, producer, broadcast on CFCN Television, Calgary, Alberta, 1977.

Index

ABC-TV, 67

Aberhart, William, 3, 10, 11, 26, 101, 102, 103, 104, 109, 111–12, 147, 153, 159, 175, 177

Adair, Boomer, 80

Alberta Advantage, 136, 151, 152

Alberta budgets: 1993–94, 102; 1994–95, 116, 153; 1995–96, 153

Alberta Colleges and Institutes Faculty Association, 119

Alberta Department of Education, 162

Alberta Department of Energy, 164

Alberta Economic Development Authority, 131, 132, 134–35

Alberta Energy and Utilities Board, 127, 134, 137

Alberta Federation of Labour, 149–50

Alberta Health Care Association, 119

Alberta Heritage Savings Trust Fund, 102, 155ff.

Alberta Hotel, 10

Alberta Human Rights Commission, 161

Albertan, the, 29

Alberta Pacific, 81

Alberta Report, 60, 102, 144, 148, 159

Alberta Special Waste Treatment Centre (Swan Hills), 82, 128, 135

Alberta Taxpayers Association, 108

Alberta Teachers' Association, 119, 141

Alberta Union of Public Employees, 119, 121

Albertville, France, 70

Alexandria Hotel, 51

Alger, Lois, 56

Alger, Ross, 35, 38–39, 41–43, 50, 56–57, 59, 63

Amoco Canada Petroleum, 125, 126

Anderson, Merv, 17

Angus Reid poll, 122

Archer, John 4

Athapascans First Nation, 2

AVRO CF-105 Arrow jet aircraft, 12

Ayers, Ella, 41

B.C. Hydro, 81

Baden Baden, 64–65, 66

Barr, John, 101

Barrhead provincial riding, 127–28

Bechtel, 5

Bell, Max, 29

Bell, Rick, 121, 145, 147

Bennett, Richard B., 4, 180

Bennett, W. A. C., 180

Bennett, William, 109

Betkowski, Nancy, 91, 92, 96–97

Bettson, Bob, 50

Biner, Mary, 16–17

Black, Patricia, 125, 126

Blackfoot First Nation, 2, 25ff., 63–64, 65, 159, 178

Blair, Bob, 88

Blood First Nation, 25

Blue Derby Café, 10

Born with a Tooth, Milton, 83

Bovar Industries, 82

Bow River, 9, 36, 80, 178

Bridgeland, 22

British Commonwealth Air Training Plan, 12

Brown & Root, 5

Buchanan Elementary School, 11

Buck, Jo, 40

Burns Building, 57

Byfield, Joanne, 159

Byfield, Link, 159

Byfield, Ted, 145, 159, 160

Calgary, 5, 8, 102; Chinatown, 30; Inglewood community, 31; Lincoln Park area, 12; Mount Royal district, 46; Nose Hill, 9, 12; Sunnyside community, 58; Tuxedo Park neighbourhood, 8, 11, 22, 88, 125; Victoria Park area, 31, 33

Calgary Brewery Malt Room, 20

Calgary Buffalo provincial riding, 61

Calgary Business College, 14

Calgary Economic Development Authority, 131

Calgary Elbow provincial riding, 77, 79

Calgary Exhibition and Stampede, 19, 25, 46

Calgary Herald, 16, 38, 66, 138, 141, 144, 147

Calgary Interfaith Food Bank, 121

Calgary Magazine, 36

Calgary McCall provincial riding, 154, 161

Calgary Mewata Armoury, 5

Calgary North federal riding, 22ff.

Calgary Real Estate Board, 46, 54

Calgary Regional Health Authority, 155

Calgary South federal riding, 23

Calgary Stampede Parade, 122

Calgary Sun, 121
Calgary Urban Party, 38
Calgary Winter Games, 57, 58, 62–71
Campbell, Kim, 180
Canada Health Act, 118, 153
Canada Manpower employment centre, 14
Canadian Airlines International, 101
Canadian Cancer Society, Alberta
    Chapter, 18
Canadian Football League, 20
Canadian Olympic Committee, 63, 65
Canadian Public Relations Society, 17
Canadian Radio and Television
    Commission, 32
Canadian Red Cross, Southern Alberta
    Division, 15ff.
Canadian Union of Public Employees,
    46, 119
Caravan Motor Hotel, 13
Cardinal, Mike, 118, 165–66
Case for Alberta, The 153
Catface, Rex, 28
CBC *Alberta News,* 144
Central Canada, 60
CFCN-TV, 21, 23ff., 38
Chadi, Sine, 142, 143, 144
Chapman, Ted, 29
China, 59, 151
Chrétien, Jean, 151, 153, 154, 165
Chumir, Sheldon, 61, 73
Churchill, Winston, 150
Clark, Gib, 78
Clark, Joe, 180
Clark, Robert, 136, 137, 138
Cockshutt Plough Company, 6
Coldwell, M. J., 159
Colin M. Brown Freedom Medal, 149,
    150
Contenta, Sandra, 150
Copps, Sheila, 165
Cornish, George, 48–49, 65, 67–68, 86,
    125
Cree First Nation, 2, 165
Crescent Heights High School, 11
Crowfoot, Chief, 28
Cunningham, Jim, 147

Dafoe, John, 23
Davidson, Mayor Andrew, 47
Day, Stockwell, 159
Dean, Carol Ann, 119, 121
Debt Elimination Act, 157
Decore, Laurence, 73, 78, 96–97, 108,
    109, 113–14, 121, 141ff., 160
Deficit Elimination Act, 102, 112, 119,
    121, 157
Department of Economic Development

and Tourism, 130
Depression, the Great, 3
Dickson, Gary, 143, 144
Diefenbaker, John G., 12, 22, 45, 177, 180
Dinning, Jim, 91, 92, 97, 102, 106, 110,
    117, 121, 122, 123, 136, 145
Doerksen, Victor, 162
Donahue, Jack, 125
Douglas, Sir Roger, 110
Douglas, Tommy, 180
Dunn, Hugh, 129
Duplessis, Maurice, 175

Eastern Canada, 60
Economic Safety League, 112
Edmonton, 10, 113
Edmonton Journal, 144, 147
Edmonton-Whitemud provincial riding,
    79
Elder, Phil, 38
Ellis, Aileen, 19
Elzinga, Peter, 91, 92–93, 94, 117
Energy Resources Conservation Board,
    82, 84, 126, 134
Environmental Protection Act, federal, 82
Evans, Art, 4

Fair Comment, 147
Financial Post, 145, 150
Financial Review Commission, 101, 106
First World War, 1
Ford, Catherine, 147
Foster Advertising, 19
Francis, Diane, 145, 150
Francis, Roger, 61
Frank's Caffé dello Sport, 51
Fraser, Brad, 163
Friedman, Milton, 109–10
Friedman, Rose, 109–10
Friends of the Oldman, 83

Gaebler, Ted, 110
Germaine, Adam, 143, 144
Getty, Donald, 11, 73, 74–76, 78, 79, 83,
    86, 90–91, 99–100, 117, 127, 155
Getty, Margaret, 76, 79
Gibbins, Roger, 148
Gilmet, Gil, 17–18
Gleichen, Alberta, 24ff., 33
Globe and Mail, 145
Golden Hawks, 12
Goldson, Gloria, 121
Grande Prairie, Alberta, 81, 102
Grant, Ulysses S., 169
Gray, Jim, 109–10, 125
Grayston, Gordon, 15, 39
Grayston, Isobel, 41, 53

Green, Bruce, 76, 125
Gzowksi, Peter, 136

Halifax, Nova Scotia, 151
Harcourt, Mike, 118
Harkness, Douglas, 22
Harper, Christine, 6, 11
Harper, Hollins (Harry), 6, 11
Harper, Ila, 6
Harper, Ralph, 6, 11, 179
Harradence, Justice Aza Milton (Milt), 44–45
Harradence, Clive, 45
Harris, Mike, 149
Hartman, Don, 77
Havel, Vaclav, 37
Henderson's Business College, 14
Henry, Michael, 163
Heritage Park, 114
Higgins, Sue, 68, 70
High Prairie, Alberta, 18
Hong Kong, 59
Hooke, Alfred, 2, 10
Horner, Dr. Hugh, 127
Howard, Grant, 30, 33, 41, 88
Howard, Judy, 14
Hudson's Bay Company, 2
Hussey, Elizabeth, 14
Hussey, Francis, 14
Hussey, Lucille, 14
Hussey, Michael, 14
Hutton, Joe, 23
Hutton, Peter, 85
Hydro Québec, 156

Immacula Hospital, 128
Inkster, David, 119
Insight into Government, 148
International Olympic Committee (IOC), 63, 65
Isley, Ernie, 91, 93–94

Jack Singer Concert Hall, 57
James Lovick & Co., 21
Janz, Darrel, 27
Jasper Avenue, Edmonton, 10
Johnson, Anthony, 141
Johnston, Dick, 110
Jonson, Havlor, 163

Karpowich, Linda, 150
Kauffman, Bill, 121
King, David, 92, 97
King, Frank, 62, 65
King, William Lyon Mackenzie, 103, 104, 153, 175
Klein, Andrew, 1, 2, 177

Klein, Angela, 13, 32
Klein, Bradley, 13, 32
Klein, Christine (Pinder), 32
Klein, Cindy, 11
Klein, Colleen Evelyn (née Hamilton), 32, 34, 44, 48, 51, 55, 56, 73, 79, 88, 94, 111, 115, 135, 146, 178, 179
Klein, Darren, 11
Klein, Florence (née Harper), 6–7, 8, 10, 43
Klein, Hilda May (née Hepner), 13, 32
Klein, Kate (née Drury), 1, 2
Klein, Lisa (Pinder), 32
Klein, Lynn, 9, 11, 13, 179
Klein, Philip, 3–7, 8, 10–11, 33, 38, 43, 77, 93, 171, 179
Klein, Ralph Philip: born, 7; boyhood, 8; Leading Aircraftsman in RCAF, 12–13; marries Hilda May Hepner, 13; teaches at Calgary Business College, 14; public relations director for Canadian Red Cross, Southern Alberta Division, 15; newsman for CFCN-TV, 23; divorces Hilda May Hepner, 32; marries Colleen Evelyn Hamilton, 32; *Calgary Magazine* columnist, 36; announces 1980 mayoralty candidacy, 38; elected mayor of Calgary, 43; sworn in, 44; hosts Olympic Winter Games, 61; campaigns for reelection in 1986, 69–70; considers Alberta Liberal Party leadership, 73; resigns as Calgary mayor, elected Conservative MLA, 77–78; appointed environment minister, 79; runs for Conservative leadership, 93; elected leader of the Conservative Party and Premier of Alberta, 96; wins 1993 provincial election, 114; awarded Colin M. Brown Freedom Medal, 149–50
Klein, Theresa, 33
Klein Gang, 14, 39, 40, 93, 124ff., 138
Klein Revolution, The, 147
Kowalski, Ken, 86, 91–94, 97, 125, 127–31, 132ff., 145, 147, 160, 161, 167
Kroeger, Arthur, 68
Kuyt, Bill, 65

Lalonde, Marc, 44
Lamond, Robert, 169
Langevin, Paul, 141–42
Laurier, Sir Wilfred, 1
Lee, Brian, 59–61, 73
Lethbridge, Alberta, 102
Liberal Party in Alberta, 61, 73–75, 99, 103, 108, 109, 113–14, 140

Liberals, federal, 22–23, 165
Light Rail Transit, 58, 63, 68
Lincoln, Abraham, 169
Lisac, Mark, 147
Little Miss United Way, 19
London, U.K., 1, 4
Lougheed, Peter, 44, 45, 56, 63, 75, 78, 92, 105, 127, 140, 155, 161, 177, 180
Love, H. Gordon, 29
Love, Rod, 40, 47, 49, 53, 64, 66, 85, 86, 106, 111, 117, 125, 129, 138, 140, 146, 160, 179
Lund, Ty, 161, 165

MacBeth, Gordon, 10,
McCaig, Bud, 155
McCall Field (Calgary International Airport), 12
McClellan, Shirley, 153
McCoy, Elaine, 92, 97, 110
MacDonald, Thompson, 26ff., 38, 43, 93
MacDonald, Webster, Jr., 125
MacDonald, Webster, Sr., 39, 125
MacDonald Cartier Club, 122
McDougall Centre, 129, 139
MacKay, Don, 72
McLean, Candi, 34
Macleod Trail, Calgary, 31
McMahon Stadium, 68
MacNichol, Vance, 85, 86, 117, 164
Main, Doug, 92, 97
Manning, Ernest C., 10, 45, 101, 102, 103–5, 111–12, 135, 158, 159, 177, 180
Manning, Preston, 105
Mannix Construction, 5
Maritimes, 60
Marleau, Diane, 153, 154
Martin, Paul, 145, 154
Martin, Ray, 113
Masterman, Bruce, 61
Meeker, John, 21
Mewata Armoury, 5
Mewata Stadium, 19
Miller, Peter, 147
Millican, Donna, 56, 168
Millican, Harold, 56, 140, 167, 168–69
Minhinnett, Tom, 125
Ministry of Technology, Research and Science, 100
Mirosh, Dianne, 161–62
Miss United Way, 20
Mitchell, Grant, 97, 142, 144
Modern Business College, 14
Modern Café, 29, 38
Montreal, 63
Moore, Sherrold, 125, 126
Morningside, 136

Mount Royal College, 14, 25, 140
Mulroney, Brian, 62–63, 73, 106
Nakiska, 66
Napi, 27
National Citizens' Coalition, 149
National Energy Program, 44, 154, 165
National Hockey League, 64
Natural Resources Conservation Board, 85
Nelson, Reuben, 92, 97
New Albertan, The, 148
New Democrats in Alberta, 83, 108, 113, 114
Newman, Peter C., 146
Nicol, Ken, 141
North Saskatchewan River, 2
Nose Hill, 9, 12
Nova Scotia, 12, 151
NovAtel, 90, 100

O'Driscoll, Herbert, 159
Of Mice and Men, 162
Oldman River dam, 82, 136
Oldring, John, 92, 97, 133
Old Sun College, 27
Olympic Plaza (Calgary), 57
Olympics, Calgary Winter Games, 57, 58, 62–71
Ontario, 60
On To Ottawa Trek, 4
Opron Construction Co. Ltd., 81–82, 85, 86
Organizing Committee for the Calgary Olympics (OCO), 63, 65, 67
Orman, Rick, 91, 92, 93, 96–97
Osborne, Donald, 110
Ottawa, Ontario, 151
Owlchild, Nat, 28
Oyen, Alberta, 6

Pacific Rim, 59
Paddle River dam, 81, 85, 135, 137
Palliser Hotel, 9, 22
Parizeau, Jacques, 156
Parliament Hill, 4
Parti Québécois, 156
Peace Country, Alberta, 18
Peace River, 81
Peigan First Nation, 25, 82
Peters, Donna, 168
Peters, Rob, 125, 168
Petrasuk, Peter, 22ff., 39, 41–43, 50
Petroleum Club, 169
Philip, Andrew (Andy), 31, 123
Pinder, Fred, 32
Planche, Bruce, 54

Political Realignment, 158
Portage-la-Prairie, Manitoba, 13, 17
Pratt, Bill, 62, 65, 67
Priddle, Tom, 32
Prince Albert, Saskatchewan, 45
Prince Charles, 25
Principal Group, the, 75, 90, 100, 142
Proctor and Gamble, 81
Progressive Conservative Party of
    Alberta, 45, 73, 90, 158
Progressive Conservative Party of
    Canada, 125
Public Utilities Board, 134

Quantz, Lloyd, 92, 97
Québec, 60
Queen Elizabeth Hotel, 64
Queens Hotel, 51

Ranchmen's Club, 169
RCAF Training Command
    Headquarters, 13
RCMP, 4, 26
Reagan, Ronald, 109
Red Deer, Alberta, 1, 2, 102
Red Knight, 12
Reform Party (federal), 114, 125–26, 141
Regina, Saskatchewan, 4ff., 21
Reid, Gordon, 19, 21
Reinventing Government, 110
Reutlingen, 1
Robin Hood Mill, 6
Roblin, Duff, 180
Rocky Mountain House, Alberta, 1, 2, 5,
    17
Rondeau, Paul, 125
Rowell Sirois Royal Commission on
    Dominion Provincial Relations, 153
Royal Bank of Canada, 14
Royal Canadian Air Force, 12ff.
Russell, David, 78

Saddledome, 65, 66, 68
St. John's, Newfoundland, 151
St. Louis Hotel, 31, 39, 51, 170ff.
Salvation Army, 3
Salvation Army citadel, 35
Samaranch, Juan Antonio, 63, 65
Sarajevo, Yugoslavia, 67
Sarcee First Nation, 25
Saturday Night, 103
Scott, Brian, 76
Second World War, 5
Shariff, Shiraz, 155
Sheraton Summit Hotel, 20
Sherbrooke, Québec, 151
Shergill, Jeet, 155

Shrake, Gordon, 59, 94, 95, 118
Sierra Club, 165
Sifton, Clifford, 1
Siksika Nation, 27, 28, 33
Silver Dart, 12
Sindlinger, Tom, 143, 144
Singer, Jack, 39–41
Smith, Art, 130, 131, 134, 135
Smith, Heather, 119
Social Credit in Alberta, 3, 10–11, 78,
    101, 102–4, 112
Sohol, Harry, 154
Somerville, David, 149
Souris, Manitoba, 5
Sparrow, Bobbie, 125
Speaker, Ray, 11
Special Places 2000, 164–65
Stanfield, Robert, 22
Star Ambulance Society, 168
Steinbeck, John, 162
Stettler provincial riding, 79
Steward, Gillian, 138, 147, 148
Stoney First Nation, 25
Summer Meditations, 37
Swan Hills waste treatment centre, 82,
    128, 135
Switzer, Sam, 20, 178
Sykes, Rod, 29, 32, 38, 42–43, 46, 51, 72

T-33 aircraft, 12
Tadman, Peter, 91
Takacs, Ted, 39, 125
Talking with Albertans, 152
Taylor, Nick, 23, 73, 74, 142
Thatcher, Margaret, 109
Thatcher, Ross, 180
Toronto, Ontario, 59, 151
Toronto Star, 150
TransCanada Airlines, 12
TransCanada Highway, 24
Treaty Flats, 25
Treaty No. 7, 25ff.
Trimac Limited, 155
Trudeau, Pierre, 23, 44, 171, 175
Trudeaumania, 22
Trynchy, Peter, 86, 91, 93–94, 96, 133,
    137, 167
Tudor jet aircraft, 12
Tupper, Allan, 148
Turner, John, 154
Tuxedo Park Elementary School, 11
Tyranny of the Status Quo, 109–10

Unfinished Business, 110
United Appeal (United Way), Calgary,
    16, 19ff., 78
United Farmers of Alberta, 177

United Nurses Association, 119
University of Calgary, 68

Vancouver, British Columbia, 59, 151
Victoria, British Columbia, 81
Vivone, Richard, 148
Voice of the Prairies, 26, 29

Wagner, Norman, 125
Walker, Hal, 78, 125
Walsh Young, 78
Watkins, Ernest C., 104
Waugh, Neil, 145, 147
West, Steve, 117
Western Canada, 3, 21

Whalen, Ed, 39
Whalen, Nomi, 39
White, Ran, 11
Whyte, Kenneth, 145
Wild Rose Foundation, 127
Winnipeg Free Press, 23
Woodsworth, James, 159
Workers' Unity League, 4
World War I, 1
World War II, 5
World Wildlife Fund (WWF), 163–65

York, Neville, 21
YWCA, 41